The Life Story Of Edward De Vere As "william Shakespeare"

Allen, Percy, b. 1872

Nabu Public Domain Reprints:

You are holding a reproduction of an original work published before 1923 that is in the public domain in the United States of America, and possibly other countries. You may freely copy and distribute this work as no entity (individual or corporate) has a copyright on the body of the work. This book may contain prior copyright references, and library stamps (as most of these works were scanned from library copies). These have been scanned and retained as part of the historical artifact.

This book may have occasional imperfections such as missing or blurred pages, poor pictures, errant marks, etc. that were either part of the original artifact, or were introduced by the scanning process. We believe this work is culturally important, and despite the imperfections, have elected to bring it back into print as part of our continuing commitment to the preservation of printed works worldwide. We appreciate your understanding of the imperfections in the preservation process, and hope you enjoy this valuable book.

THE LIFE STORY OF EDWARD DE VERE AS "WILLIAM SHAKESPEARE"

THE LIFE STORY of EDWARD DE VERE as "WILLIAM SHAKESPEARE"

By
PERCY ALLEN
Author of "*The Oxford Shakespeare Case Corroborated*," etc.

WILLIAM FARQUHAR PAYSON
598 MADISON AVENUE
NEW YORK

PR
2947
O9
A62

Made in Great Britain

AUTHOR'S FOREWORD

THE conception, construction, and writing of this book are wholly my own; but the interpretations of the plays, and the linking of them with events in Oxford's life, though also largely my own, are borrowed, in part, from the writings of my fellow-workers upon this subject, including Mr. J. T. Looney, Admiral H. H. Holland, and Mrs. E. T. Clark, whose help I gratefully acknowledge. Mrs. Clark's valuable and sagacious work, *Shakespeare's Plays in the Order of their Writing* published also in America under the title, *Hidden Allusions in Shakespeare's Plays*, has been constantly, and very usefully, at my elbow. This word of appreciation, however, should not be interpreted as implying acceptance by myself of all Mrs. Clark's conclusions.

My larger debt, however, is to my valued collaborator, Capt. B. M. Ward, who has written an introduction to this book, and from whose *Life of the 17th Earl of Oxford* I have, with his consent, and with that of Messrs. John Murray, his publishers—to whom also I express my indebtedness—taken substantially all the facts, extracts from correspondence, and so forth, which make up the biographical basis of this work. For reasons of space and economy, I have not inserted, in the following pages, the usual page-references to Capt. Ward's volume, which my own does *not* supersede; since I have, in the main, used extracts only, from the letters and other documents quoted, which, with much other information, can be read, in full, only in *The Life of the 17th Earl of Oxford*. To that book I refer my readers. Capt. Ward, when writing his biography, was fully satisfied concerning the identity of Oxford with "Shakespeare," though he rightly judged that a proclamation of the fact would, at that time, have been premature. Many years must pass before the final and definitive biography of Edward de Vere, as "Shakespeare," can be written.

I am further greatly indebted to Capt. Ward, for supplying me with transcripts, from the Record Office, of valuable and important documents, relating to the Howard-Arundel quarrel with Oxford of 1580–81, of which I have made use in my interpretations of *Much Ado about Nothing* and *Measure for Measure*; and also for sending me, from Somerset House and other sources, necessary information concerning Thomas Knyvet (Tybalt) and Anne Vavasour (Juliet), and their families. We must jointly express our warm thanks to Mr. Edgar de Knevett, of 23 St. Martin's Avenue, Epsom, Surrey, for giving Capt. Ward access to the family records in his possession.

Capt. Ward has also furnished me with valuable information concerning the connexion of the Oxford family, through the Trussells, with certain Manors in Warwickshire; thus linking de Vere, in a most interesting way, with the Forest of Arden district. It was in discussion with him, also, that I adopted the line of thought followed in this book, concerning Oxford's relations with the Essex-Southampton group.

Col. B. R. Ward, Secretary of the Shakespeare Fellowship, has also been most helpful and generous in weighing with me these difficult problems, and in placing his wide knowledge at my disposal. My collaboration with the Wards has greatly added to the pleasure of writing this book, as also to such authority as it may possess. Without their earlier studies and research, the work could not have been attempted.

I have also to thank that very learned archæologist of the "Oxford" country, Mr. L. H. Haydon Whitehead, for supplying me with a genealogy, and other valuable information concerning the de Veres and the "Oxford" country. Father C. S. de Vere Beauclerk has supplied me with many composite pictures, a group of which is reproduced in this book, proving, in a most ingenious and convincing way, that many of the portraits of "Shakespeare," including the "Ashbourne" and others, are, in fact, pictures of Edward de Vere; and the Rev. K. J. L. Donald, Vicar of Copmansthorpe, Yorks, has given me valuable hints and information concerning the Vavasour family, for all of which I am grateful. Dr. Gerald H. Rendall has also given me sound counsel and advice, for which I thank him. I gratefully thank Mr. Eustace Conway of New York, and the Executrix of the Folger Estate for permission to reproduce the "Ashbourne" portrait of "Shakespeare."

For reasons of space, I have been compelled to exclude much interesting corroborative proof of my arguments; and I have also excluded, in general, references to the literary sources of Shakespeare's plays, since these are familiar to most readers, and can be found in all the orthodox editions and text-books.

Will readers please note, that when, in this book, I use such an expression as "Claudio is Oxford" or "Feste is Oxford," I mean that Oxford had some aspect of himself basically in mind when shaping the character. The universally acknowledged many-sidedness of "Shakespeare," and his astonishing faculty for dramatiz ing, with detachment and aloofness, varying traits of his own character, alone make such feats possible. Most of these " Oxford " portraits, however—excepting, for example, Hamlet, which I take to be the most purely personal of them all—are, no doubt, composites of himself with other historical figures—e.g., Macbeth as Oxford-cum-the-Bothwells, and Orsino as Oxford with much of Alençon and Henry III of France added—and so forth.

Lastly, in launching this first Life of de Vere, as " Shakespeare," I would offer a word of tribute to Mr. J. T. Looney, that bold and far-seeing pioneer, who, in common with most of his kind, has had to wait long for that recognition, which, as I hope and believe, is coming to him at last.

PERCY ALLEN.

CONTENTS

CHAPTER		PAGE
	INTRODUCTION	xi
I.	THE DE VERES DOWN THE CENTURIES	1
II.	THE ROYAL WARD: 1550–1574	19
III.	THE BLESSED HAPPY TRAVAILER: 1575–1576	53
IV.	DE VERE AS WRITER OF VERSE AND COURT COMEDY: 1577–1578	77
V.	"THE MERCHANT OF VENICE" AND "TWELFTH NIGHT": 1578–1580	132
VI.	OXFORD'S BATTLE WITH THE HOWARD-ARUNDEL GROUP: 1581–1582	155
VII.	"ROMEO AND JULIET" AND "HAMLET": 1582–1583	185
VIII.	CROWDED YEARS: 1584–1588	215
IX.	WITHDRAWAL FROM PUBLIC LIFE: 1589–1596	251
X.	OXFORD'S LITERARY WAR WITH CHAPMAN AND JONSON; 1596–1598	291
XI.	CLOSING YEARS AND DEATH: 1599–1604	329
	APPENDIX A: THE RELATIONS BETWEEN OXFORD AND QUEEN ELIZABETH	362
	APPENDIX B: GENEALOGY	368
	,, C ,,	369
	INDEX	375

INTRODUCTION

By Captain B. M. Ward

TEN years ago, when I first read Mr. J. Thomas Looney's *Shakespeare Identified in Edward de Vere, Seventeenth Earl of Oxford*, I recognized that he had proved his case. Almost without exception, however, his book was turned down by the critics and reviewers; but it is significant that although Mr. Looney has been attacked on matters of minor detail, his main thesis and arguments have never been challenged or refuted. And, indeed, it is safe to say that they never will be, for the simple reason that they are unanswerable.

Since the publication of *Shakespeare Identified* there has been a steadily increasing output of books dealing with the Oxford theory. Each volume has added to our ever-increasing store of knowledge; and to-day Oxfordians can justly claim that the case is complete and Mr. Looney's hypothesis proved. And it is a remarkable tribute to Mr. Looney's great work that it stands to-day as unshaken and unshakable as ever, although, of course, in matters of detail—e.g., the chronology of the plays—it has been necessary to make some slight modifications.

Mr. Percy Allen, in this book, has codified the results of the "Oxford movement" from *Shakespeare Identified* to the present day. He takes us through the eventful career of the Earl of Oxford, weaving into it the story of "Shakespeare" and his plays. He presents us with a vivid, human personality—poet, courtier, traveller, bohemian, actor, dramatist, soldier, sailor, war-propagandist. He confronts us with innumerable coincidences and topical allusions connecting Lord Oxford with the "Shakespeare" plays. He brings forward play after play to explain Oxford's life; he brings forward incident after incident in Oxford's life to explain the plays. The resultant pattern from this intricate net-work of "warp and woof" is as convincing as it is unanswerable.

Now, last year Sir E. K. Chambers carried out a similar work of codification for the Stratford man by publishing his two-volume life of *William Shakespeare*. Before I had read the book I thought: "Here at last is the best possible case that can be made out for Stratfordian orthodoxy." And this is what I found:

> It is no use guessing. As in so many other historical investigations, after all the careful scrutiny of clues and all the patient balancing of possibilities, *the last word for a self-respecting scholarship can only be that of nescience.* (I, 26.)

Was there ever a clearer admission of defeat? One cannot help being reminded of the late Mrs. C. C. Stopes who ransacked the Public Record Office in an effort to find some link between "Shakespeare" and the Earl of Southampton. After eight years of industrious and painstaking research she found—nothing! And, a few months before her death, in a talk with Mr. Percy Allen, she used these words: "My life has been a failure." Yet, had she but known, the link was there all the time; for in 1593 Southampton was engaged to be married to "Shakespeare's" daughter!

Vero nihil verius! Here, then, is the choice that lies

INTRODUCTION

before the reader. He must choose between Mr. Allen's " Shakespeare," a figure pulsating with life, and making a thousand contacts with the plays and poems: or Sir Edmund Chambers' " Shakespeare," a pale, ghost-like wraith, whose life-story is wholly dissociated from the plays and poems, and concerning whom the last word is " nescience." But I am wrong to use the word " choice." There is really no " choice " whatsoever in the matter !

Mr. Allen will no doubt be told by orthodox reviewers that his book is simply a fortuitous concourse of false inferences. To which I would make reply that if all the countless coincidences and topical allusions in the plays which point relentlessly to Lord Oxford are purely imaginary, then surely the result is far more astonishing in its depth and completeness than if we make the simple and obvious assumption that Mr. Allen's inferences are true.

In conclusion, I would like to emphasize that both Mr. Allen and myself believe that " Shakespeare " can only be fully explained on the assumption that he is " a noun of multitude " (if I may take the liberty of borrowing Mr. H. T. S. Forrest's very expressive phrase). This " Group Theory," or " Disintegration Theory " —call it what you will—is vehemently rejected by orthodox scholars because its acceptance would shatter once and for all the " irrefragable testimony " of Ben Jonson and his colleagues in the preliminary matter of the 1623 Folio. Ben Jonson and his co-editors say, in effect:

1. That the thirty-six plays in the Folio are the work of a certain Mr. William Shakespeare.
2. That this Mr. William Shakespeare,
    (a) Was a fellow-actor with Heminge and Condell.

(b) Has a monument at Stratford.

(c) Is referred to as " Sweet Swan of Avon "—thus (apparently) conclusively identifying the author of the thirty-six plays in the Folio with Mr. William Shakspere of New Place, Stratford-upon-Avon, gent. But—and here is the crux of the matter—if our instinct forbids us to believe that (for example) *Hamlet* and *Henry VIII* were both written by one and the same man, then we *ipso facto* impugn the credibility of Jonson and the other Folio witnesses. And that is why all logically-minded Stratfordians are compelled to believe that the man who wrote *Hamlet* also wrote *Henry VIII*; and that is why they conduct a periodical heresy hunt in order to purge their august ranks from the contaminating influence of any " disintegrators."

This " Group Theory " is still in its infancy. But one thing is certain—the Earl of Oxford was the most important member of the Group. It also seems certain that this Group comprised three main branches: firstly in the late 'eighties and early 'nineties, the war-propagandists such as Lyly, Marlowe, Peele, and Greene, who no doubt had their share of Oxford's £1,000 a year of Secret Service money: secondly, in the late 'nineties when the war was drawing to a close, a small coterie of Oxford's personal friends and relations, such as the Earl of Derby, Francis Bacon, and Lady Pembroke: and thirdly, after Oxford's death in 1604, the " bold and skilful imitators" such as Wilkins, Chapman, and Fletcher, who met the public demand for more " Shakespeare " plays by writing, in cleverly imitated Shakesperean style, the " spurious " plays such as *Pericles, Cymbeline, Two Noble Kinsmen, Henry VIII*, etc.

The details, however, of this " Group Theory " need

not detain us here. Mr. Allen's book is concerned with the central figure of the " Shakespeare " group—Edward de Vere, 17th Earl of Oxford; and I am confident that all readers outside the sternly disciplined ranks of " self-respecting scholarship " will agree that Mr. Allen has drawn for us a fascinating and lifelike portrait of the supreme figure in English literature.

CHAPTER ONE

THE DE VERES DOWN THE CENTURIES

The de Veres Danish-Dutch by origin—Migration to Normandy—Aubrey de Vere probably crosses with the Conqueror, and fights at Hastings—The second Aubrey as Crusader, and the de Vere Mullet—third Aubrey at Hedingham Castle—Magna Charta. Robert, 3rd Earl of Oxford and King John—Robert, 5th Earl made prisoner at Evesham—John, 7th Earl at Poitiers and Crécy—Robert, 9th Earl an intimate of Richard II, and cousin by marriage of Edward III—Robert de Vere and Shakespeare's " Richard II "—Omission of Oxford's name from Shakesperean First Folio—John, 12th Earl and his son beheaded on Tower Hill, 1461—13th Earl fights for Richmond at Bosworth Field—He is Godfather to Henry VIII—Enormous landed wealth of the de Veres—John de Vere, 16th Earl is " Shakespeare's " father

DURING the early eighteen-eighties, as a youngster in whom a certain zest for rhyme and metre battled already, though unsuccessfully as yet, with the strong counter-claims of cricket and football, there came one day into my hands Lord Tennyson's poem to that daughter of a hundred Earls, Lady Clara Vere de Vere.

Such was my first introduction to the name and quality of a family which, almost half a century later, was to make pressing claims upon my time and attention, and of which the story—while in no wise dispelling the charms of " a simple maiden in her flower "—helped to implant within me traditional respect for a coat-of-arms well worn, and for that repose " which stamps the caste of Vere de Vere." My views, be it added, have altered, in these respects, very little during half a century, although I did not know then—nor indeed ever dreamed —that those same de Veres, some three hundred years before, had given to the world an enchanter, who has wielded, and will yet wield, over unnumbered millions, a spell far more healthfully potent than that of Tennyson's Clara, over her foolish yeoman, was baleful and destructive.

Nor, reading that poem at schoolboy age, could I have been expected, even by a Lord Macaulay, to know that the great glory of these de Veres had been a matter of common English acceptance so long ago as the days of Charles I, when at the close of that historic lawsuit, wherein Robert de Vere claimed successfully the Earldom of Oxford against his cousin, Lord Willoughby de Eresby—Sir Randolph Carew, the Lord Chief Justice of England, had said:

> "I heard a great Peer of this nation, and a learned, say, when he lived there was no King in Christendom had such a subject as Oxford. He came in with the Conqueror, ... made Great Chamberlain of England above 500 years ago by Henry I the Conqueror's son; by Maud the Empress, Earl of Oxford, a title confirmed and approved by Henry II. This great honour, this high and noble dignity, hath continued ever since in the remarkable surname of de Vere, by so many ages, descents and generations, as no other kingdom can produce such a peer in one and the self-same name and title.... I have laboured to make a covenant with myself that affection may not press upon judgment; for I suppose there is no man that hath any apprehension of gentry or nobleness but his affection stands to the continuance of so noble a name and house."

The author of this book, though no Lord Chief Justice of England, has likewise laboured, for another reason, to make a covenant with himself, lest his affection for the greatest of all the great de Veres press likewise unduly hard upon his judgment.

That Aubrey de Vere, whom we may call the founder of the English line, did actually, in Sir Randolph Carew's phrase, "come in with the Conqueror," seems to be probably true; but since Prince Hamlet, whose historic original, quite certainly, is in part no other than Edward de Vere—describes himself definitely as "Hamlet the Dane," it is worth considering, for a moment or two whether, or to what extent, the family of de Vere, as a matter of history, was indeed of Danish descent. The late Rev. Severne A. Ashurst Majendie, in his useful little book, *Some Account of the Family of de Vere*, from which I have already quoted, cites M. de Gerville, of the Society of Antiquaries of Normandy, as opining, from a perusal of documents to which the de Veres were parties, that the family were by origin Danes, who had settled in Normandy more than one hundred years before the conquest of England.

Now all families that can truly be designated Norman must have come, originally, from Norway, Sweden, or Denmark; and if the reader cares to glance at the pedigree, kindly compiled for me by Mr. H. L. Haydon Whitehead, which will be found at the end of this book, he will see that the line of descent, if correctly drawn, traces the de Veres down from King Charlemagne through the Counts of Flanders, who were in effect kings, and to one of whom, Arnold II, was born, in A.D. 989, a daughter, Katherine, who married Alfonsus de Vere, of the town of Veer, in the Island of Walcheren, in Zeeland. This genealogy, if accepted, points to a Flemish origin for the de Veres, but does not necessarily overthrow M. de Gerville's theory, since an earlier ancestor may well have migrated from Denmark to Holland. The connexion, whether legendary or historic, of the de Veres with the Counts of Flanders, several of whom were named Baldwin, seems to be borne out by the fact that a branch of the de Vere family, which subsequently became two branches, residing respectively at Drayton and West Addington, used, in both places, the name of Baldwin as a Christian name, while in the Drayton branch, marriages took place with ladies of Danish descent. It seems clear, therefore, that the de Veres are of Danish-Dutch-Norman descent, and that some of them maintained, in part, their Dutch and Danish connexions, long after having settled down in England. That Edward de Vere, as self-revealed in "Shakespeare," and by other contemporary writers, habitually regarded himself as a natural peer and companion of royalty, is almost beyond dispute; and many an orthodox Stratfordian, though without realizing the implication of his words, has admitted that "Shakespeare," in his plays, persistently wrote himself down a prince, and the equal of kings.

Aubrey de Vere, the first of the several Aubreys who will be named in the course of our story, probably fought beside the Norman Duke at Hastings Field, and became a large beneficiary in the distribution of lands that followed upon the Saxon defeat. Every resident in Kensington, with its Aubrey House, Aubrey Walk, and de Vere Hotel, knows, or should know, that the district round Campden Hill and the Church of St. Mary Abbots —which de Vere gave to the Abbey of Abingdon—are all remembrances of the regard in which William the Conqueror held Aubrey de Vere. To Aubrey also came

Colne—afterwards Earl's Colne, the customary burial-place of the Earls of Oxford—in the County of Essex, and Hedingham, where the de Veres erected the lordly castle, of which the Norman keep still stands, and where, " as can be said of no other," his posterity flourished for above six hundred and thirty years, " in great riches, honour, and power," though it was in no splendour of array, but in the humble cowl of a monk, at his own Priory of Colne, in the year 1088, the first of William Rufus, that Aubrey de Vere passed from this world. Eighteen years later, in 1106, King Henry I granted to de Vere's eldest son, the second Aubrey, the office of Lord Great Chamberlain of England, with right to hold it " to himself and his heirs with all dignities and privileges thereto belonging." The Lord Great Chamberlain, by virtue of his office, took precedence over all other Earls, and this seniority gave him the privileges of carrying the Sword-of-State, and also of bearing the golden canopy over the crowned head, upon great national occasions, and to which Shakespeare will refer in Sonnet 125 :

> " Were't aught to me I bore the canopy,
> With my externe the outward honouring."

In 1098 as Leland tells us, the second Aubrey fought in the first crusade, before Antioch, against " Corborant, Admiral of the Soudan of Perce," or Sultan of Persia.

> " The night cumming on yn chace of this Bataile, and waxing dark, the Christaines being 4 miles from Antioch, God willing the saufte of the Christ-taines shewed a white starre or molette of fyve pointes on the Christian Host, which to every mannes sighte did light and arrest upon the Standard of Albry, there shyning excessively.

Hence, thereafter, upon the de Vere arms, " Quarterly gules and or, in the quarter a mullet argent," appears the mullet, in French *molette*, meaning the rowel of a spur, and being a silver five-pointed star, perhaps referred to in such a line as this, from Sonnet 116:

"It is the star to every wandering bark."

Similarly the floating of that star downward from heaven above the banner of " Shakespeare's " ancestor, is referred to in Sonnet 59, written, as I believe, five hundred years later, in 1598:

" O that record could with a *backward look*,
Even of *five hundred courses of the sun*,
Show me your image in some antique book,
Since mind at first in character was done."

The third Aubrey, Lord Great Chamberlain of England, and Comte de Guisnes, served also as a Crusader before Jerusalem, and was a powerful supporter of the Empress Matilda, who offered to him, it would seem, by way of reward, any one of four Earldoms—Oxfordshire, Berkshire, Wiltshire, and Dorsetshire. His choice fell upon the first named; and Matilda's son, Henry II, confirmed the grant, creating Aubrey Earl of Oxford, with gift of " the third penny of the pleas of the County, as an Earl ought to have." It was during the lifetime of this same third Aubrey, that his benefactress, Matilda, wife of King Stephen, died at Hedingham Castle, her then host living on until 1194, when the following inscription was written upon his tomb in Earl's Colne Priory:

" Hic jacet Albericus de Vere filius Alberici de Vere, Comes de Guisney et primus Comes Oxoniae, Magnus Camerarius Angliae."

He is described, in the same inscription, as "Grymme Aubrey," a double reference—first to the ferocious temperament of the Earl himself, and secondly to his kinship in fierceness with the *Verres*, or blue boar, a beast which the de Veres—who right down to Shakespeare himself seem ever to have loved a pun—chose as a Rebus, or pictorial representation of their name.

Now we have already seen, in the Sonnets, several quite obvious references to these lordly ancestors of Edward de Vere; but such allusions are by no means confined to the Sonnets; since, as we should expect, the historical plays of Shakespeare also—though, lest their authorship be thereby betrayed, they significantly exclude direct reference to the Earls of Oxford—make frequent mention of events in which those Earls were deeply concerned. Thus, for example, the play of *King John* puts on an added interest, when it is remembered that Aubrey, the 2nd Earl, commanded John's forces in Ireland, while his brother, Robert, the 3rd Earl, succeeding in 1214, was one of the Barons who took up arms against his king in defence of British liberties, and, with twenty-four nobles, compelled John reluctantly to sign the Magna Charta, on 15 June, 1215; thereby bringing upon himself, along with others, sentence of papal excommunication. During the civil wars that followed, and before the landing of the Dauphin, who had been sent by King Philip of France to lead the French troops which he had despatched to the help of the English king, the latter, in 1216, after besieging Colchester Castle, and receiving the surrender of its French garrison, captured Hedingham Castle, which was recaptured, with great difficulty, by Louis the Dauphin, in 1217, the last year of King John's life. When one matches this sequence of events, in which the 3rd Earl of Oxford was so intimately concerned, with the eminently national, and anti-Roman Catholic, spirit of *King John*—

> "No Italian priest
> Shall tithe and toll in our dominions"—

difficulties in accepting the de Vere theory of authorship are correspondingly diminished.

Look where you will down the long roll of these great Earls, and, one after another, they emerge prominently as participants in national events. Robert, the 5th Earl, sided with the Barons in Simon de Montfort's insurrection; and after being knighted by him, in 1264, was taken prisoner, a few days before the battle of Evesham, and deprived of lands and offices, until the amnesty of 1266 restored him to his possessions again. Robert the Good, the sixth Earl, was a mighty warrior against France and Scotland in the reigns of the three Edwards; and John, the 7th Earl, fought in the first battalion beside the Prince of Wales at Crécy, and led, with great gallantry, the English archers at the Battle of Poitiers. When, in 1360, he died before the walls of Rheims, and was buried at Colne, he left landed estates of vast extent, stretching over ten English counties, and destined, in part, though burdened with debts and mortgages, to descend, by process of time, to "Shakespeare," who, for the financing of his travels, books, plays, and players, will further, and almost to extinction, alienate and charge them. We shall hear Rosalind lightly chaffing Jaques, who is Edward de Vere:

> "You have sold your own lands to see other men's: that is to have rich eyes and poor hands."

But with the advent into our story of the ill-fated Robert de Vere, the 9th Earl, we are brought still more strangely near to " Shakespeare," through the lyrical tragedy, *Richard II*, a king at whose coronation the young Earl, then a boy of fifteen, fulfilled his hereditary office of Lord Great Chamberlain, by pouring " water for the King to wash when he went to meat." At the age of sixteen, by marrying Philippa, daughter of Ingleram, Sire de Coucy, and granddaughter to King Edward III, Earl Robert became cousin to the reigning English king, and son-in-law to that line of French Barons which owned the most imposing castle, and the proudest motto, of all the nobility of France :

"Roi ne suys, ne prince, ne duc, ne comte aussi : je suis le Sire de Couci."

Is it matter for wonder, I repeat, that Edward de Vere conceived himself, habitually, as the peer and companion of kings ?

After his return from military service in Scotland, Robert de Vere was created, in 1386, " Duke of Ireland, with the domain of Ireland for life,"[1] thus adding yet another to the family estates of the Earls of Oxford, already almost fabulous in number. But, alas for the vanity of place and power ! Wealth and honours, beyond the dreams of avarice and ambition, swelled unduly a head never, it would seem, of the strongest. The Earl grew insolent, threw off all restraints, moral and other, until he had made himself an object of those hatreds and jealousies that are never difficult to arouse

[1] *Account of the Family of de Vere*, by Rev Severne A. Majendie (p 21) my principal source of information concerning the Earls of Oxford during the Middle Ages.

against the man whom the king delights unworthily to honour. When civil hostilities broke out, Robert, with four or five thousand men, marched upon London, in King Richard's cause, only to see his army scattered by Gloucester and Bolingbroke, at Radcott, near the meeting point of Isis and Thames, and himself compelled to swim for his life, leaving behind him letters of a most compromising kind, since they revealed Richard's plan to seek, in the Earl's company, the protection of the French king. By the "merciless parliament," in February 1388, de Vere himself, with other of the royal favourites, including Suffolk and the Archbishop of York, was impeached for high treason, banished the country, and reduced from semi-royal rank and riches, to dire poverty and distress. Finally, gored by a wild boar—a beast strangely symbolical of the Earl's own ungoverned passions, and symbolically to be introduced into Shakespeare's *Venus and Adonis*—Robert died at Louvain, in 1392, grievously stricken in mind, body, and estate. Three years later, Richard, still, for a brief while, monarch of England, wrought as follows for the favourite whom he had loved:

> "He caused the cypress chest wherein his body lay embalmed to be opened that he might see him"... and "caused his body to be apparelled in princely ornaments and robes, and put about his neck a chain of gold, and rings on his fingers, and so he was buried in the Priory of Earl's Colne, the King himself acting as chief mourner."

Of this Robert de Vere, Walsingham and Sir Richard Baker wrote, in Elizabeth's day, "He was valiant enough against any man, except the Earl of Derby (i.e., Bolingbroke) whom he always feared"; and such facts as these, when mentally related to the text of the Shakesperean play, become immediately pertinent to our story; for who will consider the intimate relationship of the 7th Earl of Oxford, by marriage, friendship, and similarity of character, with the Richard II of history, and of Shakespeare, and deny the probability that, when the 17th Earl wrote his dramatic poem, he had his ancestor very consciously in mind, as a part original for the character of the king, whose destiny, like his disposition, was so nearly akin to that of the royal favourite. Thus considered, it becomes a deeply significant point, that, excepting the single line spoken by Northumberland, in the closing scene (V, vi), when the Earl states that he has sent to London,

The heads of Oxford, Salisbury, Blunt and Kent—

the name of Oxford is excluded from the play. Edward de Vere, quite evidently, had not forgotten the prominent part played in Richard II's reign by Robert de Vere, but, as Mr. Looney, with his accustomed astuteness, has not failed to note,[1] the dramatist has deliberately excluded his ancestor, for the double reason, it would seem, that such deeds, and such a character, could neither redound to the credit of the de Veres, nor be drawn prominently into the drama of *Richard II*, without arousing comments concerning authorship, which, in the year of first performance, whenever that may have been, and of the publication of the First Quarto in 1597, would have been most imprudent, on the part of a secret author, deeply vowed to silence. In this connexion it is again most significant to observe that the editor of the First Folio will not permit even that single appearance

---

[1] *Shakespeare Identified*, pp. 221, 222.

of Oxford's name; but alters it to "Spencer," making Northumberland's line read:

The heads of Salisbury, Spencer, Blunt, and Kent.

Such a change—meaningless upon the assumption that Heminge and Condell were merely editing on behalf of the deceased Stratford man's executors—becomes instantly comprehensible, if it be granted that the Lady Pembroke–Bacon–Ben Jonson group was behind the publication of the Folio.[1] In *Richard II*, therefore, the silences concerning the contemporary Earl of Oxford are no whit less significant than the single, and finally suppressed, inclusion of his name.

Passing on, to consider briefly the fortunes of the Earls of Oxford under the Lancastrian kings, we find them linked more closely than ever with the themes of the Shakesperean plays; for Richard, the 11th Earl, was prominent at the battle of Agincourt; and I shall have no difficulty in showing, when we reach the life of our hero, that, in all of the Henry plays, the unregenerate young Edward de Vere himself stands, topically, for Prince Hal, both in his early misdemeanours and in his subsequent reformation.

The 12th Earl, John de Vere, succeeded to the title in 1417, at the age of ten years; was knighted by the young king, Henry VI, in 1426, and after the loss by England of all her French possessions, excepting Calais, was appointed "Captain to guard the sea," with a degree of success or failure concerning which I am ignorant. This much, however, is certain, that his own life he could not guard; for, following upon the

---

[1] This subject is fully treated in Dr. Gilbert Slater's *Seven Shakespeares*, Cecil Palmer, 1931.

accession of Edward IV, and the triumph of the Yorkists, this prominent Lancastrian Earl, with his eldest son, Aubrey, was beheaded upon Tower Hill, in February 1461, a tragedy which, I imagine, his descendant had consciously in mind, when, some one hundred and twenty years later, Edward de Vere, imprisoned within that same Tower, conceived, and, perhaps, even drafted, a tragi-comedy that he called *Measure for Measure*.[1] The Earldom descended to the second of John's sons, bearing the same Christian name as his father, and destined to be, with one exception—who is the subject of this book—the greatest de Vere that ever bore the title, Earl of Oxford. A "lion of the Lancastrian cause," was this 13th Earl, a *valentissimus miles*, and a deadly foe of the Yorkists, upon whom his father and brother will be signally avenged. When, in 1470, King Henry VI was translated from the Tower to the Throne, the Earl of Oxford, in the procession to St. Paul's, bore the sword-of-state before the monarch, and with the Earl of Pembroke, was fully restored to his lands and honours, only to forfeit them again, when, at Barnet Field, the mists of sunrise, by dimming the star upon the Oxford liveries, caused them to be mistaken for King Edward's sun; thus inducing a mistake and a panic, which resulted in the utter rout of the Lancastrians.

Deeply interesting are the strange vicissitudes of this so chequered career; and charming are the words written of, and by, this high-spirited Earl, in the Paston Letters. These many mischances by flood and field, I can, however, only epitomize—as a flight to Scotland and France; a raiding capture of the Fortress of Mount St. Michael; subsequent captivity of King Edward;

[1] See *post* pp 177-181

a twelve years' imprisonment at Hammes; attainder and confiscation of offices and lands, in the first year of Richard III, to be followed by restoration of all estates and honours, after the decisive triumph of Bosworth Field, in 1485—whereat, battling against his life-long enemies, the Yorkists, he bore himself with magnificent courage. Again, is it matter for surprise that, when the 17th Earl, or one of his group,—for I am not satisfied of the Oxfordian authorship of *Richard III*—comes, some one hundred years later, to dramatize the story, he makes of Richard a monster, to whom the English king, of authentic history, lends almost nothing of truth ?— more especially when we remember, that this same Earl John stood godfather to the baby prince, afterwards Henry VIII, who, in his turn, fathered Edward de Vere's own royal and Lancastrian queen and mistress, Elizabeth. When, on March 10, 1512, Earl John died at Hedingham Castle, where he had frequently resided, he held the following galaxy of honours and titles: Earl of Oxford, Marquess of Dublin, Viscount Bulbec, Lord Scailes, Baron Plaiz, Knight of the Bath, Knight of the Garter, Privy Councillor, Great Chamberlain of England, Ld. High Admiral of England, Scotland and Aquitaine, High Steward of the Duchy of Lancaster, Justice of the Peace, Constable of the Tower of London, and Keeper of the King's Lions at the Tower of London, " with grant for keeping of the lions, sixpence a day for each lion."[1]

Right to the close of this ancestral story do the links between the Earls of Oxford and the characters of the Shakesperean plays continue in unbroken succession; for the 14th Earl, " little John of Campes," was ward of

[1] Stowe.

King Henry VIII, as Edward de Vere was to be of Queen Elizabeth. This Earl, moreover, was present, with due splendours of retinue, at the Field of the Cloth of Gold, and at twenty-four years of age was specially ordered, by Cardinal Wolsey, to have " vigilant regard that hee use not much to drink hott wines, ne to drinke or sitte up late." As for the 15th Earl, another John, and also a " good " one, he was concerned in the divorce of Catherine, and in measures against Wolsey. Further, by marrying the heiress, Elizabeth Trussell, whose family crest was a " trussell " or candle-holder, the design of which appears clearly upon her husband's arms, and yet again, by becoming grandmother to " Shakespeare," in the person of Romeo, the lady comes directly into that scene of the tragedy of Verona, wherein Romeo declines to take part in the Capulet's ball:

> A torch for me : let wantons light of heart
> Tickle the senseless rushes with their heels ;
> For I am *proverb'd with a grandsire phrase ;*
> I'll be a *candle-holder* and look on.
> The game was ne'er so fair, and I am *done.*
> *Mer.* Tut, *dun's* the mouse, the constable's own word.
> If thou art *dun,* we'll draw thee from the mire.

Here Romeo-Oxford tells us, quite plainly, that he will take no active part in the festivities, but prefers to be what his grandmother was, a Trussell (candle-holder) or Torch-bearer, and look on. Whereupon Mercutio, picking up Oxford's " I am done," follows with a series of puns upon " done " and " dun," by way of reminder, as Mr. Kennedy-Skipton has pointed out,[1] that Elizabeth Trussell's grandfather was a Sir John Dun.

[1] In the *Morning Post*, 22 July, 1931.

Nor is this grandsire candle-holder of Romeo's the only link, hereabouts, between history and the plays; for when the 15th Earl died at Earl's Colne, on 21 March, 1540, he was buried in the chancel of Castle Hedingham Church, beneath a tomb of black marble, on which the figures of himself and his wife, Elizabeth Trussell, are carved in bas-relief, as any visitor to-day may see for himself; that tomb, I take it, being the one referred to by Gratiano, in *The Merchant of Venice*, when, standing for the lighter side of Oxford, he says to the sad Antonio, who personifies Oxford's pensive mood:

> "Why should a man whose blood is warm within
> Sit like *his grandsire cut in alabaster*!"

Antonio-Oxford's grandfather, therefore, was, in actual historic fact, that 15th Earl who is "cut in alabaster" upon the tomb at Hedingham Church—a typical English country gentleman of his day, much addicted to sports, especially hunting; and, to judge by the following episode, one endowed with a natural kindliness towards young people: for on 15 October, 1531, a certain schoolboy, Gregory Crumwell, wrote to his father:

> "Father, I besseech you whan ye meet wyth the ryght honorable lorde of Oxford, to give thaks unto hys Lordchypp, for whan he came to a town called Yeldam, to the parsons thereof to hunt the fox, he sent for me and my cossens, and mad us good schere; and lett us see schuch game and pleasure as I neer saye in my lyfe."

John de Vere, the 16th Earl, who succeeded to the title in 1540 was, like his father before him, an ardent sportsman and rider to hounds. During a stay in France, in

1544, he was the hero of the following story, told by Gervase Markham in *Honour in His perfection*:

"By reason of his warlike disposition he was invited to the hunting of a wild boar, a sport mixed with much danger and deserving the best man's care for his preservation and safety. Whence it comes that the Frenchmen, when they hunt this beast, are ever armed with light arms, mounted on horseback, and having chasing staves like lances in their hands. To this sport the Earl of Oxford goes; but no otherwise attired than as when he walked in his own private bedchamber, only a dancing rapier by his side; neither any better mounted than on a plain English Tracconer or ambling nag. Anon the boar is put on foot (which was a beast both huge and fierce), the chase is eagerly pursued, many affrights are given, and many dangers escaped. At last the Earl, weary of the toil or else urged by some other necessity, alights from his horse and walks alone by himself on foot; when suddenly down the path in which the Earl walked came the enraged beast, with his mouth all foamy, his teeth whetted, his bristles up and all other signs of fury and anger. The gallants of France cry unto the Earl to run aside and save himself; everyone holloed out that he was lost, and (more than their wishes) none there was that durst bring him succour. But the Earl (who was as careless of their clamours as they were careful to exclaim) alters not his pace, nor goes an hair's breadth out of his path; and finding that the boar and he must struggle for passage, draws out his rapier and at the first encounter slew the boar. Which, when the French nobility perceived, they came galloping in unto him and made the wonder in their distracted amazements, some twelve times greater than Hercules twelve labours, all joining in one, that it was an act many degrees beyond possibility.... But the Earl, seeing their distraction, replied. 'My lords, what have I done of which I have no feeling? Is it the killing of this English pig? Why, every boy in my nation would have performed it. They may be bugbears to the French, to us they are but servants'... And so they returned to Paris with the slain beast, where the wonder did neither decrease nor die, but to this day lives in many of their old annals."

One more hunting incident, in the life of Shakespeare's father, has come down to us. When, in 1559, Prince Eric of Sweden landed at Harwich, he visited the Lord of Hedingham, who entertained his guest after dinner with some hawking in the valley of the Stour, "and showed him great sporte killing in his sight both faisant and partridge." With such ancestry behind the dramatist, the knowledge and love of field-sports, and especially of horses, revealed in the Shakesperean plays, is at once, and completely accounted for.

CHAPTER TWO

THE ROYAL WARD: 1550-1574

Birth of Edward de Vere at Hedingham Castle, 12 April, 1550—Boyhood at Hedingham—Death of the 16th Earl—Edward goes to London as Royal Ward, September, 1562—Life at Cecil House—A Student of Law and History—His skill in Horsemanship—Marries Anne Cecil, 1571—The Norfolk Conspiracy—The Massacre of St. Bartholomew—Oxford's Rivalry with Christopher Hatton—Influence upon de Vere of Castiglione's " The Courtier "—" Cardanus' Comfort " and de Vere's Letter to Thomas Bedingfield—Its connexion with the Shakesperean Plays and Sonnets—" The Famous Victories of Henry V," 1573—De Vere " steals away " to Flanders, 1574.

JOHN the 16th Earl of Oxford, married, about 1537, Dorothy Neville, a sister of the 4th Earl of Westmorland, by whom he had one daughter, Katharine, afterwards the wife of Edward, 3rd Baron Windsor. In 1548 he married his second wife, Margaret Golding—daughter of Mr. John Golding, of Belchamp St. Paul's, one of the Auditors of the Exchequer—who presented him with a daughter Mary, Lady Mary Vere, whose future husband, Lord Willoughby de Eresby, will, as Petruchio to his wife's Katharine, enter, I think, into our story with *The Taming of The Shrew*. John de Vere's next child, the subject of this book, was born on 12 April, 1550, some three years before Queen Mary came to the throne of England, and was named Edward, probably in compliment to the then reigning king. The world, however, for many succeeding centuries, was to know him far better as " William Shakespeare " than as Edward de Vere. These pages, meanwhile, contain already enough to show that the boy was surrounded from birth with every kind of equipment, and was granted by descent all such direct connexion with the outstanding events of our history as a future national poet could desire.

Born within one of England's lordliest castles, the Norman keep of which, still standing, though burned out, was once unsurpassed in all the land; with a vassal village at its gates, and, all around, the verdant meadowlands and elm-lined hedgerows of Essex and Suffolk, the boy could, and did from his earliest days, familiarize a swift intelligence, whether in cottage or castle, with the life of his day, as lived by peasant and peer. Later on, when old enough, astride of a pony, to accompany his father upon visits to his estates or as spectator of field-sports, Edward must have made contact with other social classes as well, including the rich clothier-merchants of Lavenham, Long Melford,[1] or Sudbury, in days when, though the weaving of simple, blue broad cloth which, for hundreds of years past, had made the fortunes of East Anglia, was already being supplanted by "new draperies," such as "arras," and a dozen others—that industry had lifted the Master Weavers of Essex and Suffolk to an honoured position among the richest tradesmen of the country.

The "common of Melford," or Long Melford, in Suffolk, a thriving centre of the cloth industry during Edward de Vere's boyhood, is mentioned, by the Earl of Suffolk, in Shakespeare's play *2 Henry VI*, I, iii; and Mr. F. Haydon Whitehead of Long Melford, has pointed

---

[1] Long Melford church was partly built by the family of the Cloptons, rich Weaver-Clothiers. The 12th and 13th Earls of Oxford were friends of John Clopton. See *Holy Trinity Long Melford*, L. G. H. Haydon Whitehead, p. 4.

out to me that several names of lesser characters in the plays, such as Gurney, Bardolph, Erpingham, Gray, Lucy, Bassett, and others, are eastern county names, and not western ones, such as would much more probably have been chosen, had the man from Stratford, and not Edward de Vere, been the real "Shakespeare." In the moated Manor House of the de Veres, near Lavenham —a description that recalls at once Mariana in the moated grange who, as we shall see, is, in fact, Anne Cecil herself —lived, for a while, the 14th Earl of Oxford, "Little John of Campes," he who had been at the Field of the Cloth of Gold, and whose estate, "The Campe," is probably referred to by Imogen, when, in *Cymbeline*, IV, ii, she gives her name to Lucius, as "Richard du Champ"[1]. All these towns, one may suppose, young Edward de Vere must have visited, at one time or another, and familiar to him, at least by hearsay, and probably by sight, were the then fresh, though now weather-worn figures—as they are alleged to be—of that Lion of the Lancastrian cause, and principal builder of the beautiful Lavenham Church, his ancestor the 13th Earl, on the door-post of Garrard's House at Lavenham; or, better still, in the market-place, upon the corner-post of the Guildhall, the armoured figure, still holding a distaff, of Edward's grandsire, the 15th Earl, over whose carved tomb, cut, as we have seen "in alabaster," in the Church of St. Nicholas at Castle Hedingham, the boy may often have passed his careless hand.

Earl's Colne also, where so many of his progenitors, from the first Aubrey onward, lay buried, was, almost certainly, familiar ground to him with the church of St. Andrew showing its de Vere mullets proudly upon the

[1] See *post* pp. 91, 92

battlements of the tower, and its priory which still contains recumbent figures of the 5th, 9th, and 11th Earls.

Literature the boy loved from his early days in that family circle of which Hedingham Castle formed the ancestral and august centre, linked, as it was, in the mid-sixteenth century, with many leading scholars and poets of the day. A sister of the 16th Earl, Frances Vere, herself a writer of verse, was married to Edward's uncle, that hapless poet, the Earl of Surrey, within the influence of whose literary style our hero, beyond question, was to come. Another sister, Anne Vere, married Lord Sheffield, the musician and sonneteer, "according to the Italian fashion," who had become the Earl of Oxford's ward in 1538; and among young Edward's early tutors were the scholars, Sir Thomas Smith, and the boy's uncle, Arthur Golding, translator of Ovid's *Metamorphoses* of whom more anon. Lastly, though not least important, in this connexion, Edward's father was one of the small, increasing band of noblemen maintaining a company of actors, with whom we may be positively certain that young Edward—when, in winter-time, they were playing at the castle—was on terms of intimacy as close as the respective social positions of the parties would allow. When Hamlet—intimate, as we know, with the players—stands, with the skull in his hand, beside Ophelia's grave, soliloquizing:

> "Alas, poor Yorick! I knew him, Horatio, a fellow of infinite jest, of most excellent fancy: he hath borne me on his back a thousand times; and now ... my gorge rises at it. Here hung those lips that I have kissed I know not how oft"—

memory, I think, and not imagination, is here dictating the poet's words.

Many scholars hold, and perhaps rightly, that Shakespeare was aiming at King Henry VIII's jester, Will Somers, who died in 1560, when Edward de Vere was ten years old; but those lines, it would seem, may be read also as a wistful reminiscence of boyhood days at Hedingham, when the heir to the Earldom was just old enough to take delight in the players. That same troupe, be it noted, probably played, in Edward's presence before Majesty, when, in 1561, one year before his death, the 16th Earl entertained that dazzling twenty-eight year-old queen with whom—though little he may have foreseen it then—the boy's own personal destiny, for weal and woe, was to be long and inextricably linked.

Edward's father being one of " the reformed religion," the circumstances of Mary's reign had compelled him to retire from court-life, to the seclusion of Castle Hedingham; but the year 1558, which brought young Elizabeth to the throne, had also brought protestant John de Vere, though for no long span, back into prominence again. On 3 August, 1562, he died at Castle Hedingham, with " great moan made for him," and was buried " with a standard and a great banner of arms, and eight banner rolls, crest, target, sword and coat-armour, and a hearse with velvet and a pall of velvet, and a dozen of scutcheons, and with many mourners in black."

One month later, on the third day of September 1562, there came clattering forth from the great gate of Hedingham Castle, " out of Essex from the funeral of the Earl of Oxford his father," the young Earl, Edward de Vere, " with seven score horse all in black, through London and Chepe and Ludgate, and so to Temple Bar." Thus, amid strange paradox of pageantry and mourning, our lordliest poet, still a boy, rides, at the head of an imposing cavalcade, into the scene of his toils, his triumphs, and his doom.

He may have ridden alone, at the head of the little procession, with a couple of Hedingham men in immediate attendance, and the seven score attendants, in trappings of woe, trotting behind; but it is more probable that, at only twelve years of age, he had a companion who, if Captain Ward is right, may well have been George Gascoigne, the poet, with whom young Oxford was to have literary relations later on: for when "G.T."[1] collected the anthology, *A Hundreth Sundrie Flowres*, he wrote at the head of Gascoigne's "De Profundis":

> "The occasion of the writing hereof (as I have heard Master Gascoigne say) was this. Riding alone between Chelmsford and London his mind mused on the days past ... when a great shower of rain did overtake him; and he being unprepared for the same, as in a jerkin without a cloak,—the weather being very fair, and unlikely to have changed so—he gan to accuse himself for his carelessness; and thereupon in his good disposition compiled first this sonnet, and afterwards the translated Psalm of *De Profundis* as here followeth."

This incident of the boy Earl and his companion, overtaken coatless by an autumn storm, on the way from a father's funeral, may have begotten, some thirty years afterwards, another sonnet by "Shakespeare," namely this one (67):

> "Why did'st thou promise such a beauteous day,
> And make me travel forth, without my cloak,
> To let base clouds o'er take me in my way,
> Hiding thy bravery in their rotten smoke?"

[1] Perhaps George Turberville—Capt. B. M. Ward, *Review of English Studies*, January 1928.

It was to Cecil House, in the Strand, without the city walls—"a very fair house" of brick, "with four turrets placed at the four quarters," and superbly gardened, that young de Vere rode, by way of Chelmsford, through stormy September weather, to the London home of the Queen's minister, Sir William Cecil, lately appointed Master of the Wards, and now to take charge of this latest, greatest, and most troublesome of them all, Earl John's son, on behalf of Queen Elizabeth. Great state the minister maintained, in his London mansion, "a household of eighty persons," exclusive of those who attended him at court; and certainly this addition of an eighty-first was to prove no sinecure even to one well accustomed, as was Cecil, to the adjustment of delicate matters, and the pacification of difficult men and women. We may suppose, however, that this boy of twelve years old was easily amenable, at first, to the daily curriculum, which, beginning with dancing from 7–7.30 a.m., and including French, Latin, and Cosmography, ended with Common Prayers, "and so to supper."

Edward's tutor at Cecil House, Laurence Nowell, Dean of Lichfield, had discovered, by the summer of 1563, that his pupil, then thirteen and a half years old, was more than usually gifted; since he states, in a letter to Burleigh, written during June of that year; "I clearly see that my work for the Earl of Oxford cannot be much longer required"; and, as instancing the boy's early delight in history, it is pleasant to read, in the dedication to him by his uncle and tutor, Arthur Golding, of *Th' Abridgement of the Histories of Trogus Pompeius* (May 1564), "how earnest a desire your honour hath naturally graffed in you to read ... the historie of ancient times, and things done long ago, as also of the present state of things in our days, and that not without a certain pregnancy of wit and ripeness of understanding."

Very apposite all this, it will be agreed, to the future author of *Richard II*, and of the "King Henry" plays. Our royal ward, beyond question, was studiously inclined from the first; since five years later, in another dedication, this time by Thomas Underdoune, "To the Right Honourable Edward de Vere," we read: "I do not deny that in many matters . . . a nobleman ought to have a sight; but to be too much addicted that way, I think it is not good."

Let no reader suppose, however, that de Vere, in his youth, was a mere bookworm, consecrated overmuch to his studies, and concerning himself but little with amusement, and the outward shows of life. On the contrary, as one would insistently expect from the dramatist to be, this boy has other addictions, including, by way of example, a feministic weakness for gay, and even fantastic, clothes. There exists, endorsed in Burleigh's own hand, a document revealing the fact that "the charges of the apparel of the Earl of Oxford," for the first four years of his wardship, 1562–66, amounted to over £600, which represents, at least, £6,000 of our money, in modern purchasing power. A dandy, quite evidently, from the beginning, is this boy, impressionable to sight, sound, and sense—swift, impulsive, passionately impetuous when roused, agile, and dangerous, whether with tongue or weapon. Before he is eighteen years old, he has blood upon his hand and conscience; for Burleigh, under date July 1567, wrote in his diary, "About this time Thomas Brincknell an under-cook was hurt by the Earl of Oxford at Cecil

Hous in the Strand, whereof he died; and by a verdict found *felo-de-se* with running upon a point of the fence sword of the said Earl's."

That verdict of *felo-de-se*, however, as Burleigh subsequently wrote, seems to have been brought in unwillingly under pressure from the Queen's minister: and when one recalls that Burleigh's own daughter, Anne Cecil, who is soon to become Oxford's wife, and a part original of Ophelia in *Hamlet*, was also living in Cecil House at the time, no very powerful imagination is needed to link these events up with a certain well-known scene, in the last act of *Hamlet*, wherein, of course, the Prince of Denmark is Oxford himself. In the matter of Thomas Brincknell, be it added, the Earl had pleaded *se defendendo*, alleging that the cook, attacking him, had run upon his (the Earl's) sword.

> *First Clown.* How can that be, unless she drowned herself in her own defence?
> *Second Clown.* Why, 'tis found so.
> *First Clown.* It must be " *se offendendo* "; it cannot be else.

The analogies here are unmistakable; nor can I doubt that the First Clown's shrewd comment concerning the man's coming to the water (i.e., sword) or the water (sword) to the man, and the Second Clown's clinching answer:

> "Will you ha' the truth on't? If this had not been a gentlewoman, she should have been buried out o' Christian burial—"

paraphrased much whispered talk, in the summer of 1567, throughout Burleigh's household below-stairs, concerning the verdict that would have been delivered had Brincknell been the Earl, and Oxford the cook.

During this same year, young Oxford was making more regular acquaintance than this with those laws of his native land, concerning which other plays, besides *Hamlet*, show him to have possessed at least a superficial acquaintance: for it is in 1567 that we find the Earl's name, with those of Philip Sidney and John Manners, enrolled on the register of students at Gray's Inn, where the sons of landed noblemen and gentry were customarily sent, to acquire some knowledge of the complex statutes and procedures relating to the transfer, and general administration, of real estate. Here the young courtier probably came into touch, once more, with George Gascoigne, who, at this time, was studying for the bar, and writing plays, one of which, *The Supposes*, from Ariosto, was the first prose play to be represented in English, and seems to have provided some basic material for *The Taming of the Shrew*. Oxford, probably, though not certainly, was a spectator of these comedies.

Heavier work, however, than sitting out comedies, or dabbling in Gray's Inn law, was awaiting Edward de Vere. These were difficult and dangerous days for the Elizabethan world. Unless the Queen, already "married to England," should choose to ally herself matrimonially with a prince, as well as with a country, and thereby give to England a legitimate heir, only her own life shielded this land from the horrors of another civil war. In France, the Peace of Amboise (1563) had ended the first of a series of conflicts between Catholic and Protestant which were ultimately to devastate that unhappy country. At the head of the French Catholic party was the queen mother, Catharine de' Medici—

the Goneril of *King Lear* to be—while against her stood a part-original of King Lear himself, that noble figure, Coligny, Admiral of France. In 1567, following upon the murder of Darnley in Edinburgh, Mary Queen of Scots married the Earl of Bothwell, thus, as I believe, providing de Vere, whose young imagination thrills already to these events, with original studies for Lord and Lady Macbeth. In the same year, Philip of Spain, by entrusting the Duke of Alva with the re-establishment of Roman Catholicism in the Netherlands, initiated a policy which led, step by step, to the annihilation of the Armada in 1588, and was to shape, in part, the form, or content, of several Shakesperean plays.

That the feudal aristocracy of England, always conservative in tendency, should remain predominantly Catholic, was a circumstance naturally to be expected; and in the year 1569 the Catholic nobles, led by the Duke of Norfolk and the Earl of Arundel, and fully conscious of their numerical superiority over the Protestants, at whose head was Sir William Cecil, believed the time to be propitious for carrying out their design, which was to marry the imprisoned Queen of Scots to the Duke of Norfolk, and to set her upon the English throne. Into the story of that ineffectual " rising in the North," we cannot enter here, but must content ourselves with merely noting that, when Edward de Vere heard that his friend, the Earl of Sussex, had been appointed Lord Lieutenant of the North, with military command, he wrote to Cecil, on 24 November, 1569, begging " that you will suffer me to be employed by your means and help in the service," and reminding his guardian of an often expressed wish, to see " wars and service in strange an foreign parts."

The request was granted; and during April and May 1570, Lord Oxford, probably as one of Lord Sussex's staff officers, took part in his leader's successful campaign in Scotland, and remained, from that time onward, Sussex's devoted friend. Stowe, thinks Capt. Ward, was perhaps writing of Lord Oxford's return home from that Border campaign, when he described the Earl riding into London

> "to his house by London Stone, with four score gentlemen in a livery of Reading tawny, and chains of gold about their necks, before him; and one hundred tall yeomen in like livery to follow him, without chains, but all having his cognizance of the Blue Boar embroidered on their left shoulders."

In this connexion, it is worth remembering, that scene six of the fourth act of *2 King Henry VI*, set in Cannon Street, shows us Jack Cade seated upon London Stone, and striking his staff upon it, while proclaiming "Mortimer lord of this city." London Stone, led me add, is still to be seen in the City of London, built into the south wall of St. Swithin's Church, just south of the Mansion House.

On 2 April, 1571, Oxford, with precedence, as Lord Great Chamberlain, over all other Earls, took high ceremonial part in the opening, by the Queen, of the first Parliament in which he sat; and a month later, on 3 May, 1571, we find him putting to use his skill in arms and horsemanship, by winning "at Westminster before the Queen's Majesty, a solemn joust at the tilt, tourney and barriers. The challengers were Edward Earl of Oxford, Charles Howard, Sir Henry Lee, and Christopher

Hatton, Esq., who all did very valiantly; but the chief honour was given to the Earl of Oxford."[1]

Ten years later, in January 1581, at the second of the two great tournaments in which de Vere competed, on the occasion of the Earl of Surrey's succession to the Earldom of Arundel, Oxford, this time as a defendant, was the winner. Concerning this prowess of his, at the joust and the tournament—" far above the expectation of the world"—George Delves, himself a defendant in the tourney of 1571, wrote: " There is no man of life and agility in every respect in the court but the Earl of Oxford"; and towards the end of the century, Ben Jonson, in Act II of that anti-Shakesperean burlesque, *Every Man Out of His Humour*, will make Carlo speak thus of the Knight, Puntarvolo, who is Oxford himself and also Romeo:

> " Why he loves dogs and hawks and his wife well; he has a good riding face, and *he can sit a great horse*: he will taint a staff well at tilt; *when he is mounted he looks like the sign of St. George*.[2]

Little, in their lifetimes, did either George Delves or Ben Jonson think how " far above the expectation of the world " Edward de Vere was destined to climb, in a vocation then despised, but now grown to greater credit than that of dancer or jouster.

The young Earl has no wife, as yet; but long before this spring of 1571, marriageable daughters, and not less so their mothers, within the circle of the court, must have dreamed dreams and seen visions of this observed of all observers. Guardian Burleigh, however, is laying his plans, and so also are the Guardian's wife,

---
[1] Stowe.
[2] See Chapter II of my *Oxford-Shakespeare Case Corroborated*, p. 46.

Lady Burleigh, and their pretty daughter, Anne, formerly betrothed, or nearly so, to Philip Sidney, who, throughout his career, is destined to stand, occasionally, in Oxford's way, and to be lampooned in consequence, in plays yet to be written. Anne Cecil and Sidney, as Mr. Looney first pointed out, are the Anne Page and Slender of *The Merry Wives of Windsor*, with Fenton for the successful lover, Oxford. The girl was fifteen years old in 1569, the same year which—enhancing her maiden prestige—saw the elevation to the peerage of her father, as Baron Burleigh. Thus Lord St. John, to the Earl of Rutland in Paris:

> "The Earl of Oxford hath gotten him a wife— or at the least a wife hath caught him; this is Mistress Ann Cecil; whereunto the Queen hath given her consent, and the which hath caused great weeping, wailing, and sorrowful cheer of those that had hoped to have that golden day."

But could the curtain that shrouds the coming years have been, for an instant, drawn, those doleful maids, and disappointed mothers would have wept, not for the loss of that golden day, but rather for pity of her upon whom it shone, poor Anne herself, doomed to union with a genius, among whose magnificent endowments were included, alas, but few of those that go to the fashioning of a model husband. Burleigh himself, as the play, *Troilus and Cressida*, indisputably proves, will live to curse an ambition that pushed him into " pandering " the ill-starred marriage.[1]

Anne Cecil, then, is affianced to Edward Earl of Oxford, whom she loved from the first; and for good or ill—it will be mainly for ill—the marriage takes place,

---

[1] See *post* pp. 99-112.

THE ROYAL WARD

in the Queen's presence, at Westminster Abbey, and is followed by a great feast at Cecil House, whereof La Môthe Fénelon, the French Ambassador, wrote to the King of France, telling how, at that dinner, he talked long with the Earl of Leicester, concerning another marriage—the proposed alliance between the English Queen and the Duke of Anjou—events which, read together, put on deep significance and interest, when it is remembered that the host, Lord Burleigh, becomes Polonius in *Hamlet*; that Anne Cecil will be, in part, Ophelia; and that Oxford himself will stand, in person, for the Prince of Denmark. As for the projected union between England and France, what is it but the theme of *Twelfth Night*, with the Queen herself as Olivia, and Anjou, with his younger brother Alençon, as the originals of Orsino, in this same comedy of Illyria? Thus, from the fabric of his most vital and intimate experiences, will our Shakespeare fashion his plays.

Big with decisive events in the history of Europe, and in the lives of those with whom, for eighteen years to come, the Earl's destinies will be interwoven, was this first year of Oxford's marriage. One of those whom destiny struck was Oxford's first cousin, the Duke of Norfolk, who, throughout 1571, had carried on treasonable correspondence with the Queen of Scots, for which, and for complicity in Catholic plots and risings, the Duke was sentenced to death in January, and executed on 2 June following. Oxford, who had been a warm friend of his cousin's, was greatly distressed by the sentence, and engineered a coup for the condemned man's rescue, which, though it failed utterly, is, for our purpose, important, since it seems to foreshadow a bitter feud between Oxford and his cousins Lord Henry Howard and Charles Arundel, who, irritated, it may be by indiscreet remarks dropped, upon occasion, by Edward, concerning Norfolk, endeavoured, thenceforth, secretly to turn the Queen against her Lord Great Chamberlain and ward, of whom, unquestionably, she was becoming fond, and with whom, the while, Howard and Arundel remained ostensibly upon terms of intimate friendship. Jealousy, combined with natural readiness for intrigue, may have bred the sequel; but whatever the cause, or causes, it is indisputable that, at last, openly hostile relations between Oxford and his two cousins will exert a determining, and deeply sinister, influence upon the whole of de Vere's subsequent career, and, as a direct consequence, upon the themes and qualities of the Shakesperean drama.

On 12 August, 1572, the Queen, accompanied by many noblemen and officials, among whom was her Lord Great Chamberlain, visited Warwick Castle, to which, after a short stay with the Earl of Leicester, at Kenilworth, she returned. There, on Sunday, 18 August, "it pleased her to have the country people resorting to see her dance in the court of the Castle ... so it seemed her Majesty was much delighted and made very merry."

Elizabeth's merriment, however, was not fated long to endure; for on 27 August, the day on which that gallant young Frenchman, La Môle, the historic prototype of Viola, returned, as nuncio, wooing Elizabeth, the Olivia of *Twelfth Night*, on behalf of Alençon (Orsino) his master, there landed at Rye two couriers from Paris one of whom bore to England the first, and fearful, news of the Massacre of St. Bartholomew, that, spreading fast across England, does soon, in Oxford's own phrase, ring, like a dirge, " dolefully in the ears of every man." Immediately all rejoicing over the marriage negotiations ceased; La Môle—reluctantly dismissed, just as Viola was by Olivia—hastened home; the government went into anxious council, the court into deep mourning; and when the Queen, on her way to Windsor, received the French ambassador at Woodstock, Olivia, as also she traditionally is, at the opening of Shakespeare's play, was veiled, " like a cloistress," in black—

> " all this to season
> A brother's dead love, which she would keep fresh
> And lasting in her sad remembrance."[1]

We have seen the Queen's marriage, not to Alençon, but to his elder brother, Anjou, discussed with Leicester at Lord Oxford's own wedding feast; and it is to the strains of nuptial music that Walter Pater—though he dreamed not of any connexion between *Twelfth Night*, and the Tudor and Valois courts—conceived, in " Gaston de Latour," the anomalies, at once lovely and terrible, of this exotic Valois world:

> " He (Gaston) saw them (the Valois) irresistibly. moving, to the sound of wedding music, through a world of dainty gestures, amid sonnets and flowers, and perhaps the most refined art the world has ever seen, to their surfeit of blood."

Edward de Vere will not be " Shakespeare " for many years yet; but already the vital experiences of his life, and especially the nation-wide clash of personalities, policies, religions, and interests, which issued in Saint Bartholomew, is shaping within his soul the essential

[1] Valentine: *Twelfth Night*, I, 1.

themes of his plays, and determining the types of character that shall inform and interpret them. The Queen, La Môle, Alençon, we can already recognize in *Twelfth Night*. Philip Sidney, as Aguecheek, will soon become charmingly visible in the same play; and at this very time there has also " danced his way into the Queen's favour in a galliard," yet another fantastic Illyrian figure, best known to us as Malvolio, and to history as Sir Christopher Hatton, now, in 1571, Captain of the Queen's Body-guard, inditer of fervid love-letters to his royal lady, and a deadly rival of de Vere, whom he hates " in the Queen's understanding for affection's sake." Will not Her Majesty, begs Hatton, " reserve her gracious favour " to " the sheep " (himself), who " hath no tooth to bite, where the Boar's tusk may both rage and tear."

The " Sheep " was the Queen's pet name for Hatton, that " niggardly rascally sheep-biter," hated of Sir Toby Belch; and the " boar," of course, is the blue boar of the Oxford crest—Oxford himself, in the comedy, being that other bitter opponent of Malvolio, namely the Lady Olivia's " allowed fool " and " corrupter of words," Feste—privileged nobleman-clown, singing in his gilded cage, the court, and using, with devastating effect, upon rival or hostile courtiers, his deadly tusk, or tongue.

Catholic or Protestant?—that is still, for many, the predominant question. The doleful peal of St. Bartholomew may well have drawn even young Oxford, for a while, closer than ever before, or afterwards, to that stalwart of the Protestant faith, his father-in-law, Burleigh; and St. Bartholomew, it may be, seconded somewhat the last efforts of his Puritan uncle, Arthur Golding, to draw his beloved erstwhile pupil back towards the narrow path of Calvinism, by dedication to him, as "greater things" than Conquests, Common Weals and Chivalry, "true Religion, true Godlinesse, true Virtue." Golding's efforts, however, were made in vain; for already at the young courtier's heart-strings—precisely as, some two hundred and fifty years later, in the case of another poet-peer, Lord Byron[1]—were pulling, not these aridly insoluble religious problems, but two other forces equally conflicting, yet far more hopeful and attractive—letters, and the call of active service abroad. Again and again, during this year 1572, Oxford is pressing his father-in-law; "If there be any service to be done abroad, I had rather serve there than at home, where yet some honour were to be got," and especially, "if there be any setting forth to sea, to which service I bear most affection." But in any event, whether by land or water, let it be some active service, "in Defence of his Prince and Country."

Not yet awhile, however, was the Earl to be released from the empty and tedious trivialities of court-life and royal attendance; perhaps because the Queen, with good cause, did not yet sufficiently trust her young ward's discretion, or, possibly, for a more personal reason, hinted at in Gilbert Talbot's letter to his father, the Earl of Shrewsbury; "The queen's Majesty delighteth more in his (Oxford's) personage and his dancing and his valiantness than any other. If it were not for his fickle head he would pass any of them shortly."

No whit less significant is the sequel:

"My lady Burghley has declared herself, as it were,

---

[1] The analogies of birth, circumstance, character, genius, and career between George, Lord Byron, and Edward de Vere as "Shakespeare" are surprisingly close.

jealous, which is come to the queen's ear: whereat she hath been not a little offended with her, but now she is reconciled again. At all these love matters my Lord Treasurer winketh, and will not meddle in any way."

My Lord Treasurer might wink and wag his head, and my Lord Treasurer's lady wax jealously spiteful, over the gallantries of their exalted son-in-law; but the fact, nevertheless, is of great import to our story; for I am convinced that a passionate love-affair, mutual or one sided, quasi-actual, upon de Vere's part, it may be, or, perhaps, merely imagined or pretended, was already, in this year 1572, kindling itself between the Queen and her Great Chamberlain, and was later, as we shall see, to exercise a profound effect upon Oxford's destiny, and noticeably to colour the Shakesperean plays. Meanwhile, inexorably denied any much coveted foreign adventure, whether upon sea or land, he turned, in fulfilment of God's high pleasure, and for the world's inestimable benefit, towards the ruling passion of his life, literature.

The third and fourth decades of the sixteenth century had produced, in particular, two books fated to exercise powerful influence upon the aristocracies of that day. These were *The Courtier*, by Baldassare Castiglione, an Italian statesman and man-of-letters, published at Venice in 1528; and *The Prince*, by Machiavelli, which appeared in 1532. This last, modernistic in tendency, absolving, as it did, the state from all curbs of moral law; and openly advocating force and fraud as legitimate, and even essential, instruments of government, could not greatly appeal to a mind steeped, as Oxford's was, in the romantic cast of mediaeval chivalry, and the æsthetic idealism of the Renaissance. But in *The Courtier*, which with equal propriety might also have been entitled *The Prince*—since Lord Julian therein makes interchangeable the courtier-prince and the princely courtier—all de Vere's own personal ideals of princely behaviours found perfect expression. The book, quite evidently, delighted him; and when, in 1572, his former tutor, Bartholomew Clerke, translated Castiglione's work from Italian into Latin, the Earl contributed, in the same language, a preface which, as Capt. Ward has phrased it, "seems to have been his first serious incursion into literature," and which, since it expresses literary ideals almost every phrase of which finds perfect expression in the plays of " Shakespeare," we will borrow from thus freely here.

"For what more difficult, more noble or more magnificent task has anyone ever undertaken than our author Castiglione who has drawn for us the figure and model of a courtier ... a portrait which we shall recognize as that of the highest and most perfect type of man. And so, although nature herself has made nothing perfect in every detail, yet the manners of men exceed in dignity that with which nature has endowed them; and he who surpasses others has here surpassed himself, and has even outdone nature which by no one has ever been surpassed ...

"I will say nothing of the fitness and the excellence with which he has depicted the beauty of chivalry in the noblest persons. Nor will I refer to his delineations in the case of those persons who cannot be Courtiers, when he alludes to some notable defect, or to some ridiculous character, or to some deformity of appearance. Whatever is heard in the mouths of men, in casual talk and in society ... that he has set down in so natural a manner that it seems to be acted before our very eyes.

"Again to the credit of the translator of so great a work a writer too who is no mean orator, must be added a new glory of language. ... All this my good friend Clerke has done, combining exceptional genius with wonderful eloquence. For he has resuscitated that dormant quality of fluent discourse ... For this reason he deserves all the more honour, because that to great subjects ... he has applied the greatest lights and ornaments.

"For who is clearer in his use of words? Or richer in the dignity of his sentences? Or who can conform to the variety of circumstances with greater art? If weighty matters are under consideration, he unfolds his theme in a solemn and majestic rhythm; if the subject is familiar and facetious, he makes use of words that are witty and amusing. When therefore he writes with precise and well chosen words, with skilfully constructed and crystal-clear sentences, and with every art of dignified rhetoric, it cannot be but some noble quality should be felt to proceed from the work.

"Lastly, if the noblest attributes of the wisest Princes, the safest protection of a flourishing commonwealth ... in the opinion of all continually encompass her (Queen Elizabeth) around; surely to obtain the protection of that authority, to strengthen it with gifts, and to mark it with the superscription of her name, is a work which, while worthy of all monarchs, is most worthy of our own queen, to whom all alone is due all the praise of all the Muses and all the glory of literature."

It is surely undeniable that every one of these ideals,

including naturalness, the "acting before our very eyes" of the deformities or notable defects of persons, ridiculous or otherwise, who can, or cannot, be perfect courtiers; the outdoing or surpassing of nature, in the presentment of the loftiest or most perfect types of princely men, is wholly realized in the characters of the Shakesperean plays, from Lear and Hamlet, down to Falstaff and Armado; no less so than are the further ideals of adding a "new glory of language" to our literature, "combining exceptional genius with wonderful eloquence," and resuscitating "that dormant quality of fluent discourse," while reserving for weightier themes, such a "solemn and majestic rhythm" as we find in the most exalted and transcendent passages of *Macbeth*. Even the "protector of that (royal) authority," the Queen herself, "to whom alone is due all the praise of all the Muses, and all the glory of literature," finds its counterpart in the royal, though secret, authority and reward, under which, as we shall see, the Shakesperean plays were passed on, from the court to the country.

The already accomplished skill wherewith, in this preface to *The Courtier* the young Earl adumbrates, thus early, the exact method, scope, and aim of his life's work to be, did not pass unnoticed. The preface was reprinted in all subsequent editions of Clerke's translation, and was referred to, six years later, by Gabriel Harvey, as witnessing "how greatly thou dost excel in letters."

That the text of Castiglione's *The Courtier* suggested ideas to Shakespeare is, of course, no new theory of my own. Dr. Mary A. Scott, in her *Book of the Courtyer*

(1901) supposed that the misogynist, L. Gaspar Pallavicino and the Lady Emilia, with whom he spars, suggested Benedick and Beatrice in *Much Ado About Nothing*; while Mr. Drayton Henderson, in his " Note on Castiglione," in the Everyman edition of that work, echoes the same idea. These conclusions are very suggestive; for although we cannot point, with absolute certainty, to the historic original of Beatrice, upholders of the Oxford theory of authorship are generally agreed that Benedick is de Vere himself: and when we further remember that, whoever " Shakespeare " may have been, he is, by common consent, in great measure Hamlet, Mr. Henderson's conclusions, concerning Castiglione's connexion with the Prince of Denmark, put on a peculiar pertinence.

> " We may even venture to say, if a trifle hyperbolically, that without Castiglione we should not have Hamlet. The ideal of the courtier, scholar, soldier developed first in Italy, and perfected in the narrative of Il Cortegiano was Castiglione's gift to the world . . . Hamlet is the high exemplar of it in our literature."

The courtier's, soldier's, scholar's eye, tongue, sword.

> " According to Bradley . . . Hamlet . . . is almost paralysed by the shock arising from his mother's hasty and dishonourable second marriage. From what was he paralysed?—From the ideal of courtiership; and especially from that phase of it which regarded women as the inspiration and mainstay of courtliness. He believed that beauty and goodness were one . . . He was 'the Courtier,' he was *the* Prince. . . . . Hamlet, in addition to the endowments of physical strength, courage, and comeliness, and

to the acquirement of skill in fence and the like . . . adds certain characteristics which are purely of Castiglione's school. He is a scholar—of Wittenberg University—much given to the classics. He knows how to use puns and jests, is a master of the retort courteous and the retort discourteous, and can twist words into whatever ironies he will. . . . He is a passionate friend . . . . He is the 'sweet prince' through most of his life. But he is capable of violence, of that dramatic sort which Castiglione advises. . . . He dresses his part. 'Customary suits of solemn black' are not mourning garments only. They are what Castiglione recommends for the Courtier's ordinary wear. . . . For peace, 'methinks a black colour hath a better grace in garments than any other.' He is a musician. At least he fingers a pipe as though accustomed to its stops and ventages. . . . More than musician he is potentially painter. He plays with cloud shapes as no other of Shakespeare's heroes does, except Antony. He regards the external world with that appreciation of line, form, mass, chiaroscuro, without which Castiglione says, man cannot be great. 'And in very deed who so esteemeth not this art (of painting) is, to my seeming, far wide from all reason.' The succeeding words in praise of the beauty of the earth should be compared with Hamlet's 'This most excellent canopy the air,' and Hamlet's celebration of the masterpiece man, with such passages from *The Courtier* as that beginning, 'Think now of the shape of man' . . . Hamlet's manner of speech, the range of his vocabulary, his freedom and dignity of utterance, are what we should expect . . . from the suggestions in *The Courtier*. All his doings are, besides, marked by that 'certain recklessness' or nonchalance which is Castigilone's hall mark of gentility. But it is not only Shakespeare's Hamlet that seems to follow Castiglione. Shakespeare himself does so."

Many more personal instances can be adduced, in respect to Hamlet, and also a whole sequence of ideas, that are lifted, I think, straight from Castiglione into the Beatrice and Benedick scenes of *Much Ado About Nothing*, as any intelligent reader of the play, and of the book, can see, in a moment, for himself. I will pass on, therefore, merely mentioning, by the way, Thomas Twyne's dedication to the Earl, in 1573, of his English version of Humphrey Lhuyd's *Breviary of Britain*, wherein, expressing a general English hope that the young Earl would " become the chiefest stay of this your commonwealth and country," the translator uses, concerning his patron, a phrase very suggestive of the words of Claudius to Hamlet:

Our chiefest courtier, cousin and our son.

It was during this same crucial year, 1573—which seems definitely to have turned Oxford's mind towards literature; probably, at first, as a mere distraction from the tedium of court life—that the Earl determined to publish, against its author's expressed wish, an English translation of *Cardanus Comfort*, done by his friend Thomas Bedingfield, a gentleman pensioner of the Queen, and one of the Defenders opposed to Oxford in the tournament of 1571—prefacing the book with a letter and a poem, from the former of which I will presently quote. This piece of Elizabethan prose is one of the most gracious that even those days of exquisite writing have bequeathed to us, from the hand of a great nobleman, to a worthy commoner. Thus, in brief, Lord Oxford excuses himself, to his diffident friend.

"I do confess the affections that I have always borne toward you could move me not a little. But when I had thoroughly considered in my mind, of sundry and diverse arguments, whether it were best to obey mine affections, or the merit of your studies: at the length I determined it were better to deny your unlawful request than to grant or to condescend to the concealment of so worthy a work. Whereas you have been profited in the translating, so many may reap knowledge by the reading of the same that shall comfort the afflicted, confirm the doubtful, encourage the coward, and lift up the base-minded man to achieve to any true sum or grade of virtue, whereto ought only the noble thoughts of men to be inclined.

"And because, next to the sacred letters of divinity, nothing doth persuade the same more than philosophy, of which your book is plentifully stored, I thought myself to commit an unpardonable error to have murdered the same in the waste bottom of my chests, and better I thought it were to displease one than to displease many: further considering so little a trifle cannot procure so great a breach of our amity as may not with a little persuasion of reason be repaired again. . . . What doth avail the tree unless it yield fruit unto another? What doth avail the vine unless another delighteth in the grape? What doth avail the rose unless another took pleasure in the smell? . . . So you being sick of so much doubt in your own proceedings . . . are desirous to bury and insevill your works in the grave of oblivion . . . yet I as one that is willing to salve so great an inconvenience, am nothing dainty to deny your request ... for in your lifetime I shall erect you such a monument that, as I say ... you shall see how noble a shadow of your virtuous life shall after remain.

"Thus earnestly desiring you in this request of mine (as I would yield to you in a great many) not to repugn the setting forth of your own proper studies, I bid you farewell. From my new country Muses of Wivenhoe ....

"your loving and assured friend
"E. Oxenford."

No reader, I think, sensitive to nobility of character, and grace of literary style, will withhold admiration from this page of self-excuse; with its friendship that never condescends, its intimacy that is never familiar, its persuasive logic, its harmonious rhythms, its gentle and compelling charm. Such qualities alone are enough to make the Bedingfield letter memorable always to lovers of beauty; and who, moreover, with the ideals of *The Courtier* still in mind, will deny, any more than in the earlier case, the mental affinities of its writer with Hamlet. Here, surely, speaks the veridical Prince of Denmark, though the connexion be but subtly discernible whereas connexion here with Shakespeare's Sonnets is, indisputably, verbal and direct. Compare, for example, Oxford's, "an unpardonable error to have murdered the same in the waste bottom of my *chests*," followed by the words, "considering so little a *trifle*," and "a mass of *gold*," with 48 and 65:

Shall time's best jewel from *time's chest* lie hid?

But thou, to whom thy *jewels trifles* are,
Most worthy comfort ...

and it will be seen that thought and phrasing, of letter and sonnets, are almost identical—" chest," " gold " (jewels), " trifle," and " comfort " (*Cardanus Comfort*) being common to both writings.

Such facts, surely, are immensely meaningful ; yet the parallels do not end here ; for Sonnet 94 :

> The summer's flower is to the summer sweet,
> Though to itself it only live and die—

is just a variant of the above-quoted line from the letter, concerning the scent of roses ; " What doth avail the rose unless another took pleasure in the smell."

Turning now to a comedy, *Much Ado About Nothing*, wherein, as we have seen, Shakespeare uses material from *The Courtier* for Benedick, who stands probably for Oxford himself, we read, in V, ii :

> If a man do not *erect* in this age *his own tomb* ere he dies, he shall *live no longer in monument* than the bell rings—

words that have appeared thus in the Bedingfield letter :

> By *erecting* then of *tombs* . . . make we them *live* as it were again *through their monument*. . . . But with me behold it happeneth far better : for in your lifetime I shall erect you such a monument.

Once more the thought and its terminology—" erect," " tomb," " monument," are identical in both passages. " Shakespeare," even thus early, is practising a habit that will become lifelong, of borrowing from himself. There remains to be considered, in this letter, one more important and interesting analogy, which is, that here, as early even as 1573, in this his first glow of literary impulse, the Earl was already concerning himself though, in this instance, upon another's behalf—with the problem—unavoidable by an Elizabethan author of the courtier-class—whether, by declining to publish, or by publishing anonymously, or under a pseudonym, it were better "to bury and insevill your works in the grave of oblivion," or whether, "knowing the discommodities that shall redound to yourself thereby," it were best, by printing them, "to erect a monument for posterity." The plan finally adopted by the Earl was, as we shall see, to delay publication for many years, before doing so under a pseudonym which, however, he made transparent by the insertion of a thousand clues, some of which this book, among many others, brings to light. Already, indeed, this remarkable fact emerges, that, through many subjects which we have considered or shall be considering, there runs recognizably, as a common theme, this deliberate concealment of personal identity, or of individual character. Prince Hamlet dons "an antic disposition"; Prince Henry—who is again Oxford—disguises himself as a "drawer," and bids Falstaff "stand for me," while "I play my father," and both make allusions to their temporary mental metamorphosis.

Here let the mention of Prince Hal introduce a play that touches upon our story—*The Famous Victories of Henry V*, a crude history-drama, generally supposed to have been drawn from Holinshed's *Chronicles*, first published in 1578, but now shown, by Capt. Ward[1], to have come, by way of Holinshed, from an earlier Chronicler, Hall, who published his book in 1548. This important discovery cleared the way, at once, for a new hypothesis—

[1] *Review of English Studies.*

namely, that the play was first written before, not after, the publication of Holinshed in 1578. Capt. Ward's next step was to notice that, in defiance of history, Edward de Vere's ancestor, Richard, the 11th Earl of Oxford, though mentioned once only by Holinshed, and twice by Hall, is allotted, in the play, no less than eighteen speeches—more than are given to any other character, excepting only the two kings, and the Lord Chief Justice. Oxford, moreover, is the nobleman entrusted by Henry V with charge over, and protection of, the palisade of stakes erected against the French cavalry at Agincourt.

Now is it not a very curious and significant thing that the author of the *Victories* should thus, with complete disregard of historic fact, "write up" the 11th Earl of Oxford, who fought at Agincourt? Certainly; but this fact is stranger still—that in scenes one and four of the old play, on 20 May, in "the fourteenth yeare of the raigne of our soveraigne Lord King Henry the fourth," Prince Hal and three of his wild companions are recorded to have ambushed and robbed, at Gads Hill, on the Rochester Road, in Kent, two of King Henry IV's Receivers, on their way to the Exchequer, when, as a matter of plain fact, there was no such date as a 20th of May in the fourteenth year of that king, since that year under the old style, terminated with the king's passing, on 20 March, 1413.

What is the answer? Obviously this, that the author of *The Famous Victories of Henry V* must have been thinking of an incident that occurred, not in Henry IV's reign, but in Queen Elizabeth's; and it is historically true that, in May 1573—the very year in Oxford's life which, as we have seen, is marked by these first literary activities—at that same spot, Gads Hill, upon the road to Rochester, as we have seen—an incident took place precisely similar to that recorded in the play, when two servants of Oxford's own father-in-law, Lord Treasurer Burleigh, were shot at by "thre of my L. of oxenforde's men."

When therefore we find that in *The Famous Victories of Henry V*, a former Earl of Oxford is, of set purpose, magnified out of all historic actuality; and that an incident of May 1573, is slipped back to May 1413, wherein, apart from date, the change is merely from the King's servants, and the King's son, to the Lord High Treasurer's (Burleigh's) servants, and his son-in-law, Edward de Vere—what other inferences can we draw, except that the author of *The Famous Victories of Henry V* was either the young Earl of Oxford himself, or some scribe, under his patronage, glorifying therein de Vere's own ancient and noble house, and inserting into this patently immature work, a topical incident from Oxford's own immediate family-story, which happened when the Earl was twenty-three years old, and not long before he first conceived his play, probably in the form of a court masque! The sequel we shall see in a few moments.

Il Cortegiano, with his alluring laudation of Italy, as soul and centre of European culture; and the large rumours from the world without, ever floating through the galleries of Whitehall, are augmenting de Vere's inward urge towards foreign travel; yet never can he wring the necessary permission from reluctant guardian or Queen. It is always "too young," and "next year," until which distant future he must continue to "dance attendance upon a smock," and neither wear nor wield any sword, save that court-weapon in which, for the last ten years, he has been dancing his way into the royal lady's favour. Ever hot-headed, impetuous, he can endure it no longer. Already young de Vere is whispering in Lord Seymour's ear; "By heaven, I'll steal away"; and gets his answer, "There's honour in the theft."[1]

Loud was the buzz of talk throughout the court-circles of London, when, in July 1574, the news reached Walsingham that "My Lord of Oxford and Lord Seymour are fled out of England, and passed by Bruges to Brussels," in which city the Earl of Westmorland, attainted for complicity in the rebellion of 1569, was still in exile! What! has the boy turned Catholic then, and traitor? Jubilation among the Romans: wrath and dismay among loyal Protestants. Burleigh, however, did not panic. Writing to Oxford's friend, Sussex, the Lord Treasurer showed that he knew his man:

> "My Lord, howsoever my lord of Oxford be for his own part (in) matters of thrift inconsiderate, I dare avow him to be resolute in dutifulness to the queen and his country."

Burleigh proved to be right; for when the enraged Queen at once despatched Thomas Bedingfield, with orders to bring his friend home, upon the instant, the translator of *Cardanus Comfort*—the philosophy of which de Vere may have found use for on the occasion—brought the truant Earl back within a fortnight; when, upon making full submission, he was, by 7 August, wholly reconciled with the Queen, "restored to Her Majesty's

---

[1] The words in this paragraph in inverted commas are all spoken by, of, or to, Bertram (Oxford) in *All's Well that End's Well*.

favour," and pardoned for his grievous "contempt," in going without licence overseas.

Here, following Capt. Ward, we come upon a very plausible, and interesting, sequel, which is this, that the wayward young nobleman, having made his royal peace, proceeded, in his own fashion, to offer further and final amends, when, on the following Christmas day, which opened the dramatic season at court, he presented, before the Queen, his newly written *Famous Victories of Henry V*, wherein he portrayed himself as Prince Hal, in the Gads Hill escapade of 1573; the prince's subsequent repentance and reconciliation with the king, and the somewhat hazardous promise, for the future, of irreproachable and valorous life, being dramatic means of pointing the obvious moral to his royal mistress and Queen. Already it would seem, Elizabeth's Lord Great Chamberlain is becoming her court dramatist. Before long he will make use of this truant adventure, delivering it, in detail—

"both in time,
Form of the thing, each word made true and good"—

as a Shakesperean comedy, of which the swifter-minded among my readers will, assuredly, already have guessed the title, *All's Well that Ends Well*.

CHAPTER THREE

THE BLESSED HAPPY TRAVAILER: 1575–1576

Portraits of De Vere and "Shakespeare"—Travels in France and Italy—De Vere the Traveller, and Harvey's "Speculum Tuscanismi"—Rome and the Jubilee of 1575—De Vere returns to London—The Crisis of 1576—Breach with Burleigh and Anne Cecil—Its Causes—Links with Hamlet and Ophelia.

ALL'S Well that Ends Well, indeed; but, as we know from a letter in the Domestic State Papers, "The desire of travel is not yet quenched in him"; and, for months afterwards, if Charles Arundel—no very truthful witness—be not altogether lying, the Earl, during convivial evenings with his cousins, as also, no doubt, in that more bohemian and literary company referred to by Lord Burleigh as his son-in-law's "lewd friends," would harp at length upon that subject, prating vaingloriously of those valiant deeds in Flanders, under the Duke of Alva, so unkindly put an end to by royal behest, when "Master Bedingfield, as the devil would have it, came in upon his swift post horse, and called him from this service by Her Majesty's letters, being the greatest disgrace any such general received."[1]

The thing is likely enough. De Vere, in his cups, must have been facile, even to fecundity, in *Traveller's Tales*; and "The Traveller," in fact, is to be one of the names by which contemporary London will later pseudonyse the mature "Shakespeare."

[1] *State Papers Dom. Add. Eliz.* Vol. 27 A. Papers relating to Lord Henry Howard: Charles Arundel, (1580–1581).

The coming year, however, was at last to provide fulfilment of his unsatisfied longing; for, whether as an act of faith in the implied promise of *The Famous Victories of Henry V*, or to silence an importunate and biting tongue, the Queen granted him his desire, and his licence; so that, the necessary family arrangements having been made, including some provision for the payment of his debts, which were formidable—Oxford, having taken his leave of the Court, is free now to start for Paris, accompanied by a retinue of " two gentlemen, two grooms, one payend, a harbinger, a housekeeper, and a trenchman."

In the French capital, where he stayed for some time, Valentine Dale, the English Ambassador, presented the Earl to King Henry III and his Queen. When the King asked Dale whether the Earl was married, and heard that he had "a fair lady," the royal comment was, "Il a donc ce un beau couple." One after another, de Vere was making acquaintance with that sinister Medici-Valois group, who are to figure so largely in the plays.

It was, probably, during this stay in Paris, at the age of twenty-five years, that Oxford's portrait was painted by a Flemish artist, concerning whom Dale wrote to Burleigh:

> "God send him (Oxford) a Raphael always in his company, which I trust he verily so hath. . . . If the skill of the painter here be liked, I suggest he would be induced to come thither, for he is a Fleming and liketh not overwell of his entertainment here."

Oxford, apparently, sent the picture direct to his Countess with a further present of two horses, and its reproduction

THE BLESSED HAPPY TRAVAILER

in this book[1] gives the reader opportunity to challenge or endorse King Henry's favourable opinion of the original. It reveals, at a glance, an unusually sensitive face; so feminine in expression as to account, at once, for the charge of womanishness, which is one of the stock criticisms to be levelled against Oxford by Harvey, Jonson, Chapman, and others.

The picture in question, now the property of the Duke of Portland, and known as the Welbeck portrait, is, I think, not the only portrait of de Vere painted when he was a young man. There exists another, painted at the age of twenty-four, and known as the Grafton portrait, not of Oxford, but of " Shakespeare," and strongly resembling the Welbeck picture, as a comparison of the pair will show. This Grafton portrait, now in the John Ryland's Library at Manchester, was originally hung, it would seem, in Grafton House, Northamptonshire, prior to the capture and burning of that mansion by the Parliamentary troops in 1643. It is painted upon wood, as portraits of the fifteen-seventies often were, and is thus described by Mr. Thomas Kay, in his account of the picture, written in 1915. " The collar and dress, which latter is a slashed doublet, is of an elegant and sumptuous quality, but rather bizarre," which is exactly what we should expect of Oxford, whose attire always verged upon the fanastic—but should certainly not look for in the young man from Stratford, who, at the age of twenty-four, had been living only for a year or two in London—and at a period when all men dressed, just as clergymen or sailors do to-day, according to their station in life!

All this is remarkable enough; but stranger still is

[1] Facing title page.

the fact, that the Grafton portrait, besides its obvious resemblance to the Welbeck portrait of de Vere, recalls also the "Droeshout" portrait of "Shakespeare." Further, as Mr. Looney has pointed out, beneath the four of the age (twenty four) upon the Grafton portrait, there had apparently been a three, and under the eight, it would seem, another three; to controvert both of which alleged alterations, authorities have been called in; and very significantly so, when we remember that, as the Earl of Oxford would be twenty-three in 1573—these are two out of the three precise alterations necessary to make the age and date, of a portrait of de Vere, fit in with the particulars concerning Will Shakspere of Stratford.[1]

Again, Mr. Kay holds that the style of the Grafton picture is "allied to Zuccaro's early manner"—an interesting opinion, when we remind ourselves that, if the portrait shows him as twenty-four years of age, and not twenty-three, the resulting year, 1574, is precisely that during which London was visited by Zuccaro, to whom also is attributed the "Bath" Shakespeare, which again I take to be a portrait of the Earl of Oxford. Zuccaro, moreover, was working, in 1575, at Florence, where also Oxford will be found during that same year. I cannot here enter fully into this immensely important question of the Oxford-Shakespeare portraits; but my readers will note that already, by the mid fifteen-seventies, portraits of, or closely resembling, de Vere in his twenties, are already linking themselves with the "Shakespeare" that is to be; my own conclusion being that the remarkable

[1] The "Ashbourne" portrait of Shakespeare-Oxford, as we shall see (p. 328), provides a precisely identical example of the manipulation of dates to make it fit in with the Stratford authorship.

scarcity of portraits of the Earl of Oxford, having regard to his importance and position, is accounted for by their mysterious transference—sometimes with slight alteration and manipulation of age, date, and even of appearance—to fit in with an ascription of the plays to the Stratford actor.

We left Oxford in France; and must now follow him, very briefly, into Germany and Italy, because, though the results of this tour are vitally important, in their effects upon Oxford's subsequent work, we know, unfortunately, but little of the journey itself.

From Paris, Oxford went to Strasburg, where he visited Sturmius, the *Rector Perpetuus* of Strasburg University, an institution famous then and now, as a centre of learning in western Europe. On April 26, 1575, in the company of Ralph Hopton, a son of the Lieutenant of the Tower, he left Strasburg for Padua; this, I suppose, being the journey referred to by George Chapman, when, in his tragedy, *The Revenge of Bussy*, which is a counterblast to *The Revenge of Hamlet*,[1] teeming with attacks upon Shakespeare—he set among obvious comments upon, and borrowings from, Hamlet these words in the mouth of Clermont d'Ambois, who is Chapman's version of the Prince of Denmark:

> "I overtook coming from Italy,
> In Germany, a great and famous Earl
> Of England, the most goodly fashion'd man
> I ever saw; from head to foot in form
> Rare and most absolute; he had a face
> Like one of the most ancient honour'd Romans,
> From whence his noblest family was derived;
> He was besides of spirit passing great,

---

[1] See my *Shakespeare and Chapman as Topical Dramatists*, Chapter VII.

> Valiant, and learn'd, and liberal as the sun,
> Spoke and writ sweetly, or of learned subjects,
> Or of the discipline of public weals;
> And 'twas the Earl of Oxford."

By September the Earl had reached Venice, where he was "grieved with a fever," and received news that, on July 2, the Countess, his wife, had given birth to a daughter. In a letter to Burleigh, after mentioning his illness, he adds:

> "For my liking of Italy, my Lord, I am glad to have seen it, and I care not ever to see it any more, unless it be to serve my prince and country.... I thought to have seen Spain but by Italy I guess the worst.

This "worst," I think, is a word dictated to the Earl, not by his sober opinion of Italy, which, beyond question, greatly impressed and influenced him, but by sickness— including, perhaps, a little home-sickness, and the black mood induced by the financial troubles and difficulties, that followed him wheresoever he went. He writes to Burleigh, September 24:

> "By reason of great charges of travel and sickness I have taken up of Master Baptiste Nigrone five hundred crowns ... hoping by this time my money which is made of the sale of my land is all come in."

Whether it had "all come in," I know not; but this is certain, that out of the fifty-six separate sales of his lands, which Oxford effected between 1572 and 1592, no less than six were made during this period of foreign travel; these sales, quite certainly, being those referred to by Rosalind, when, in *As You Like It*, IV, 1, she chaffs that mournful traveller, Jaques, who, with Touchstone as a composite, is Oxford himself:

> *Jaqu.* The sundry contemplation of my travels, in which my often rumination wraps me in a most humorous sadness.
> *Rosa.* A traveller! By my faith, you have great reason to be sad. I fear you have sold your own lands to see other men's; then, to have seen much, and to have nothing, is to have rich eyes and poor hands.
> *Jaqu.* Yes, I have gained my experience.
> *Rosa.* And your experience makes you sad ... and to travel for it too! ... Farewell, Monsieur Traveller; look you lisp and wear strange suits; disable all the benefits of your own country; be out of love with your nativity, and almost chide God for making you that countenance you are; or I will scarce think you have swam in a gondola.

All this, even, probably, to the lisp, is pure Oxford, from first to last. Gabriel Harvey likewise chaffs this " passing singular odd man," the " Travailer," in *Speculum Tuscanismi;* and Jonson, in *Cynthia's Revels*, I, i, and elsewhere, again and again, mocks at Oxford-Shakespeare as " Amorphus, or the deformed, a traveller that hath drunk of the fountain," as all readers of my earlier books well know.[1] " The Traveller," indeed, seems to have been one of the familiar names by which Oxford, after his return to London, was known.

Widely scattered throughout this Italian journey of his are easily traceable links with the Shakesperean plays. For instance, in that letter to Burleigh, written shortly before the Earl's arrival in Padua, we have just

---

[1] *Oxford-Shakespeare Case Corroborated*, Chapter III.

read of a borrowing from "Master Baptiste Nigrone five hundred crowns"; and straightway are reminded of *The Taming of the Shrew*, a comedy much concerned with crowns, and with one Baptista therein, a rich gentleman of Padua, who is father to Katharina, just as Burleigh is father to Oxford's first wife. Of *Two Gentlemen of Verona*, also, we shall have cause to speak in due place.

The needful cash being, at last, forthcoming, Oxford left Padua for Florence, the Tuscan capital and home of the Medicis, who, with their Valois connexions, are to loom large in the plays; and, despite the interminable financial difficulties, necessitating yet further sales of land, he determines to continue his travels, even though it be at the price of Burleigh's friendship—"*Ut nulla sit inter nos amicitia.*"

January 1576 finds the Earl in Sienna, where, in 1929, I heard directly of an individual, then iving in that city, who, apparently, claims to be descended from Oxford, and to possess a ring, with the de Vere arms upon it! For the next three months, we lose sight of Oxford while —as I think probable, though it cannot be proved—he visited, as we shall see, and was greatly impressed by, Rome, more especially so because the eternal city was in Jubilee in the year 1575. Jubilees, in the Roman Catholic Church, are held every twenty-five years; and it was probably to this one, and to the following one in 1600, that Jonson refers, when in the second act of *Every Man Out of His Humour*, first acted in 1599, he makes Puntarvolo-Oxford say:—"I do intend this year of Jubilee (1600) coming on to travel." Puntarvolo refers, immediately afterwards, to a projected visit to "The Turks' Court in Constantinople," the very court to which, when the Earl was in Paris, King Henry III had given him letters of recommendation. To Turkey, however, de Vere, it seems, did not go; though he roamed as far as Sicily, where Master Gunner Edward Webbe gives us a vivid and characteristic picture of him, thus aggressively championing his queen:

"One thing did greatly comfort me which I saw long since in Sicilia in the city of Palermo, a thing worthy of memory, where the Right Honourable the Earl of Oxford, a famous man of Chivalry, at what time he travelled into foreign countries, being then personally present, made there a challenge against all manner of persons whatsoever, and at all manner of weapons, Tournaments, Barriers, with horse and armour, to fight a combat with any whatsoever in the defence of his Prince and Country. For which he was very highly commended, and yet no man durst be so hardy to encounter with him, so that all Italy over he is acknowledged the only Chevalier and Nobleman of England."

This chivalric patriotism is wholly characteristic of the courtly traveller of 1576; and, in connexion with what is to come, we must remember that, though Palermo is not mentioned in the plays, the more ancient and historic capital of Sicily, "quadruplices Syracusa," or Syracuse, is repeatedly referred to, in that early farce, *The Comedy of Errors*, which he probably drafted at this time. *A Winter's Tale*, also, is set partly in Sicily, and Illyria of *Twelfth Night* was across the Adriatic, almost upon the opposite shore.

From Sicily, by way of Lyons, the Earl returned to Paris at the end of March, where we leave him, apparently in good spirits, while the story returns, for a time, to London, where, it will be remembered, Lady Oxford had given birth to a daughter, on 2 July, 1575, to he delight of Oxford himself, then in Venice, and of the English Queen. Elizabeth hearing from one of her physicians, Dr. Richard Masters, at Richmond, that the Countess of Oxford was to become a mother, sprang up from her cushion, exclaiming; "It is a matter that concerneth my Lord's joy chiefly; yet I protest to God that next to them that have interest in it, there is nobody that can be more joyous of it than I am."

This was natural and womanly upon the Queen's part; and one might have supposed the expectant mother to be, at least, as pleased as was her Queen; yet the letter in which Masters communicates these news to Burleigh continues:

> "Her Majesty asked me how the young lady did bear the matter. I answered that she kept it secret four or five days from all persons and that her face was much fallen and thin with little colour, and that when she was comforted and counselled to be gladsome and so rejoice, she would cry, 'Alas, alas, how should I rejoice seeing that he that should rejoice with me is not here' ... and bemoaning her case would lament that after so long sickness of body she should enter a new grief and sorrow of mind. At this Her Majesty shewed great compassion ... and repeated my Lord of Oxford's answer to me, which he made openly in the presence chamber of Her Majesty, viz. that if she were with child it was not his. I answered that it was the common answer of lusty courtiers everywhere, so to say. ...
> Severally she (the Queen) showed herself unfeignedly to rejoice, and in great offence with my Lord of Oxford, repeating the same to my Lord of Leicester after he came to her."

THE BLESSED HAPPY TRAVAILER

Mystery, doubt, suspicion, grief, and jesting are abroad. On 3 January, 1576, Lord Burleigh writes:

> "He (Oxford) confessed to my Lord Howard that he lay not with his wife but at Hampton Court, and that the child could not be his because the child was bornin July which was not the space of twelve months."

The reasoning here is somewhat beyond me; but if the reader will bear in mind the close analogies of circumstance, situation, and character, with those of *Measure for Measure*, especially the story of Mariana, as told in that play, and also the first three acts of *A Winter's Tale*, we shall, I think, be able somewhat to fathom the inner meaning of what Capt. Ward, in his Life of the Earl, calls "The Crisis of 1576," concerning which, however, his own views have undergone modification, since the appearance of that work in 1928, and still more so since the discovery that the poems on *Loss of Good Name*, hitherto supposed to refer to these matters, and to have been written by Oxford himself, are just parodies of the episode, and of Oxford's style in versification, probably written by another courtier. The fact is, I think, that this whole business of Oxford's paternity was, from the first, and probably with malicious intent made a joke of at Court; the idea being initiated by the Earl's own remark, also first made as a stock court-jest, that, if his wife should bear him a child, in his absence, it could not be his. During de Vere's sojourn abroad, this merely flippant speech, made, be it remembered, by the Queen's most inveterate jester, was evidently repeated against him in Court—as though it had been said seriously—most probably by Lord Henry

Howard, who, with his cousin, Charles Arundel, soon to come still more prominently into our story, we have already seen, at the time of the Norfolk conspiracy, endeavouring to enrage the Queen against the Earl. Further, the charge against Conrad and Borachio, who are Arundel and Howard, that they " have belied a lady," Hero, who as we shall see, is Anne Cecil, makes their guilt in this matter practically certain.

Oxford, in Paris, hears that his name is being bandied about the precincts of Richmond Palace as that of a cuckold; and, having by this time, perhaps, wholly forgotten his previous denial of possible paternity, his ever fecund imagination begins to brood over the business, until, large already with other griefs against the Cecils, it pictures him to himself as a much wronged man, and hurries him home, in a towering rage, to sift the matter to the bottom.

Yet, all the while, behind all his rage, genuine, even to violence though it was, as the plays arising out of it demonstrably show, there lurked, I think—and Capt. Ward agrees with me—another and subtler motive; namely that—vile and humiliating to his pride though it was, to be cackled over, throughout London, as a cuckold husband—this latest villainy of Howard, or of Arundel, did, at least, give him an opportunity to get quit, once for all, with the Cecils, of whom Burleigh himself as we shall see when we reach *Measure for Measure*, has " come short of composition "—that is, of agreement in the matter of financing husband and daughter. Oxford, it must be admitted, was, at this point of his career—despite all his charm and genius—an excessively unsatisfactory and intransigeant son-in-law and husband—unstable, fickle, wayward, passionate, financially extravagant, and too overweeningly proud to overlook the fact, that—as Angelo, who stands for the unregenerated Earl, in *Measure for Measure*, tells us—his wife's reputation was publicly "disvalued in levity." He could not, and would not, live longer with a woman who was made the subject of jesting tales at Court; such, in kind at least, as that which Shakespeare tells of Mariana in his play—namely substitution, under cover of darkness, of man for man, or of woman for woman, in the marital bed. Lastly, though no courtier of them all dare breathe a hint of it, the Queen's own position relative to her Lord Great Chamberlain must not altogether be forgotten. Elizabeth, I feel positively sure, was as much in love with Oxford as she was capable of being with anyone; and if he did not reciprocate, he pretended to, just as did most other young courtiers of his day. This difficult and delicate subject we will return to later on, with the text of *Two Gentlemen of Verona* before us; meanwhile it must never be forgotten that Oxford, an idealist in his regard for women, if ever there was one, deeply loved his wife, as the plays *Hamlet*, *Troilus and Cressida*, and *Every Man Out of His Humour*—"He loves his wife well"—to name no others, will make positively certain; nor can there be any doubt that Cressid-Ophelia's "falsity"—concerning which more anon—outraged not merely the Earl's overweening personal pride, but also a far nobler phase of his character—a passionate consciousness of, and deep regard for, the potential loveliness, physical and spiritual, of the nobleman-courtier's lady.

For the moment, however, the plays that all these events foreshadow are not so much *Two Gentlemen of Verona*, nor even *Measure for Measure*, nor *All's Well that*

End's Well, but *Hamlet*, *Troilus*, and *A Winter's Tale*, the first of which, though not drafted, I think, before 1583, is now historically in the making, and may briefly be considered here. Between Hamlet's position at the court of Elsinore and Oxford's position at the court of London the analogies are inescapable: for although Oxford was not precisely a prince, he descended, as we have seen, from a long line of illustrious and quasi-royal ancestors, while his relations with Burleigh and Anne parallel closely those of Hamlet with Polonius and Ophelia. Indeed, the very name *Corambis*—by which Polonius is called in the First Quarto—would seem to be aimed, with satirical intent, directly at Burleigh's motto, *cor unum via una* [1]; and, further, the name Polonius seems to be taken straight from "Pondus," which was, apparently, a nickname for Burleigh at Elizabeth's Court. Again, Burleigh's notorious addiction to the employment of spies is adumbrated in the use of Ophelia, by Polonius, as a spy upon Hamlet; an inference which undoubtedly accounts for a part of the friction between husband and wife. There is also an obvious connexion traceable between the baseless taunts concerning the paternity of her daughter, which we have seen aimed at Anne, and the scornful-pitiful words of Hamlet to Ophelia:

> "Be thou chaste as ice, as pure as snow, thou shalt not escape calumny."

Oxford, it will be remembered, was in Paris when the news reached him, of court rumours concerning the legitimacy of his daughter. Furiously angry, he started at once for England; but, on the way, his ship was

---

[1] Implying that Polonius was less single-hearted than might be gathered from his motto.

THE BLESSED HAPPY TRAVAILER

attacked by pirates, who stole his baggage—a mischance that seems to be echoed in *Hamlet*, IV, vi—" Ere we were two days at sea a pirate of very warlike appointment gave us chase." Landing in the Thames, he was met by Burleigh and his countess, but declined to speak with them, and went, on 20 April, straight to the Queen, to whom, three days later, Burleigh made piteous appeal, in a letter of which the garrulous prolixity was, I suggest, directly parodied by his irate son-in-law, in the speeches of Polonius, concerning Hamlet, and his relations with Ophelia. Thus Burleigh, as I have cut him :

" Most sovereign lady, As I was accustomed from the beginning of my service to your Majesty until of late by the permission of your goodness and by occasion of the place wherein I serve your Majesty, to be frequently an intercessor to your Majesty or rather an immediate petitioner for myself and an intercessor for another next to myself for others to your Majesty, and therein did find your Majesty always inclinable to give me gracious audience ; so now do I find in the latter end of my years a necessary occasion to be an intercessor for another next to myself, in a *cause* godly, honest and just ; and therefore, having had proof of your Majesty's former favours in *causes* not so important, I doubt not but to find the like influence of your grace in a *cause* so near touching myself as your Majesty will conceive it doth ...

" To enter to trouble your Majesty with the circumstances of my *cause*, I mean not for sundry respects but chiefly for two ; the one is that *I am very loth to be more cumbersome to your Majesty than need shall compel me* ; the other is for that I hope in God's goodness, and for the reverence borne to your

Majesty, that success thereof may have a better end than the beginning threateneth. But *your Majesty may think my suit will be very long where I am long ere I begin it*; and *truly* most gracious sovereign lady, *it is true* that the nature of my *cause* is such as I have no pleasure to enter into it, but had rather seek means to shut it up for them to lay it openly not for lack of the soundness thereof on my part, but for the wickedness of others from whom the ground work proceedeth. . . . in the *cause* betwixt my Lord of Oxford and her (Lady Oxford), whether it be for respect of misliking in me or misdeeming of hers whereof I cannot yet know the certainty, I do avow in the presence of God and of his angels whom I do call as ministers of his ire, if in this I do utter any untruth . . . though nature will make . . . to speak favourably; yet now I have taken God and His angels to be witnesses of my writing, *I renounce nature*, and protest simply to your Majesty. I did never see in her behaviour in word or deed, nor ever could perceive by any other means, but that she hath always used herself honestly, chastely and lovingly towards him.

Compare this with Polonius' words to the King and Queen, concerning his daughter and the Prince. (II, iii.)

> My liege, and madam, to expostulate
> What majesty should be, what duty is,
> Why day is day, night night, and time is time,
> Were nothing but to waste night, day and time.
> Therefore, since brevity is the soul of wit
> And tediousness the limbs and outward flourishes,
> I will be brief. Your noble son is mad.
> Mad call I it, for, to define true madness,
> What is't but to be nothing else but mad?
> But let that go.

THE BLESSED HAPPY TRAVAILER

Queen. More matter with less art.
Polo. Madam, I swear I use no art at all.
That he is mad, 'tis *true*. 'Tis *true* 'tis pity,
And pity 'tis 'tis *true* : a foolish figure ;
But farewell it, for *I will use no art.*
Mad let us grant him then : and now remains
That we find out the *cause* of this effect,
Or rather say, the *cause* of this defect,
For this effect defective comes by *cause.*
Thus it remains and the remainder thus.
Perpend.
I have a daughter—have while she is mine—

Now if Burleigh's letter be carefully collated with Polonius's speeches, with remembrance, at the same time, of the almost identical similarities of circumstances and characters, in the two writings, no one, I submit, gifted with any sense at all of literary style, can deny, for an instant, that Polonius' lines are simply a parody of the Lord Treasurer's letter. Burleigh's epistolary style is a platitudinous, humourless, tedious, garrulous prolixity, emphasized by perpetual repetition of names and phrases ; and he is writing, remember, to a queen, concerning his own daughter's intimate relations with his son-in-law, the Queen's ward, a student, just returned from France and Italy ; while Polonius speaks also to a queen, about the queen's son, just returned from Wittenburg, concerning his own daughter, the young couple having, evidently, had intimate relations together.

Oxford, then, some seven years later, with Burleigh's letter, or a copy of it before him, ruthlessly ridicules both content and style, by making the circumstances of the play correspond most closely with historic fact, and twisting the actual phrases, and style, of the epistle into speeches only slightly more ridiculous than the original. Borrowings and parody alike are unmistakable, and undeniable.

VERE AS SHAKESPEARE—POLONIUS TO QUEEN GERTRUDE CONCERNING HAMLET AND OPHELIA	BURLEIGH TO QUEEN ELIZABETH CONCERNING OXFORD AND ANNE CECIL
Hamlet, II, ii.	
To expostulate ... what duty is, Why day is day ... Were nothing but to waste night, day and time.	*Cf.* Burleigh's preliminary time-wasting "expostulation" with its triple repetition of the word "cause."
Therefore since brevity is the soul of wit, And tediousness the limbs and outward flourishes, I will be brief.	I am very loth to be more cumbersome to your Majesty than need shall compel me ... your Majesty may think my suit will be very long when I am so long ere I begin it.
Your noble son is mad.	Burleigh probably hinted as much to the Queen. Oxford was not her son, but her ward, as Bertram (Oxford) says in *All's Well that Ends Well* " to whom I am now in ward."
Queen. More matter with *less art*.	*Truly* most gracious sovereign lady, *it is true* that the *nature* of my cause is such ....
Polon. Madam, I swear I use no art at all. That he is mad, 'tis true. 'Tis *true*	though *nature* will make me ... to speak favourably; yet now I ... *renounce*

THE BLESSED HAPPY TRAVAILER 71

'tis pity, And pity 'tis 'tis *true*, a foolish figure; But farewell it, for *I will use no art*.	*nature* and protest simply to your Majesty

One conclusion only is here possible, whether you take the parallels concerning tediousness and brevity, or the repetitions of the word true or truly; or whether you set Polonius', "Madam I swear" against Burleigh's, "I protest simply to your Majesty," or whether you take the bored Queen's request for less "art," followed by Polonius' "I will use no art," and set it against Burleigh's prolix determination—art, obviously, being beyond him—to renounce even nature! Oxford's obvious meaning is, that Burleigh and Polonius are equally ridiculous, since both were equally false and unnatural. Compare also the lines that follow:

Polo. now remains That we *find* out the *cause* of this *effect*, Or rather say, the *cause* of this *defect*, For this *effect defective* comes by *cause*	*Burl.* or rather an immediate petitioner... in a *cause* godly honest and just, and therefore having had proof of your Majesty's former favour in *causes* not so important, I doubt not but to *find* the like influence of your grace in a *cause* so nearly touching myself.

These analogies are striking as any; for here we have the old courtier saying to his queen, in the play; "Now remains that we find out the cause," and, in the letter, "I doubt not but to find the like," the word "cause," moreover, being here thrice repeated in each passage.

Again the words "touching myself" are compared with Ophelia, in I, iii, "touching my Lord Hamlet."

But we have not finished yet. In the penultimate paragraph of Burleigh's letter, occur these lines, not quoted as yet:

> "When at his (Oxford's) arrival, some doubts were cast to his acceptance of her, that innocency seemed to make her so bold as she never cast any care of things past, but wholly reposed herself with assurance to be well used of him. And ... she went to him and there missed of her expectation."

Compare those words—preceded, as they are by Burleigh's protestation that his daughter has "always used herself honestly, chastely, and lovingly towards him" (Oxford), with *Hamlet*, III, ii, wherein Ophelia coming to her prince, missed cruelly of her expectation, in hearing spoken to her such words as these:

> "Are you honest? ... If you be honest and fair your honesty should admit no discourse to your beauty ... for the power of beauty will transfer honesty from what it is to a bawd ... the time gives it proof. I did love you once.
> *Ophe.* Indeed my lord, you made me believe so ...
> *Haml.* Be thou chaste as ice, as pure as snow, thou shalt not escape calumny.

Parallels of situation and phrase are here again obvious; and lastly we find Lord Burleigh's letter terminating upon another "expostulation," concerning his service to the Queen, as being but "a piece of my duty"—words which reappear in the play as:

To *expostulate* what Majesty should be, what *duty* is.

Hamlet, alone, in my judgment, provides sufficient evidence to prove the identity of " Shakespeare." But to our story.

A thousand times Burleigh must have cursed the day, when pushed by personal ambition, and solicitude for a beloved daughter, he failed to stand to words, perhaps uttered by him in real life, as they are by Polonius in the tragedy :

Lord Hamlet is a prince out of thy star.
This must not be—

and how often, I wonder, did the lady also, who is Helena, as well as Ophelia, whisper to herself in Helena's own words :[1]

That I should love a bright particular star
And think to wed it—

Wedded, however, and more for woe than weal, they are. On 27 April Burleigh received, at last, from the hitherto resolutely silent son-in-law, a letter containing these phrases :

" Until I can better satisfy or advertise myself of some mislikes, I am not determined, as touching my wife, to accompany her. . . . Some that otherwise discontented me I will not blaze or publish until it please me. And last of all, I mean not to weary my life any more with such troubles and molestations as I have endured, nor will I, to please your lordship, only discontent myself."

His reasons, so far as I can tell, he will blaze and publish to the world in the plays, as we shall see—particularly in *All's Well that Ends Well* and *Measure for*

[1] *All's Well that Ends Well*, I, i.

Measure; and then from beneath a double disguise—that of "Shakespeare," and his two characters, Angelo and Bertram. *Troilus* and *A Winter's Tale* will dramatize the same sad story again.

Egotistical, you say? I grant you. Smouldering beneath the gentle courtesies, and the irresistible charm, of the young courtier, who, four years earlier, had written the gracious letter to his friend Bedingfield, and who, seven years later, is to write *Hamlet*, there lay, fused within his kindling genius, an overweening pride, a petulant fury, that opposition, and the crosses of a difficult world, can cause readily to flame out, whenever these are further blown upon by an imagination more vivid and fecund than any yet—for posterity's pleasure, and its possessor's misery—bestowed upon us children of men. Real or unreal, the griefs that Oxford alleged against his somewhat bewildered father-in-law, seem to have been substantially these—slowness in raising ready money for the settlement of the Earl's always formidable debts, failure to supply Anne with as large a dowry as had been promised and agreed, failure to obtain renewal of Oxford's licence to travel; with probably—by Burleigh's command—a little quiet spying, and tale-bearing, by the lady; and, lastly, a general incompatibility, arising from the fact, made perfectly clear in *Hamlet*, even though we did not know it from history, that the already ageing statesman was a puritan, bereft of any liking for, or appreciation of, art, and convinced that France and Italy, regarded by de Vere as the living homes of the renaissance, intellectual and æsthetic, were—which is partly true—haunts of iniquity and vice. The Earl, moreover, intensely resented Burleigh's openly garrulous way of handling questions, as between himself and his countess, which, as he wrote, " might have been done through private conference before, and had not needed to be the fable of the world, if you would have had the patience to have understood me."

Since when has the plain man-of-affairs " understood " the romantic artist ? Oxford, therefore, will no longer live with his wife.

> " If it standeth with your liking to receive her into your house . . . it doth very well content me : for then, as your daughter or her mothers, more than myself, you may take comfort of her."

The Earl, meanwhile, peremptorily forbade his father-in-law to bring the Countess to Court ; but after another appeal from Burleigh, in which the statesman protested that " unkindness in me towards him (Oxford) was grounded upon untrue reports of others, as I have manifestly proved them "—meaning, I suppose, Lord Henry Howard and Arundel—Oxford consented to meet Burleigh, on 12 July, and wrote to him, on the following day, he " could eft bring her (Lady Oxford) to Court, with condition that she should not come when I was present, nor at any time have speech with me . . . for always I have, and will still, prefer mine own content before others,"—all this, alas, in respect of a wife, who, whatever her failings, had certainly never been unfaithful to her husband ; since the legitimacy of the daughter, whose arrival had heralded all this domestic trouble, had never been, nor ever was, called seriously in question, or challenged in any court-of-law.

Oxford further attempted, though in vain, to nominate as his successors in the Earldom, his favourite cousins,

Francis and Horatio de Vere, afterwards famous as "the fighting Veres"—this fine pair of men being, in my judgment, the historic originals of Francisco and Horatio in *Hamlet*.

Lord and Lady Oxford did not, in fact, live together again, for some five or six years; but they seem to have been reconciled by 1581—a son, whose stay in this world was of the briefest, being born to them in 1583. That year or the next, saw, if I am right, the drafting of *Hamlet*; but, before then, there were to befall many events of equally vital import to our story, and to the shaping of the Shakesperean plays.

CHAPTER FOUR

DE VERE AS WRITER OF VERSE AND COURT COMEDY: 1577-1578

De Vere's courtly predecessors in Song; Surrey, Wyatt and Vaux—Some anthologies of the day—Oxford's Echo Song and its links with " Hamlet " and " Romeo and Juliet "—Vero Nihil Verius and de Vere Puns—De Vere's early Plays, " Comedy of Errors " and " Two Gentlemen of Verona "—Oxford as the Queen's " Allowed Fool " and " Corrupter of Words "—" Historie of the Solitary Knight " (Timon) 1577—" Titus Andronicus "—" Pericles "—Early version of " Cymbeline," 1578—Marriage of Lady Mary Vere, 1577—" The Taming of the Shrew "—Rumours of De Vere's impending Withdrawal from Court—Lady Anne and a Stratagem—" All's Well that Ends Well "—Oxford as Bertram in " All's Well that Ends Well "—" Troilus " and " A Winter's Tale " as Dramatizations of the Oxford-Anne Cecil rupture—Early version of " Love's Labour's Lost."

WE have already seen that de Vere, in 1573, perhaps wrote, or caused be written, *The Famous Victories of Henry V*, and, after his truant escapade of 1574, presented the comedy at court, as a pledge of amendment and a promise, the implication of which would be more binding still, did Lord Oxford, as is most probably the case, appear in person as the scapegrace, though now repentant, prince. There exists, however, so far as is known, no definite record of Oxford as an actor, before the year 1578, when, with the Earl of Surrey and other lords, he appeared in a masque before the Queen; but that he did play the leads in his own early comedies is, I think, most probable. Later on I shall bring evidence pointing that way. At the moment, however, we must consider the Earl, not as actor, but as poet and comedy-writer, during the fifteen-seventies.

In the last year of the preceding reign, when de Vere was in his eighth year, were published the *Songs and Sonettes* of Lord Henry Howard, late Earl of Surrey, and Oxford's uncle—a work which, as Mr. Looney has pointed out[1], was, until 1576, for nearly twenty years, almost the only volume of its kind, and likely, therefore, to be much in evidence, when young Edward, as royal ward, was passing care-free days, during the fifteen-seventies, in attendance upon the Queen at Windsor. Now the exact topographical accuracy of Shakespeare's knowledge of Windsor has been remarked upon by Hepworth Dixon and others; and it was at Windsor also that Surrey, when a boy of twelve, in 1529, had passed close upon three years, as companion to Henry VIII's natural son, Henry, Duke of Richmond, enjoying hours whose all too brief happiness is wistfully recalled in Surrey's lines, written shortly before his execution:

> " So crewell prison ! How could betyde, alas !
> As proud Wyndsour, where I, in lust and joy,
> With a king's son my childish years did passe."

Imagine then young de Vere walking the castle corridors, and the Great Park of Windsor, with his uncle's book in his hand, and his uncle's memory in mind; and, later on, putting into Slender's mouth, in the very first scene of *The Merry Wives of Windsor*:

> I had rather than forty shillings I had my book of Songs and Sonnets here—

words that are mindful both of Surrey's book, and of

---

[1] *Poems of Edward de Vere*, pp. xliv, xlv.

Philip Sidney also, who, undoubtedly, is the historic original for Slender.

Lord Surrey's, however, was not the only herald of Elizabethan lyricism. Two other pioneer volumes were the *Miscellany* published by Tottell in 1557, including poems from the pens of Lord Surrey, Sir Thomas Wyatt, and Lord Vaux; and later, in 1573, the first of the many anthologies published during Queen Elizabeth's reign, *A Hundreth Sundrie Flowres*, both of which books are linked with Oxford personally, or with the Earl as " Shakespeare "; for it is a remarkable fact that the grave-digger's song commented on by Hamlet—" Has this fellow no feeling of his business that he sings at grave-making ? "—is taken from a song—*The Aged Lover renounceth Love*—written by Lord Vaux, who was a contributor not only to Surrey's *Book of Songs and Sonnets*, in which it appeared, but also to a third pioneer anthology, *The Paradise of Dainty Devices* (1576), which contains a number of interesting parodies of Oxford's own songs. As for *A Hundreth Sundrie Flowres*, an annotated edition of which was published by Capt. B. M. Ward in 1926, this is also an anthology, made up of contributions by Oxford's aforetime friend, George Gascoigne, and also by Sir Christopher Hatton, Oxford's rival and foe, whose posy, or motto, with which he signed his work was " Si Fortunatus Infœlix " or " The Fortunate Unhappy," which is the signature of the famous forged letter, from Olivia-Elizabeth to Malvolio-Hatton, upon whom the whirligig of time, in the shape of " Shakespeare's " pen, is, at last, to " bring in his revenges."

A detailed consideration of Lord Oxford's admitted poems, some of which were probably written before the crisis of 1576, is outside the scope of this book, the central purpose of which must be narrative. They can be examined in Mr. Looney's edition, and in my earlier books upon Oxford; but I must set down enough here to show how rash and unfounded is the statement, credited to Sir Edmund Chambers in *The New York Sun*, that Oxford's songs have no connexion with Shakespeare. My answer is that in theme, mentality, and allusion, as also in verbal and metrical style, they abound with such connexions, though allowance must, of course, be made for their immaturity, when compared with the versification of the matured "Shakespeare," as exemplified, for example, in *Macbeth*, written at least a quarter of a century later. I shall content myself with quoting, in part, one crucially important lyric, the famous "Echo" song of 1576, intimately linked, once more, with *Hamlet*, as also with *Romeo and Juliet*, and crammed with those Vere echo puns which, when we reach closer contact with the plays, we shall find to be one of Oxford's chosen methods of revealing his concealed identity as author.

Verses made by the Earl of Oxforde

Sitting alone upon my thought in melancholy mood,
In sight of sea,[1] and at my back an ancient hoary wood,
I saw a fair young lady come her secret fears to wail,
Clad all in colour of a nun, and covered with a veil;
Yet (for the day was calm and clear) I might discern her face,
As one might see a damask rose hid under crystal glasse.
Three times with her soft hand, full hard on her left side she knocks,

---

[1] Oxford's country house, "Wivenhoe," is at the mouth of the Colne, not far from Colchester. The poem may have been written there.

And sigh'd so sore as might have mov'd some pity in the rocks;
From sighs and shedding amber tears into sweet song she brake,
When thus the echo answered her to every word she spake.

Anne Vavesor's Eccho

Oh Heavens! who was the first that bred in me this fever? Vere.

Who was the first that gave the wound whose fear I wear for ever? Vere.

What tyrant, Cupid, to my harm usurps thy golden quiver? Vere.

What wight first caught this heart and can from bondage it deliver? Vere.

Already the reader will be asking who was this Anne Vavasour, obviously in love with Oxford, and pursuing him with her attentions? She is a daughter of Henry Vavasour, of the ancient family of Vavasours, whose seat was at Tadcaster, Copmansthorpe, close to York, and who gave most of the stone for the building of the Minster. Further, she is to become, as we shall discover, the Juliet of *Measure for Measure*, and of the Verona tragedy; but, for our immediate purpose, she seems to be—with Anne Cecil, as chief partner—a part original of Ophelia, as the following comparisons seem conclusively to show.

OXFORD	SHAKESPEARE
I saw a fair *young lady come*, her secret *fears* to wail.	*Ophe.* He *comes* before me. *Polo.* Mad for thy love. *Ophe.* My lord, I do not know, but truly I do *fear* it. (*Ham.*, II, 1.)

Clad all in colour of a *nun*.	*Ham.*, Get thee to a *nunnery*, go. (*Ham.*, III, i.)
I might *discern her face*.	*Ophe.* He falls to such *perusal of my face*. (*Ham.*, II, i.)
As one might see a *damask rose* hid under crystal *glass*.	*Ophe.* The *rose* of the fair state. . . . *the glass* of fashion. (*Ham.*, III, i.)
Three times with her soft *hand*.	He took me by the *wrist* and *thrice*. (*Ham.*, II, i.)
And, *sighed* so sore as might have mov'd some *pity* in the rocks.	He raised a *sigh so piteous* and profound.
From sighs and shedding amber *tears*, into *sweet song* she brake.	I cannot choose but *weep*. (cf. also *Ophelia's songs* in *Ham.*, IV, v.)
Who was it first that *bred* in me this fever? Vere.	*Ham.* Would'st thou be a *breeder* of sinner? (*Ham.*, III, i.)

The verbal links revealed by the words in italic, make it quite certain, to my mind, that Anne Vavasour, who, as we shall see, was to become Oxford's mistress, stands for the less chaste side of Ophelia, and also for both the Juliets, as will appear, when we come to examine the remainder of the "Echo" poem, in the light thrown upon it by the Verona tragedy; meanwhile, since we are upon the verge of some necessary exercises in Elizabethan word-play, I would here call attention to an interesting little relic belonging to about this date, 1576, preserved among the Hatfield MSS. It is a Latin poem of ten lines, stated to have been copied from the fly-leaf of a Greek Testament, once in possession of

VERSE AND COURT COMEDY

the Countess of Oxford, and probably given to her by Oxford himself, who, as Capt. Ward thinks, may have written the lines in the Testament, upon hearing of the birth of his daughter, Elizabeth. In English they run thus:

> "Words of truth are fitting to a Vere; lies are foreign to the truth, and only true things stand fast, all else is fluctuating and comes to an end. Therefore, since thou, a Vere, art wife and mother of a Vere daughter, and seeing that thou mayest with good hope look forward to being mother of an heir of the Veres, may thy mind always glow with love of the truth, and may thy true motto be *Ever Lover of the Truth*. And that thou mayest better attain to this, pray to the Author of all Truth that his Word may teach thee; that his Spirit may nourish thy inner life. So that, thus alleviating the absent longings of thy dear husband, thou, a Vere, mayest be called the true glory of thy husband.

Now in view of the fact that the plays, as I hope to prove, reveal throughout, but especially in the early ones, this trick of disclosing identity by means of reiterated punning upon the words, Vere, Veritas, Vérité, and so forth, and of making much play with the punning family motto of the Veres, "*Vero Nihil Verius*," the above lines become very significant, and the more so if indeed written by Oxford himself—because they show that, already in 1575, he, or a relative of his, used, elsewhere than in the Echo song, the words "Ever," "Lover," "Very," and their like, as puns upon the family name; just as did Gilbert Talbot when, on 28 June, 1574 (probably), he wrote to his mother, the Countess of Salisbury, concerning "The young Earl of

Oxford of that ancient and *Very* family of the *Veres* "—so that when, as not infrequently happens, my opponents deride the suggestion that such puns can be anything other than coincidences, they are merely revealing complete ignorance of the euphuistic methods of word-play already in use in this country, some four or five years before the publication of *Euphues* early in 1579. That Oxford was about to insert identically similar puns into the two plays, which, it would seem, we owe to his travels, and to events immediately following thereupon, I will now proceed to show; the two plays in question being *The Comedy of Errors*, alluding frequently, among other topicalities, to Syracuse, from which, probably, Oxford had just come, and *Two Gentlemen of Verona*.

The first named of these—a farce comprising doubled identities, married estrangements, and ultimate reconciliation, as its theme, I take to be reminiscent in part of Oxford's misunderstandings with, and estrangements from, his own wife, and to have been first drafted about this time, but rewritten after the reconciliation of 1581-82; my theory being that the two Antipholus, and the two Dromios are simply a quadruple presentation of varying sides, and circumstances, of Oxford himself, just as Adriana and Luciana are of his wife. Even the title, *The Comedy of Errors*, I take to be topically descriptive, as are several of his titles to come, and akin, in word-play, to the closing couplet of Sonnet 116, which is one of the most elaborately punning and meaningful of them all:

> If this be error and upon me prov'd,
> I *never* writ, nor no man *ever* lov'd.

Both the words in italics I take to be deliberate **Vere**

puns.[1] The "two gentlemen," then, in the *Comedy of Errors* stand for one Vere, while in the second play, which we owe to Oxford's Italian travels, he repeats that fact in his title, *Two Gentlemen of Verona*—the last three letters spelling, approximately, the Italian word for "one"—wherein Valentine and Proteus are again Oxford himself, twice over, as is indeed openly hinted in the second, or interchangeable, Protean name (Proteus). Launce and Speed, correspondingly, also represent the comedic sides of Oxford's own character. Whether *Two Gentlemen of Verona* was, as Admiral Holland thinks, first drafted in 1576, or as Mrs. E. T. Clark believes, written three years later, at the close of 1579, cannot be definitely determined; but no one can intelligently deny that, in addition to an Italian setting, the comedy smacks strongly of events and situations of 1576. Further the opening references by Valentine to the benefits of foreign travel, and the line :

That art a votary to fond desire—

at once recall Oxford's "Desire" Poems, and his keen traveller's zest; while the pointed references to *Metamorphoses* suggest the translation from Ovid made by Oxford's uncle, Arthur Golding, in 1575. Again, the chatter concerning sheep and shepherd, and Launce's references in III, i—"she hath no teeth to bite"—are all aimed symbolically at the plays, with direct reference to Hatton, "the sheep's," letter to Queen Elizabeth of 1573, "Reserve (your favours) to the sheep, he hath no teeth to bite where the boar's (Oxford's) tusk may both raze and tear." Such allusions, "kept together

---

[1] Meaning, of course, "I, E. Ver, never wrote, nor did any one ever love E. Ver."

and put to use," are more than enough to fix the crucial date at some time in the mid fifteen-seventies. Lastly, and to conclude, as Dogberry would put it, the duologue between Valentine and Speed, at the opening of II, i.

> *Speed* (*picking up a glove*). Sir, your glove.
> *Vale.* Not mine, my gloves are on.
> *Speed.* Why, then, this may be yours, for this is but one.
> *Vale.* Ha, let me see: ay, give it me, it's mine
> Sweet ornament that decks a thing divine!
> Ah, Silvia, Silvia!—

is a patent reference to the return of Oxford from Italy with gloves for Silvia, who is Queen Elizabeth—as recorded by Stowe in his *Annals*.

> "Milliners or haberdashers had not any gloves embroidered, or trimmed with gold or silk, neither gold nor embroidered girdles nor hangers, neither could they make any costly wash or perfume; until about the 14th or 15th year of the Queen the right honourable Edward de Vere, Earl of Oxford, came from Italy and brought with him gloves, sweet bags, a perfumed leather jerkin, and other pleasant things; and that year the Queen had a pair of perfumed gloves trimmed only with four tufts, or roses of coloured silk; the Queen took such pleasure in those gloves that she was pictured with those gloves upon her hands, and for many years after it was called the Earl of Oxford's perfume.

Thus, with *Two Gentlemen of Verona* already either simmering in his mind, or actually written, and possibly played at court, in some early form, the year 1577 opens without any improvement in the unhappy relations between the Earl and his Countess. Burleigh is much distressed; and with that flat and heavy prolixity of style which we have already shown to be pitilessly ridiculed in *Hamlet*, he makes to his son-in-law a pathetic appeal for himself, as well as for his daughter,

> "whose grief is the greater and always shall be inasmuch as her love is most fervent and addicted to you, and because she cannot or may not, without offence be suffered to come to your presence, as she desireth, to offer the sacrifice of her heart.

Burleigh asks for a private interview, in the presence of a third party, if the Earl so desire. De Vere, so far as is known, did not reply; he being, we may assume, much more interested in dramatizing, than in corresponding over, these very events, and was, besides, ardently prosecuting a suit to the queen, for the grant to himself of the fee simple of the Manor of Rysing, originally held by the Duke of Norfolk, and confiscated to the Crown, after that nobleman's attainder and execution. In 1578 Elizabeth granted her ward's request, "in consideration of the good, true and faithful service done and given to Us before this time by our most dear cousin Edward, Earl of Oxford, Great Chamberlain of England."

What kind of service was it, in reward for which the Queen thus acceded to her dear cousin and Great Chamberlain's request? There was, of course, nothing unusual in the receipt of rich gifts of land, by such men as Leicester, Essex, and Hatton, all of whom had filled, or were filling, highly responsible posts in the royal household; but the Great Chamberlainship—the only office then held by Oxford—though an exalted one, was a sinecure, calling for almost no duties at all, excepting at coronations. Elizabeth, moreover, was not accustomed to grant, even to favourites, such as her " cousin " Oxford, so large an additional revenue as £250, without ample return. What was that return? We cannot positively say; but I feel certain, as does also Capt. Ward, that the concession represents Oxford's first salary, as unofficial playwright to the court, granted to him by a queen who genuinely liked the stage, and derived much amusement, and pleasure, from her ward's clever comedies. From this time forward, he became, as Mrs. Clark cleverly suggests, Elizabeth's " allowed fool " and " corrupter of words," privileged to set down upon paper, and to present upon court-stages, secret matters and daringly satirical allusions, both topical and personal, which, had they been penned by the youth from Stratford—at this time, by the way, about thirteen years old—would, assuredly, have cost him his liberty, if not his life.

But were they comedies alone—these masques and entertainments already streaming continuously from that facile and gifted pen? The majority of them, undoubtedly, were so; but although, at this period of his career, despite matrimonial and financial troubles, Thalia was more often his guiding Muse than Melpemone, de Vere, a temperamental man of moods, if ever there was one, could, I think, already attempt tragical drama, when fallen into the melancholy fit; and Mrs. Clark certainly makes out a good case for her contention that *The Historie of the Solitarie Knight*,[1] played at Whitchall on Shrove Sunday, 17 February, 1577, was the early form of a play known to us as *Timon of Athens*, in which Oxford realizing that his financial embarrassments were alienating

[1] *Shakespeare's Plays in the Order of their Writing*, pp. 25-42.

VERSE AND COURT COMEDY

fair-weather friends, and that loneliness, and soul solitude, were not incompatible with prominence in Gloriana's court, sketched out this tragedy of cynicism, later to be rewritten, for the Folio, by some other hand. Certainly such lines as the Senator's (II, i)

> I must serve my turn
> Out of mine own. . . . Immediate are my needs—

are remarkably close to the wording of, for example, Oxford's letter to Burleigh, January 3, 1576, "I have no other remedies, I have no help but of mine own, and mine is made to serve me and myself, not mine." "Auditors," moreover, are referred to, both in "Timon" and in the letter, while Timon's, "Let all my land be sold," may well have come straight from Oxford's letter (1576), "to authorize your lordship to sell any portion of my land."

Two days only after the above recorded performance of *The Solitary Knight*, on Shrove Tuesday, 19 February, the Children of Paul's performed *The historye of Titus and Gisippus*, words held by Mrs. Clark to be a mistranscription for *Titus Andronicus*,[1] a tragedy which, in her opinion, is Oxford's first conscious attempt in the larger patriotic sense, "to serve his queen and country by means of the drama"; the play being, it is argued, an immediate reflection of the massacre at Antwerp, known as "The Spanish Fury," of 4 November, 1576, and a warning as to the grievous danger to which

---

[1] Mrs. Clark's contention was attacked in *The Times Lit. Sup.*, May 28, 1931; but Col. B. R. Ward has no difficulty in showing in *The Shakespearian Pictorial*, August, 1931, that the documents now available in the Record Office are not originals but fair copies and Capt. Ward has supplied him with evidence of a mistake precisely analogous to that cited by Mrs. Clark.

England was subjected by Roman Catholic conspirators. Lavinia thus becomes a composite character, symbolizing Queen Elizabeth and the ravished city of Antwerp; Saturninus is Philip of Spain (Saturn); Tamora, the captive Queen, is Mary Stuart; and Aaron the Moor, her lover, is Charles Arundel (Aarondel) the English traitor in the pay of Spain, who will soon be coming prominently into our story. The analogies here are most remarkable; the safe sending of "both thy sons alive," in return for a severed hand, immediately suggesting the name Antwerp or "Hand-werper," of which the legendary origin, as attested by the two hands upon the city's escutcheon, was the custom of the giant Antigonus to hew off the right hands of all navigators passing his castle on the Scheldt, unless they met his claim of one half their merchandize. Meaningful also are these lines:

> *Titus.* Lucius, what book is that she turneth so?
> *Young Luc.* Grandsire, 'tis Ovid's *Metamorphoses.*
> My mother gave it me—

seeing that the story of Lavinia's mutilation is taken from Ovid's *Metamorphoses*, the very book which the Earl's mother's brother, Arthur Golding, had translated, while acting as tutor to his nephew. Young Lucius, by such a reading, would seem to become Oxford himself.

Pericles though, in my judgment, a wholly spurious Shakesperean play, written by George Wilkins,[1] is, nevertheless, linked, by many qualities, with the group we are considering; and Mrs. Clark[2] has pointed out that such lines as:

---

[1] See my *Shakespeare, Jonson and Wilkins as Borrowers*. Chapter IX.
[2] *Op. cit.*, pp. 74-94

VERSE AND COURT COMEDY

>1 *Fish.* Why, wilt thou tourney for the lady?
>*Peric.* I'll show the virtue I have borne in arms—

and the description of Pericles "the music master's" victory in the tournament, all fits exactly with Oxford, who was a skilled musician, as well as jouster, and who won the prize at all the three tournaments at which we know that he competed, in 1571, 1581, and 1584.

On Sunday, 28 December, 1578—writes the same authoress—*An history of the crueltie of a Stepmother* was played by the Lord Chamberlain's men at Richmond; and since the cruelty of a stepmother is precisely the theme of *Cymbeline*, Mrs. Clark infers that we have here the first performance of *Cymbeline*, in its original form, as a comedy of the French Queen Catharine de, Medici's effort to marry her son Alençon (Cloten) to the English Queen. Posthumus' phrase, that he is in "Cambria at Milford Haven," does not, it is suggested refer to the Welsh port, but to Long Melford, the town mentioned in *2 Henry VI*—wherein Elizabeth received the French envoys of Alençon in 1578; Posthumus' "Cambria," being, in fact, Cambridge, where Oxford actually was at the time of the Queen's progress there, during the last mentioned year: in all of which surmise, I fully concur, holding Posthumus to be Oxford, and Hedingham Castle, near Long Melford, to be "the residence of Posthumus," which, according to Pisano in the play, is near Milford Haven, just as are other homes of the Earls of Oxford, in that district, including Earl John of Campes' house at Lavenham, near Melford, and Wivenhoe at the mouth of the Colne, near Colchester. It is most significant that Imogen, in *Cymbeline*, when asked her name, answers that she (disguised as a man) is Richard du Champ (Campes)—Richard being a Christian name common among the de Veres.

With Mrs. Clark's main interpretation of the play, as another comedy of the Alençon marriage, I cannot, however, agree, preferring, with Capt. Ward, to read the play, *Cymbeline*, as a dramatic allegory probably inspired by another succession play, *Gorboduc* (1562)— from which Cloten's name is borrowed—and devised, as Capt. Ward has argued, for political-dramatic propaganda, on behalf of the Suffolk succession, in the form of an appeal to the queen, to legitimize the two sons of Lord Hertford and Lady Katharine Gray, whose mother, Lady Katharine, was a prominent candidate for the royal succession, in the event of Elizabeth dying childless. These two children of a clandestine marriage had been declared illegitimate in May 1563, by a specially appointed Commission of inquiry.

Secondly Capt. Ward regards *Cymbeline* as an attack upon the Dudley family's design to capture the English throne; the Earl of Leicester being an inveterate opponent of Oxford and a bitter enemy of Sussex, whose company of actors first presented *The Cruelty of a Stepmother*. Several points of direct evidence can be advanced to show that Oxford was friendly with the Seymours during the 'seventies; one being that Lord Hertford's brother, Lord Edward Seymour, was, almost certainly, the Lord Seymour with whom de Vere had played truant to the Continent, in 1574. The story of Iachimo's wager with Posthumus, that he would seduce Imogen, does not touch the theme of the Suffolk succession; but, while based upon a story in the Decameron, dramatizes yet again the quarrel between Lord and Lady Oxford in 1576, thus linking Imogen, or Anne, once more with one or other of these moated granges, in the Suffolk and Essex counties, that were evidently in the mind of the writer of *Cymbeline* and *Measure for Measure*.

That all these plays last analysed, including *Timon of Athens*, *Titus Andronicus*, *Pericles* and *Cymbeline* were drastically rewritten, by another hand, or hands some six or seven years after Oxford's death, I take to be positively certain; the most active of those revisers being George Wilkins.[1]

It is high summer, 1577. Lady Mary Vere, Lord Oxford's sister, and Maid of Honour to the Queen, is engaged to marry one of her Majesty's best swordsmen, "the brave Lord Willoughby"—brave enough even to marry a shrew. Lord Willoughby is Peregrine Bertie, son to the Duchess of Suffolk, who, not unnaturally, is in some dread lest Mary married to Peregrine should prove as difficult a mate as Edward married to Anne. Thus the Duchess writes to Burleigh, on 2 July:

> "If she (Lady Mary Vere) should prove like her brother, if an empire follow her I should be sorry, to match so. She said that she could not rule her brother's tongue, nor help the rest of his faults, but for herself she trusted so to use her (self) as I should have no cause to mislike her.

Possibly, nevertheless, the Duchess did "have cause to mislike her"; for during the September following the marriage—which took place at Christmas 1577—Burleigh's son, Sir Thomas Cecil, writes to his father concerning "unkindness" that has grown up between the

---

[1] For my analysis of *Cymbeline*, from this view-point, see my *Oxford-Shakespeare Case Corroborated*, Chapter IX.

pair, and opines that hapless Lady Mary will "be beaten with that *rod which heretofore she prepared for others.*"

The discordant couple, however, in common with Edward and Anne, were ministering, though unwittingly, to the diversions of posterity; for the marriage of Mary certainly gave Edward ideas for one of the most popular farces in our language, The Taming of the Shrew, first played at court, as Mrs. E. T. Clark suggests, on 1 January, 1579, as a *A Morrall of the Marryage of Mynde and Measure*, by the Children of Paul's. Oxford, who had dramatized comically his own marital misunderstandings, in *The Comedy of Errors*, a year or so earlier, did the same for those of his sister, in 1578. The Bianca scenes of this early version he took from the *Suppositi* of Ariosto, translated by his old acquaintance, George Gascoigne, who had died on 7 October, 1577: but that Petruchio and Katharina are Lord Willoughby and Lady Mary Vere— the lady destined, as was also the other shrew "to be beaten with that rod which heretofore she had prepared for others"—I take to be reasonably certain; in which connexion it is worth remembering that the name of Oxford's half-sister, Lady Windsor, was Katherine de Vere. I think, however, that the play, as we know it, contains something of Oxford's later experiences with his second wife, Elizabeth Trentham, which appear also in certain of the later Shakespearean Sonnets.

Oxford's letter to Lord Burleigh, from Padua, mentions two Italians, named, respectively, Baptista Nigrone and Benedict Spinola, with the first of whom, it will be remembered, the Earl had some dealing over "crowns"; and Mr. Looney in "*Shakespeare*" *Identified*, plausibly concludes that "the rich gentleman of Padua, Baptista Minola," Katharina's father, is a composite of the two

VERSE AND COURT COMEDY

names, so familiar to Oxford when he was in Italy. Mrs. Clark thinks that the name Petruchio derives from the Italian, Patruchius Ubaldinas, who was engaged, by the Lord Chamberlain, to assist in the production of plays, during this very season, 1578-79, when *The Taming of the Shrew* was first produced at court. The lines in III, ii,

> Wherefore gaze this goodly company,
> As if they saw some wondrous monument,
> Some comet or unusual prodigy—

have been noted, by Admiral Holland, as an allusion to the large comet, which appeared in 1577 and 1578. With the Induction, which I take to be of at least ten years later date, I will deal when the time comes.

Right down to the close of 1577, the Earl, still alienated and living apart from his wife, chafes at the restricted idleness of court routine, and, to judge by the Duchess of Suffolk's letter to Burleigh, written on 15 December, is already contemplating withdrawal.

> " I hear he is about to buy a house here in London about Watling Street, and not to continue a courtier as he hath done ; But I pray you keep all these things secret "—

and there follows in the same letter a device for bringing together Oxford and his baby daughter ; it having come to the Duchess's ears that the Earl though very willing to see his child, was, presumably, too proud to send for her. Thus the lady.

> " An you will keep my counsel we will have some sport with him. I will see if I can get the child hither to me, when you shall come hither ; and

whilst my lord your brother is with you, I will bring in the child as though it were some other, and we shall see how nature will work in him to like it, and tell him it is his own after.

Whether or no the old Duchess's device was ever practised upon that proud and recalcitrant father, history does not relate; but Wright, in his *History of Essex*, tells us that Burleigh arranged to do with his own daughter, Oxford's wife—whom also Oxford would not meet—very much what Her Grace of Suffolk suggested should be done with Oxford's baby girl:

> The father of Lady Anne (Cecil) by stratagem contrived that her husband should unknowingly sleep with her, believing her to be another woman, and she bore a son to him in consequence of this meeting.

Already the alert among my readers may name the play that slips next into this life-story of de Vere; since this incident of substituted infant, or mother, whether actual or invented, epitomizes, in part, the plot of *All's Well that Ends Well*, the first draft of which I assign to 1578, holding it, again, with Mrs. Clark, to be the play *The Rape of the Second Helen*, which was played at the court in the fifteen-seventies, and was, perhaps, known under yet a third title, *Love's Labour's Won*.

Bertram, in *All's Well that Ends Well*, is ward to the Countess Rousillon, as Oxford is to Queen Elizabeth; and Helena, lowly born, as also was Anne Cecil, is in love with a " bright particular star," Bertram, but can hardly, without undue presumption, " think to wed it, he is so far above me." Helena's lines in I, iii:

> I am from humble, he from honour'd name
> No note upon my parents, his all noble.
> My master, my dear Lord he is ; and I
> His servant live and will his vassal die—

not only describe exactly the relative social positions of the Earl and his Countess, before their marriage ; but also use, in the last line, the exact words, almost, of Oxford's own " Echo " song :

> May I requite his birth with faith, then faithful
>   will I die : ay—

which, though written to or about Anne Vavasour recall intimately, as we have seen, the Ophelia (Anne Cecil) scenes of *Hamlet*. *All's Well that Ends Well*, indeed, directly harbingers *Hamlet*; for a glance makes it obvious that the early talk, concerning Bertram's dead father, was paraphrased by Shakespeare, in the corresponding early passages of *Hamlet*[1] ; while the Countess's speech, " Be thou blest, Bertram," in I, i, is just a first draft for Polonius' speech to Laertes. Further, the Corambus, of IV, iii, differs only by a single letter from the name Corambis, of the first Quarto Hamlet, who is Polonius, who is Burleigh. It was to Burleigh, moreover, that the Earl first wrote from Italy, that he has " made an end of all hope to help myself by Her Majesty's service considering that my youth is objected unto me "—words which reappear thus in *All's Well that Ends Well*, II, i.

> *Sec. Lord.* O 'tis brave wars. . . .[2]
> *Bertr.* I am commanded here, and kept a coil with " Too young," and " the next year," and " 'tis too early."

[1] See my *Case for Edward de Vere 17th Earl of Oxford as " Shakespeare,"* pp. 288–290.
[2] The war between Spain and Holland, in the Low Countries, 1578.

> *Parol.* An thy mind stand to't, boy, steal away bravely.

That Bertram took Parolle's hint and did " steal away bravely " in 1574 my readers know ; and also that " the next year " he—this time with leave and licence—did actually visit " those Italian fields Where noble fellows strike " (II, iii). As for Bertram's words, " No sword worn, but one to dance with "—this same year, 1578, saw the Spanish ambassador writing about Elizabeth's entertainment of Alençon's viceroy :

> " The next day the Queen sent twice to tell the Earl of Oxford, who is a very gallant lad, to dance before the Ambassador ; whereupon he replied that he hoped Her Majesty would not order him to do so, as he did not wish to entertain Frenchmen.

Readers who may be still unsatisfied can find further evidence from the clown. " He (Bertram) will look upon his boot and sing . . . pick his teeth and sing. I know a man that had this trick of melancholy sold a goodly manor for a song." All this again is pure Oxford, for his addiction to music we already know ; and his trick of tooth-picking is laughed at by Jonson and others again and again. As for the melancholy individual—going by the name of Jaques, who " sold a goodly manor for a song"—several of them, I suppose—Rosalind, as we shall discover, will chaff him for us, in *As You Like It*.

Oxford, at this period of his life, was rarely, I think, in the dumps for very long periods together ; and we shall soon find him busy upon so effervescent and sparkling a comedy as *Love's Labour's Lost* ; but, nevertheless, during these late 'seventies, until the poignancies of anger, grief, disillusionment, and remorse are swept from his mind by the bursting of a far more devastating storm, the rupture with his wife continues to provide by far the most fecund of his dramatic motives or inspirations; and is now being exploited by de Vere in two of the most interesting, because most intimately revealing comedies of his nonage, namely the Troilus and Cressida portions of the satire still so entitled, and the first part, as far as the end of III, ii, of *A Winter's Tale*. Both of these we must now consider.

Troilus and Cressida, as it has come down to us, seems to be a composite of two plays—an early one upon the subject of the two lovers, with which I am about to deal, and, fitted on to it, a later play, probably the *History of Agamemnon and Ulysses*, which, as we know from the Revels Accounts, was acted at court by the Earl of Oxford's boys, on 27 December, 1584. This last will be examined in its right place in our story.

For a long while, though realizing that both Troilus and his lady, in common with other characters of the plays, must stand for actual Elizabethan personages, I could not identify them, even conjecturally, until, prompted by Capt. B. M. Ward, I perceived that the Troilus and Cressida episodes are simply another dramatization of the Oxford-Anne Cecil marriage and estrangement, with Pandarus standing for Burleigh, Troilus for the Earl, and Cressida for the lady his wife, who, he is led to believe, has played him false.

This discovery, intensely interesting, as at once weaving the play autobiographically into the patterns of its fellows, is historically valuable also, as throwing vivid light upon the inner history of the marriage, with the scandal of 1576 following, and upon the respective attitudes thereto of the three parties principally concerned. It became apparent, from the first, that, precisely as in similar dramatizations of determining incidents in de Vere's life-story, each scene is built up from actual conversations or letters, and retains, in its dramatic dialogue, the dominant individual characteristics as well as the style of the various speakers. Pandarus' speeches, in particular, are so obvious an imitation of Burleigh, whose letters, as we have already seen, are pitilessly burlesqued in *Hamlet*, that I was surprised at my long failure to identify Pandarus as Pondus—Burleigh's nickname at court—or to grasp the significance of an attack even more malicious than that to which Oxford would treat his audiences, when he came to fashion Polonius upon the same model—Pondus, Pandarus, Polonius! Who, with the clues in his possession, will read such lines as (I, i)

> *Pand.* Faith, I'll not meddle in't. . . . I have had my labour for my travail; ill-thought on of her, and ill-thought on of you: gone between and between, but small thanks for my labour. . . . for my part I'll meddle nor make no more in the matter—

and not recognize instantly the tautogical, repetitive style of de Vere's garrulous father-in-law? By content, as clearly as by characteristic manner, the Lord Treasurer is here proclaimed—he who had written to Rutland, on 16 August, 1571, a few months only before the ill-starred marriage:

> At his own motion I could not well imagine what to think, considering I never meant to seek it nor hoped of it.

Oxford, however, was evidently of opinion that Lord Burleigh—and not Lady Burleigh, as I used to hold—did, in fact, seek, and earnestly work for, the marriage, and was the actual Pandar through whom the alliance was brought about. Meanwhile, let any reader disposed to deny that Troilus, in the play, here stands for de Vere, read these following lines:

> *Troil.* I cannot come to Cressid but by Pandar;
> And he's as tetchy to be woo'd to woo
> As she is stubborn chaste against all suit,
> Tell me, *Apollo*, for thy *Daphne*'s love—

and compare them with those admittedly written by de Vere in *The Forsaken Man*, to the same occasion, it may be, though probably earlier in point of time:

> The more I followed one, the more she fled away,
> As *Daphne* did full long agone
> *Apollo's* wistful prey.

Further we have Troilus saying, in the same speech:

> Let it be call'd the wild and wandering flood,
> Ourself the merchant—

words to be made good when Oxford, perhaps only a few months later, will indeed, as I shall show, write of himself as the Merchant, Antonio, in *The Merchant of Venice*.

In the next scene (I, ii) are more typical repetitive babblings from Pandarus-Polonius, bent upon encouraging Cressida.

> Troilus will not come far behind him (Hector) ... Troilus is the better man of the two ... I say Troilus is Troilus ... Hector is not Troilus ... Himself! Alas, poor Troilus—

and at this stage of the play it has become obvious that the father, though "tetchy to be woo'd to woo," when so requested by the hoped-for son-in-law, woos willingly in the son-in-law's absence; as also that Anne-Cressida, while pretending indifference towards the royal ward of her father's household, is, nevertheless, deeply in love with him, and—"won with the first glance"—has loved him "night and day for many weary months."

Swiftly shine out these revealing high-lights, upon history, and upon the identities of our players; the next to appear being a characteristic stream of *Vero nihil Verius* puns, with interesting hints upon Oxford's complexion:

> *Pand.* Faith, to say *truth*, brown and not brown.
> *Cres.* To say the *truth*, *true* and not *true*.

Meaningful also is this, from Pandarus:

> I'll be sworn 'tis true; he will weep you, an twere a man born in April—

when we remember that de Vere's birthday was 12 April. "He (Troilus) never saw three-and-twenty," exclaims Pandarus—words that are again historically correct, since, at the time of his marriage, in December 1571, was well into his twenty-second year. Poor Anne, like Viola to be, still conceals her passion:

> Then though my heart's content firm love doth bear,
> Nothing of that shall from mine eyes appear.

The opening of the third act, and the statement:

> I am the Lord Pandarus . . . honour and lorship are my titles—

with the old Lord's words to the servant:

VERSE AND COURT COMEDY

> We understand not one another. I am too courtly
> and thou art too cunning—

introduces a scene which Oxford seems to have used as a basis for *Hamlet*, II, ii, where the Prince is far too "cunning" for the courtly Polonius,[1] and wherein the old lord expends his tedious tautology upon Claudius and Gertrude, who, in *Troilus*, are Helen and Paris.

Thus Pandarus, to Helen and Paris in III, i:

> *Pand.* Fair be to you, my lord, and to all this fair company! fair desires, in all fair measure, fairly guide them! especially to you, fair queen! fair thoughts be your fair pillow!
> *Hele.* Dear lord, you are full of fair words.
> *Pand.* You speak your fair pleasure, sweet queen. Fair prince, here is good broken music.
> *Par.* You have broke it, cousin: and, by my life, you shall make it whole again; you shall piece it out with a piece of your performance. Nell, he is full of harmony.
> *Pand.* Truly, lady, no.

Compare these lines with the "brevity is the soul of wit," and the "'Tis true, 'tis pity, pity 'tis 'tis true" speeches of Polonius; and it will become clear, I think, that the latter are, in part, a development of this scene from *Troilus*, which, in addition to the "broken music" phrase, that reappears in *Hamlet* as Ophelia's,

> Sweet bells jangled out of tune and harsh—

teems throughout with Hamlet motives.

---

[1] Similarly the talk between Pandarus and the Servant, concerning the "Musicians" whom the Servant "wholly knows," is paralleled by that between Polonius and Hamlet concerning the "Players," whom Hamlet likewise "wholly knows."

The second scene of Act III, after opening with a number of interesting themes that will later be developed, to much advantage, in *Romeo and Juliet*, introduces a triologue between Pandarus, Troilus, and Cressida, that is packed with ideas subsequently made use of in the Polonius-Ophelia and Hamlet-Laertes scenes of the Danish tragedy, as the following parallels show:

Pand [*to Cressida*]. What need you blush? shame's *a baby*.

Pand. You shall fight your heart out ere I part you. The *falcon* as the *tercel* . . . *go to, go to.*

Troil. In all Cupid's pageant there is presented no *monster* . . . nothing but *our undertakings*; when we vow to *weep* seas, live in fire, eat rocks, *tame tigers*; thinking it harder *for our mistress* to devise imposition enough.

Polo. [*to Ophelia*]. Think yourself *a baby.*

Polo. Go to, go to . . . . Ay, springes to catch *woodcocks*.

Haml. (V, i). I loved Ophelia. . . . What wilt thou do *for her?* . . . . Woo't *drink* up Eisel, *eat a crocodile?*

Here are parallels unmistakable, and of immense importance in linking the two plays; while hard upon, to make assurance doubly sure, follows another stream of Vere puns:

Troil. A mock for his *truth*, and what *truth* can speak *truest*, not *truer* than *Troilus*—

the name Troilus here, like Verius, in the Vere motto, being equivalent to the word Truth. Another notable passage follows (III, ii.):

Pand. Nay, I'll give my word for her too: our kindred, though they be long ere they are wooed, they are constant being won: they are burrs, I can tell you: they'll stick where they are thrown.

Cres. Boldness comes to me now, and brings
    me heart,
Prince Troilus, I have loved you night and day
For many weary months.

Troi. Why was my Cressid then so hard to win?

Cres. Hard to seem won, but I was won, my lord
With the first glance that ever—pardon me;
If I confess much, you will play the tyrant.

These lines become doubly pathetic in their strict truth to history; for Anne, whose only fault was weakness or "frailty,'" not falsity, did, indeed, through good and evil report, stick like a burr to her lord, whom she had secretly loved so long, while they were living as boy and girl together, under the same roof, and who—to his own subsequent bitter regret—did indeed play the tyrant upon his devoted and unoffending wife. The puns and word-play, upon "true" and "false," continue until almost the close of the scene (III, ii.).

The second scene of Act IV, opening with a love-duologue between Troilus and Cressida, recalls, at once, a still better known meeting between the pair, as Romeo and Juliet—I mean the beautiful aubade in III, v—"Wilt thou be gone?"—wherein the boy is implored by the girl to tarry—a lover's debate which, in Troilus, appears thus:

Troi. O Cressida! but that the busy day,
Waked by the lark, hath roused the ribald crows,
And dreaming night will hide our joys no longer,
I would not from thee.

>   *Cres.*   Night hath been too brief.
>   *Troi.*   Beshrew the witch! with venomous wights
>   she stays
> As tediously as hell, but flies the grasps of love
> With wings more momentary swift than thought.
> You will catch cold, and curse me.
>   *Cres.*   Prithee tarry.
> You men will never tarry.

One line in the above,

>   *Cres.*   [Night] flies the grasps of love
> With wings more momentary swift than thought,

will, later on, be re-spoken thus, by Hamlet:

>   with wings more swift
> Than meditation or the thoughts of love—

every immature early play thus becoming a preliminary sketch or study, for the travailed masterpieces of later years.

Scene iv, 2, closes upon a motive which will again be developed in *Romeo and Juliet*:

>   *Cres.* I'll ... tear my bright hair ... break
>   my heart
> With sounding Troilus.   I will not go from Troy.

Troi, or Troy, here means as we have seen, simply True, or Vere; and Juliet, likewise, will tear, not indeed her "bright hair," but

>   the cave, where Echo lies
> With repetition of my Romeo's name—

the Echo of Romeo being E.O., the initials of Oxford's own name, upon the last syllable of which, as my readers know, he has repeatedly punned, in his Echo Song.

VERSE AND COURT COMEDY

Scene iv, 3, opens significantly with the entry, among others, of Paris, who is seeking Cressida, just as another Paris will presently seek Juliet; and the fourth scene continues the Romeo-and-Juliet theme, when Pandarus urges the " banished " Cressida to be " moderate," precisely as the Friar does the banished Romeo, in the Verona tragedy (III, iii). There follows, besides another stream of puns, from Troilus and from Cressida, upon True and Troy, a dialogue which again seems to have supplied many ideas for *Romeo and Juliet*, including the balcony-scene, since Æneas, " from within," calls twice for Cressida, just as the Nurse does for Juliet; while Cressida, when she warns her lover that he will be " exposed to dangers," is simply foretelling her own line, as Juliet to Romeo:

If they do see thee, they will murder thee.

Still the Romeo continues; since the dialogue, in IV, v,

> *Men.* I'll have my kiss, sir Lady, by your leave.
> *Cres.* In kissing do you render or receive?
> *Patr.* Both take and give.
> *Cres.* I'll make my match to live,
> The kiss you take is better than you give;
> Therefore no kiss.
> *Men.* I'll give you boot, I'll give you three for one.
> *Cres.* You're an odd man; give even, or give none—

written, as it is, in the early rhyming manner, palpably reappears in another first meeting—that between Romeo and Juliet, wherein the same kissing motive—

Give me my kiss again. You kiss by the book—

is handled in a far more skilful though, at bottom, identical style.

Thenceforward the Hamlet motives dominate again; for Ulysses' speech runs thus:

> The youngest son of Priam, a true knight,
> *Not yet mature,*[1] yet matchless, firm of word,
> Speaking in deeds and deedless in his tongue,
> Not soon provoked nor being provoked soon calmed;
> His heart and hand both open and both free;
> For what he has he gives, what thinks he shows;
> Yet gives he not till judgment guides his bounty,
> Nor dignifies an impair thought with breath;
> Manly as Hector, but more dangerous.

and its tenour is very close to the advice of Polonius to Laertes, while the speeches of Troilus, in V, ii, thus strung together, as follows, form an obvious quarrying ground for Hamlet, though not indeed applicable to Ophelia, who is Cressid's counterpart, but to Gertrude, in the closet-scene.

> *Ulys.* Why stay we then?
> *Troil.* To make a recordation to my soul
> . . . how these two did co-act.
>
> Sith yet there is a credence in my heart,
> An esperance so obstinately strong
> That doth invert the attest of eyes and ears.
>
> Why my negation hath no taste of madness.

---

[1] Notice that Oxford is conscious of his own personal immaturity, as well as of the crudity of his verse. Observe, too, how in early life he always regards himself as a man of action, not of words.

> Let it not be believed for womanhood!
> Think, we had mothers; do not give advantage
> To stubborn critics, apt without a theme
> For depravation, to square the general sex
> By Cressid's rule, rather think this is not Cressid.
>
> This is she? no, this is Diomed's Cressida.
> If beauty have a soul, this is not she;
> If souls guide vows, if vows be sanctimonies
> If sanctimony be the gods' delight,
> If there be rule in unity itself,
> This is not she. O madness of discourse
> . . . where reason can revolt
> Without perdition, and loss assume all reason
> Without revolt: this is, and is not, Cressid!
>
> The fraction of her faith, orts of her love,
> The fragments, scraps, the bits and greasy relics
> Of her o'er-eaten faith, are bound to Diomed.

All this is pure Hamlet, alike in general outlook, and in phraseology—" a recordation to my soul " becoming, " My tables, meet it is I set it down," and the inversion of " the attest of *eyes* and *ears* " reappearing as :—

> *Eyes* without feeling, feeling without sight,
> *Ears* without hands or eyes, smelling sans all
> . . . And reason *pandars* will.

Let the reader run his own seeing eye down the extracts above quoted, then compare them with

> Lay not the flattering unction to your soul,
> That not your trespass but my madness speaks

> What judgment would step from this to this?

> Nay, but to live
> In the rank sweat of an enseamed bed,
> Stew'd in corruption, honeying and making love
> Over the nasty sty
>
> A king of shreds and patches—

and he will not, I think, feel disposed to deny, that—not forgetting the use of the word "Pandar," in a crucial scene of *Hamlet*—*Troilus and Cressida* is an immature and tentative dramatization of Oxford's intimate experiences with Anna Cecil and Burleigh—experiences that will be handled again, in fuller maturity of his genius, as to part in *Romeo and Juliet*, but more completely in the tragedy of Denmark.

The sequel makes assurance doubly sure (V, iv).

> *Pand.* Here's a letter come from yond poor girl.
> *Troi.* Let me read.
> *Pand.* A whoreson tisick, a whoreson rascally tisick so troubles me, and the foolish fortune of this girl; and what one thing, what another, that I shall leave you one of these days: and I hope a rheum in mine eyes too, and such an ache in my bones that, unless a man were cursed, I cannot tell what to think on't. What says she there?
> *Troi.* Words, words, mere words, no matter from the heart;
> The effect doth operate another way [*tearing the letter*].
> Go, wind, to wind, there turn and change together.

Here we have nothing else than a preliminary sketch for the duologues between Hamlet and Polonius, in II, concerning Ophelia. The parallels are unmistakable.

VERSE AND COURT COMEDY

Troilus and Hamlet are both reading; and when asked about the " matter " by Pandarus, Troilus answers:

Words, words, mere *words,* no *matter* from the heart—

while Hamlet, when set the same question by Polonius, replied, "*Words, words, words,*" whereupon Polonius asks, "What is the *matter*, my Lord?" Further, Pandarus, in the approved repetitive and tautological style of Polonius-Burleigh, groans over the infirmities of old age, the " rascally tisick," the " rheum " in his eyes, and the " ache " in his bones—Burleigh suffered much from gout—all of which, but thinly disguised, reappears in Hamlet's quotations from the satirical remarks made by the author of the book he is reading—which, in *Troilus,* is a letter from Cressida—concerning the " wrinkles " and " grey beards " of old age, its lamentably " weak hams," and its " eyes purging thick amber and plum-tree gum."

No proofs more finally conclusive than these could possibly be found of the identities of Burleigh, Oxford, and Anne with the three corresponding individuals dramatized in *Troilus* and *Hamlet*. Scene v, 5, opening with Diomed's remark:

Go, go my servant, take thou Troilus' horse,
Present the fair steed to my lady Cressid—

recalls the significant coincidence that, about the same time that Anne will be supposed to have played false, in London with some man, not her husband, Oxford, leaving Paris on 17 March, 1575, sent to Anne his picture —probably the Welbeck portrait reproduced at the opening of this book—accompanied by a present of two horses! In April 1576, it will be remembered, upon his return to Paris from Italy, he first learned of what he believed to be his wife's infidelity.

Troilus' last long speech in the play:

> Hector is gone.
> Who shall tell Priam so, or Hecuba . . .
> Make wells and Niobes of the maids and wives—

introduces three names—Priam, Hecuba, and Niobe—all of which are used in *Hamlet*; and the play closes upon a last bitter thrust, by Oxford, at his father-in-law, when Pandarus is made to epilogue:

> O world, world, world, thus is the poor agent despised.
> As many as be here of Pandar's hall,
> Your eyes, half out, weep out at Pandar's fall;
> Or if you cannot weep, yet give some groans,
> Though not for me, yet for aching bones.[1]

Troilus and Cressida, it will be generally agreed, is eloquent enough of the profound effects produced upon Oxford's ultra-sensitive mind, by what, for a time, he honestly, though mistakenly, believed to be the unfaithfulness of his wife; but our realization of the overwhelming dominance in his thought of this dark suspicion is doubled, when we perceive that, in the first three acts of *A Winter's Tale*, himself, as I believe, or possibly some other writer closely connected with him, dramatizes once more the same episode, with Leontes and Hermione taking the parts of Edward and Anne, originally represented

[1] I cannot think that *Troilus*, with its vicious attacks upon Burleigh, was played during the seventies in open court. It may have been privately done, as amateur theatricals, in Oxford's house, or at some friend's.

by Troilus and Cressida; the differences, in this case, being, that Burleigh, apparently, is excluded; and that Anne is here portrayed as the innocent wife that she actually was, slandered and deeply wronged by a too easily jealous husband, who, towards the close of the third act (III, ii)—which I take to mark the end of the play, *A Winter's Tale*, as first drafted—recognizes, and at last atones for, his disastrous mistake. Thus read together, the two immature comedies become absorbingly interesting for the light they throw upon the history of these lovers, and upon Oxford's astonishing faculty for thus detachedly, and yet with extreme intimacy, dramatizing, from various view-points, calamitous episodes in the careers of himself and his lady; wherein the Earl portrays himself as dupe, or villain, or hero, just as poetical urge or dramatic necessity may seem to require.

Swiftly the theme of *A Winter's Tale* develops, when Leontes, looking darkly about him, upon Hermione, Mamilius, and Polixenes, is heard murmuring:

> Too hot, too hot!
> To mingle friendship far is mingling bloods.
> I have *tremor cordis* on me.

Whereupon doubts concerning the legitimacy of his son, Mamilius, come stabbing at his peace of mind, just as, in 1576, did similar thoughts concerning the legitimacy of Oxford's daughter; though, if we guess the age of Mamilius at five years, Leontes' words:

> methought I did recoil
> Twenty-three years, and saw myself unbreech'd—

would suggest 1555 plus 23 years, or the date 1578, as the year of drafting this play. Three speeches further on, in this same pregnant scene, Leontes speaks yet more strikingly topical words.

> Go, play, boy, play, *thy mother plays, and I*
> *Play too*; but so disgraced a part, whose issue
> Will hiss me to my grave : contempt and clamour
> Will be my knell. Go, play, boy, play. There have been,
> Or I am much deceived, cuckolds ere now ;
> And many a man there is, even at this present,
> Now, while I speak this, holds his wife by the arm,
> That little thinks she has been sluiced in's absence.

Here is a palpable reference, not only to Oxford as being already by the late 'seventies, an actor—we know that he played in a device before the Queen, at Shrovetide, in this very year, 1578—but also to his wife's unfaithfulness, as he believes, during her husband's absence—most significant words, when it is remembered that, although Leontes and Hermione have not been parted in this play Elizabeth de Vere's birth synchronizes, approximately, with Oxford's visit to Sicily, the very country of which Leontes is king ; and when, a few moments later, he murmurs :

> They're here with me already : whispering, rounding Sicilia is a so-forth—

his dread of mockery in the court, as a cuckold, is expressed in words very close to those which he wrote to Burleigh, on 27 April, 1576, concerning the rupture with his wife.

> This might have been done through private conference before, and had not needed to have been the fable of the world—

an idea which we shall find repeated later on, when Oxford, dramatizing himself as Angelo, alludes, in *Measure for Measure*, to her reputation being " disvalued in levity," as a primary reason for his break with Mariana, who is Anne Cecil once more.

Leontes now suggests to Camillo, that poison may best rid him of Polixenes :

> bespice a cup,
> To give mine enemy a lasting wink
> Which draught to me were cordial.

Whether Oxford did actually incite one of his fellow-courtiers to poison the man—if there was one—with whom he suspected his wife to have played false, I cannot say ; nor—though I suspect both to be of the Howard-Arundel faction—can I hazard a name for either Polixenes or Camillo ; but as the sequel will show, when we reach the feud between de Vere and his Catholic cousins, in 1580-81—" Butcherly bloodiness " will be one of the long catalogue of charges made against Oxford by Arundel, who will write :

> No day without practise to draw blood among his own friends. . . . He set myself upon Southwell, my Lord Howard upon me.

One wonders, consequently, how much of precise historic truth there is in these scenes ; and how much, likewise, in Camillo's consent to do the deed,

> Provided that, when he's removed, your highness
> Will take again your queen as yours at first,
> Even for your son's sake—

thereby, of course, to seal the injury of babbling tongues. Again, we ask how much of actual talk, concerning de Vere, there may be in (I, ii):

>   This jealousy,
> Is for a precious creature: as she's rare,
> Must it be great; and, as his person's mighty,
> Must it be violent; and as he does conceive
> He is dishonour'd by a man which ever
> Profess'd to him, why, his revenges must
> In that be made more bitter.

All this, past question, fits closely de Vere's recognizable character at this period of his life; and just as we have observed, in *Troilus and Cressida*, matter that is used again, and more effectively in *Hamlet*, so here Leontes' words to Hermione (II, i):

> To say, " She is a goodly lady . . .
> 'Tis pity she's not honest . . . these pretty hands
> That calumny doth use. . . .

at once recall Hamlet to Ophelia:

> Are you honest? . . . Are you fair? . . . be thou chaste as ice, as pure as snow, thou shalt not escape calumny.

With the close of the scene, and the opening of II, ii, in the prison, we are less in the atmosphere of *Hamlet* than of *Measure for Measure* again.

> *Leon.* . . . this business
> Will raise us all
>   *Anti* [*aside*]. To laughter, as I take it.

VERSE AND COURT COMEDY

this laughter being the identical "levity" at court, which, as we shall see, so fatally cheapened Mariana in Angelo's eyes.

Again, when Emilia, represented, I think, in history by Oxford's sister, Lady Mary Vere, already dramatized as Katharina the shrew—visits, in the prison, Paulina, who, as we shall see, is the Duchess of Suffolk—that lady, speaking of the new-born daughter, says:

> the queen receives
> Much comfort in't; says "My poor prisoner,
> *I am innocent* as you are—"

in which connexion it becomes pertinent to know that Anne wrote to her husband, in 1581, during the swirl of events that will issue dramatically in *Measure for Measure*—"I appeal to God *I am utterly innocent,*" as unquestionably she was. "I dare be sworn," replies Paulina, and continues with these lines:

> Pray you, Emilia,
> Commend my best obedience to the queen.
> If she dares trust me with her little babe,
> I'll show't to the king and undertake to be
> Her advocate to the loudest.

Here again is authentic history; for in December 1577, the Duchess of Suffolk propounded to Burleigh exactly such a trick, when she wrote:

> On Thursday I went to see my Lady Mary Vere. After other talks she asked me what I would say to it if my Lord her brother would take his wife again. "Truly," quoth I, "nothing could comfort me more, for now I wish to your brother as much good as to my own son." "Indeed," quoth she,

"he would very fain see the child, and is loth to send for her." "Then," quoth I, "an you will keep my counsel we will have some sport with him, I will see if I can get the child hither to me, when you shall come hither; and whilst my Lord your brother is with you I will bring in the child as though it were some other child of my friend's, and we shall see how nature will work in him to like it, and tell him it is his own after." "Very well," quoth she, so we agreed hereon.[1]

Quite obviously, then, the Paulina-Emilia scene, in *A Winter's Tale* (II, ii), is just a dramatization of an innocent plot, the historic sequel to which, unfortunately, has not come down to us, unless, as is quite probable, we find its issue also dramatized here.

> *Leon.*   Force her [Paulina] hence.
> *Paul.* Let him that makes but trifles of his eyes
> First hand me. . . . The good queen,
> For she is good, hath brought you forth a daughter
> Here 'tis; commends it to your blessing.
>   [*Laying down the child.*]
> *Leon.* A mankind witch! Hence with her, out
>   o' door. Out!
> A most intelligencing bawd!
> *Paul.*   Not so.
> I am as ignorant in that as you
> In so entitling me, and no less honest
> Than you are mad; which is enough, I'll warrant,
> As this world goes, to pass for honest.
> *Leon.* Traitors! . . . Take up the bastard!
> Take't up, I say; give it to thy crone
> . . . He dreads his wife.

---

[1] Part already quoted in connexion with *All's Well* See *ante*, p. 95.

> *Paul.* So I would you did; then 'twere past all doubt
> You'll call your children yours!
> *Leon.* A nest of traitors.... A callat
> Of boundless tongue, who late hath beat her husband
> And now baits me! This brat is none of mine;
> It is the issue of Polixenes.
> Hence with it, and together with the dame
> Commit them to the fire.
> *Paul.* It is yours.

Again it would be deeply interesting to know the right proportions of fact and fiction here. Some, at least, of this talk, I suppose to be veridical at bottom, though written up for dramatic effect.

Beyond question the biographic quality of the comedy continues, for the stage direction, at the opening of Act III, is, "A Seaport in Sicilia"; and it was from a Sicilian seaport, namely Palermo, that Oxford, in 1576, issued his famous challenge, to fight as champion of his royal mistress, Elizabeth. Had the Earl extended the same solicitude to that other Elizabeth, the queen's namesake, his daughter, it would have been well for him, even though *A Winter's Tale* had not then been written, or had been written differently. Hermione's speech in III, ii:

> You, my lord, best know,
> Who least will seem to do so, my past life
> Hath been as continent, as chaste, as true,
> *As I am now unhappy*; which is more
> Than history can pattern, though *devised*
> *And play'd to take spectators*—

is again worded very closely to Anne's letter to her husband of 7 December, 1581, already quoted from:

> My Lord. *In what misery I may account myself to be,* that neither can see any end thereof, nor yet any hope to diminish it.

and readers will further observe that this play, *A Winter's Tale*, thus "devis'd and play'd to take spectators," is no other than a dramatic extension by something "more than history can pattern," of the actual life-stories of Oxford and of Anne.

Breaking up the seals, we apply our own key to the cipher, and read the Oracle's pronouncement.

> Hermione is chaste; Polixenes blameless; Camillo a true subject; Leontes a jealous tyrant,[1] his innocent babe truly begotten; and the king shall live without an heir, if that which is lost be not found.

This lost child, Perdita of the play, is, in historical fact, the Lady Elizabeth Vere, destined to be affianced, though not married, to the Earl of Southampton, to whom "Shakespeare" will dedicate "the first *heir*" of his invention. In dramatic allegory, however, that child stands, as also do many other characters of the plays, for the whole heritage of Shakespeare's invention the plays themselves, whose writer, Oxford-Leontes, must indeed live "without an heir," if his identity, in common with that of his daughter, be not, at last, discovered. Some 350 years later that discovery has come about.

---

[1] Cressida had expressed a fear lest Troilus should turn "tyrant," if she confessed too much.

VERSE AND COURT COMEDY

Meanwhile, the topical and characteristic allusions continue.

> *Leon.* I have too much believed mine own suspicion
>
> For being transported by my jealousies
> To bloody thoughts and to revenge, I chose
> Camillo for the minister to poison
> My friend Polixenes.

lines suggesting that there may even have been some hint of truth behind Arundel's charges, against Oxford, of subornation to murder, that lie not far ahead in our story.[1] Moreover, Paulina's words, that follow:

> To have him kill a king; poor trespasser,
> More monstrous standing by: whereof I reckon
> The casting forth to crows thy baby-daughter
> To be or none or little—

are strangely close to Arundel's description of Oxford, as "a monstrous earl," and as being guilty of nameless offences. It may be, however, that such dramatic ideas were merely suggested by charges that were mainly calumnious. The truth cannot now be known; but I take it as positively certain that the closing words of the first portion of the play—since III, iii, with Antigonus, though very important, is no more than a connecting link—express Oxford's self-condemnation

> *Leon.* Prithee bring me
> To the dead bodies of my queen and son.
> One grave shall be for both; upon them shall
> The causes of their death appear, unto
> Our shame perpetual. Once a day I'll visit

[1] See *post*, pp. 159, 160.

> The chapel where they lie, and tears shed there
> Shall be my recreation. So long as nature
> Will bear up with this exercise, so long
> I daily vow to use it. Come and lead me
> To these sorrows.

Dramatically he admits a guilt for which the piteously tragical, yet always noble, dramas lying ahead shall be his amends and his *recreation*, when the Earl withdraws, at last, finally from court-life. Relative to these tragedies, as yet unwritten, I would point out, that scattered among the three acts which we have examined, are lines clearly foretelling, besides Hamlet, already referred to, the three other outstanding characters of Shakespeare's tragical quartette—Macbeth, Othello, and Lear. Set such lines as these, by Leontes:

> whose issue
> Will hiss me to my grave
> Contempt and clamour will be my knell
> . . . There have been,
> Or I am much deceived, cuckolds ere now—

be set beside Macbeth's:

> And that which should accompany old age,
> As honour, love. . . . I must not look to have,
> But . . . curses . . .
> Blood hath been shed ere now, y' the olden time—

and who can doubt that, although Macbeth be founded historically upon Bothwell's part in the murder of Darnley, as well as upon the murder of Duff in Holinshed's *Chronicles*, yet, for the vital experience which shaped the character, Oxford returns to his unregenerate days of the 'seventies, when—reacting, with characteristic violence and impetuosity, to the stimuli of untoward events—his imagination teemed with vindictive, and sometimes even murderous, thought. Passage after passage suggests the origins of Macbeth; whether you take Camillo's:

> To do the deed
> Promotion follows. If I could find example,
> Of thousands that had struck anointed kings
> And flourish'd after, I'll not do it—

which is almost an epitome of the Scottish tragedy, or whether you take Paulina's:

> These dangerous unsafe lunes i' the king, beshrew them!
> He must be told on't—

words that match closely the vacillations and indecisions for which Lady Macbeth will upbraid her husband. Similarly, Leontes' lines (II, iii):

> *Nor night nor day no rest;* it is but weakness to bear the matter thus; mere weakness—

and Paulina's in the same scene:

> I do come to bring him sleep . . . I
> Do come with words as medicinal as true,
> Honest in either, to purge him of that humour
> That presses him from sleep

supply the sources of the "sleep no more" lines in *Macbeth*. Further, the Doctor's words, in *Macbeth*, V, iii, concerning the

> thick coming fancies,
> That keep her [Lady Macbeth] from her rest

and Macbeth's longings, expressed to that same Doctor, for some " sweet oblivious antidote," that shall

> Cleanse the stuff'd bosom of that perilous stuff
> Which weighs upon the heart—

are all, it would seem, topically derived, in part, from these Paulina scenes in *A Winter's Tale*, that were themselves suggested, as I suspect, by words which actually passed, in 1577, between de Vere and the Duchess of Suffolk. Even the references we have noted, to Leontes' instigation of secret murder:

> To have him kill a king; poor trespasses,
> More *monstrous* standing by.

recalls the catalogue of crimes committed by that " rarer monster," the " secret'st man of blood "—Macbeth.

Hamlet, again, tells Ophelia, who is Anne Cecil, that it is such as her who " make *monsters* " of men. Othello is jealous Leontes once more, though ennobled and exalted to the tragical plane of the mature dramas; and as for Lear, not only have we Paulina using, concerning Leontes' daughter, the words:

> Whose sting is sharper slander than the sword's.—

which is near to Lear's,

> How sharper than a serpent's tooth it is
> To have ungrateful daughters;

but also, in III, ii, the same lady says to Leontes:

>   A thousand knees
> Ten thousand years together, naked, lasting,
> Upon a barren mountain, and still winter
> In storm perpetual, could not move the gods
> To look that way thou went.

VERSE AND COURT COMEDY

This closing picture of a king, wandering naked, and in winter, over a barren mountain swept by perpetual storm—what is it but a forecast of the titanic tragedy, with which Oxford, some twenty years after writing these early scenes of *A Winter's Tale*,[1] will close, in 1598, his career as a creative dramatist?

Manifestly then, *Troilus* and its companion play, thus read together, and linked, as they have been, and will be, with plays that come before them and after, supply unanswerable evidence that this life-story, now opening to the reader, is actually that of the young courtier whose transcendent genius—now at first, as in other instances a quasi-morbid phenomenon—will clarify itself, with the passing of years, into the more spiritual, and relatively serene, faculties of the mature "Shakespeare," out of whom the offending Adam has been whipped and scourged by Consideration.

We have seen Oxford, some few pages back, stubbornly declining the Queen's request, that he would dance before de Bacqueville, who, as Alençon's ambassador for the Duke's marriage with the Queen, was being royally entertained by Elizabeth; but the Earl's plea, that he did not wish to amuse Frenchmen, was just an excuse; his much more probable, though unavowed, reason being that he was angry with the Queen who had scolded his particular friend, the Earl of Sussex, for neglecting—as she alleged—to supply enough plate for the side-board. De Vere, in fact, ever since his

---

[1] Greene's novel, *Pandosto*, printed in 1588, and generally supposed to be the source of *A Winter's Tale*, I take to have been written from the play, or from some other source common to both, and now lost. Paulina (Lady Suffolk), Autolycus and Antigonus—both of them Lord Oxford—do not appear in *Pandosto*, nor does the shepherd's son, who is William of Stratford

return from overseas, has been warmly sympathetic towards France, and is already dramatizing those French sympathies into one of the most verbally pleasing of all his early comedies, *Love's Labour's Lost*.

Mrs. E. T. Clark, in her study of the Revels Accounts,[1] has shown that, on 11 January, 1579, there was presented before the Queen and the French ambassador—probably de Simier, who had arrived on 5 January—*A Double Mask* comprising *A Mask of Amazons* and *A Mask of Knights*, in imitation of a tournament between six ladies, and a like number of gentlemen, who surrendered to them.[2] This imitation of a tournament, thinks Mrs. Clark—and I wholly concur—was a first representation of the comedy now known as *Love's Labour's Lost*, a tournament of poetical wit, in which the word wit occurs over forty times; this being done within a few weeks of the publication of the first volume of *The Anatomy of Wit*, by John Lyly, who is soon to be Oxford's private secretary and actor-manager, right through the fifteen-eighties.

For *Love's Labour's Lost*, as has often been observed, the commentators have never been able to discover any literary source; for the simple reason that the Earl, as usual, went direct to contemporary events, choosing for his characters persons whom he but thinly, and quite transparently, disguised; the two principals being King Henry of Navarre and Marguerite de Valois, married at the time of the Massacre of St. Bartholomew, only to be separated shortly after.

On 2 October, 1578, there was held, within Navarre's dominions at Nérac, as also in the play, a meeting between

---

[1] *Op. cit*, pp. 106–08.
[2] Hume, *Courtships of Queen Elizabeth*, p. 200.

Navarre and his nobles—who are the " Knights " of the " Double Mask," on one side, and, on the other, Margaret's mother, Queen Catherine—Katharine in the play—with the Maids of Honour as the Amazons. The purpose of the meeting was to discuss Queen Margaret's dowry, which had not been paid, and for which Navarre held, as sureties, certain cities in ancient Aquitaine, outside the borders of his kingdom—a state of affairs that is outlined in the opening scene of Act II of *Love's Labour's Lost*, where the topical allusions come pelting one upon another. England, however, and English characters, are aimed at in what, after all, is just a topical revue; for, as Mrs. Clark has observed, Holinshed, in 1577, describes the City of Leicester as standing " upon the river Sore," whence it surely follows that the lines below quoted must be aimed at the Earl of Leicester, who, though high in the Queen's favour, and much her " dear " or " deer," was hostile to the French marriage, and a resolute antagonist of Oxford at court.

> Put L to sore, then sorel jumps from thicket;
> Or pricket sore, or else sorel; the people fell a-hooting
> If sore be sore, the L to sore makes fifty sores one sorel!

The word sorel, be it added, was sometimes used of a chestnut horse—and Leicester was Elizabeth's Master of the Horse—while the three terms " pricket," " sorel " and " sore " were used of a buck, in its second, third, and fourth year, respectively. Leicester, therefore, a Sore L, when envisaging the French marriage, was not soothed by Oxford's attack upon him in the court-comedy of the Double Mask.

Here are more topical allusions. Costard's " Moth,

I will speak that l'envoy," is probably aimed at La Môthe Fénelon, who was then French ambassador to England; while the following passes of pate

Arma. Sirrah Costard, I will enfranchise thee.
Cost. O, marry me to one Frances—

simply means that Costard can be "enfranchised," or made a Frenchman of, by marriage with a "Frances," a feminized version of Francis of Alençon's name. Oxford, who, on the courtier side, is Biron, and, on the non-courtier side, Armado, inserts fewer references to himself than one might expect; though Biron's line:

Some men must love my lady, and some Joan—

recalls his poem *Fortune and Love* (1571), with its "Joan herself is she"; while the duologue between Biron and the King, in IV, iii, concerning the schools of day and night, is aimed, principally, at Chapman, the rival poet of the Sonnets, that still lie some fifteen years or more ahead, when Oxford will be rewriting *Love's Labour's Lost*. As Biron, the Earl enjoys himself hugely; but Armado—sure that he shall "turn sonnet" and ready now "for whole volumes in Folio"—prophecies that will be duly fulfilled, in print, by 1623—is no whit less vivacious; and, as usual, cannot resist an occasional fling at his rival, Hatton, in the lines:

"Yet was *Sampson* so tempted, and he had an excellent strength, yet was *Solomon* so seduced, and he had a very good wit. Cupid's butt shaft is too hard for *Hercules'* club.

The chances must be a thousand to one against its being mere coincidence that Master F. I. otherwise "Fortunatus Infelix," the "Fortunate Unhappy," who is

Hatton, who is Malvolio, had written lines containing the same three historic names and treating also of strength's weakness before love in *A Hundreth Sundrie Flowres*, of which Oxford was the original editor.

And *Salomon* himselfe, the source of sapience,
Against the force of such assaultes could make but small defence.
To it the stoutest yield, and strongest feel like woo,
Bold *Hercules* and *Sampson* both, did prove it to be so.[1]

With *Twelfth Night* thus already in our minds, and looming upon the horizon of our story, it is worth noting that this same scene I ii, of *Love's Labour's Lost* has just given us a stream of lines that foreshadow the opening of the Illyrian comedy.

> *Moth.* A woman, master.
> *Arma.* Of what complexion? ...
> *Moth.* Of the sea-water green, sir. ...
> *Arma.* Green indeed is the colour of lovers. ...
> *Moth.* ... for she had a green wit.
> *Arma.* My love is not immaculate white and red

The duologue between Orsino (Alençon) and Viola who is Alençon's first nuncio, La Môle, concerning " complexion " and the secretly love-sick girl's " green and yellow melancholy," joined to Viola's apostrophe over the red and white of Olivia's beauty, reveal one of Oxford's original sources for *Twelfth Night*, as surely as the business of the *Nine Worthies*, later in the Double Mask play, foreshadows the making of *A Midsummer Night's Dream*.

Precisely at what time, whether at first draft, or during revision, the Earl began to slip into his texts cipher-

---

[1] Admiral Holland first discovered this interesting allusion.

scenes indicating himself as secret author, with his plays symbolically dramatized under guise of a woman or a dog, it is impossible now to determine; but I think it more than probable that such words as Armado's "Truer than truth itself," followed by "veni, vidi, vici" are intended to recall the de Vere motto, "Vero Nihil Verius"; and that Armado, as King Cophetua, marrying the beggar-maid, directly symbolizes the princely author, married to a Jaquenetta who stands for the humble plays.

> "The conclusion is victory: on whose side? the king's. The captive is enriched: on whose side? the beggar's. The catastrophe is a nuptial: on whose side? the king's: no, on both in one, or one in both. I am the king; for so stands the comparison: thou the beggar; for so witnesseth thy lowliness. Shall I command thy love? I may: shall I enforce thy love? I could: shall I entreat thy love? I will. What shalt thou exchange for rags? robes; for tittles? titles; for thyself? me."

Here you have an almost exact analogy with Launce and his dog, in *Two Gentlemen of Verona*, II, iii.

I am the dog: no, the dog is himself, and I am the dog. Or the dog is me, and I am myself; ay, so, so—

the "catastrophe," in both instances, being a "nuptial" or merger of identity between king, or owner, on one side, and maid, or dog, on the other. We shall come across similar instances, in the other plays, of both a dog and a woman symbolizing the Shakesperean drama; and Jonson, who, of course, was behind the scenes in all this business, will repeatedly use the same "dog" metaphor, for the plays, when satirizing Oxford-Shakespeare, as Puntarvolo, in *Every Man Out of His Humour*. In the last quoted passage from *Love's Labour's Lost*, the line, "Shall I command thy love? I may," is almost echoed in the forged letter to Malvolio; "I may command where I adore."

Did Oxford himself take part, as actor, in these early performances of *Love's Labour's Lost*? My own belief is that he did; since Gilbert Talbot's letter to his father, the Earl of Shrewsbury:

> "It is but vain to trouble your Lordship with such shows as were showed before Her Majesty this Shrovetide at night. The chiefest was a device presented by the person of the Earl of Oxford, the Earl of Surrey, the Lords Thomas Howard and Windsor. The device was prettier than it happened to have been performed—

proves that Oxford was already a player in the entertainments at court. If the "device" was that Double Mask, which we now call *Love's Labour's Lost*, the Lord Great Chamberlain was then what, no doubt, he continued always to be—more skilled at writing comedies than at acting in them.

CHAPTER FIVE

"THE MERCHANT OF VENICE": AND "TWELFTH NIGHT" 1578–1580

"The Merchant of Venice" and Frobisher's Expedition to the New World—"The History of Portio and Demorantes"—Queen Elizabeth as Portia—She is a Loser, with Oxford, in the Cathay Company—Lock as the Original of Shylock—"The Merchant" is another Comedy of the Alençon Marriage Negotiations—Sidney and Oxford as Rivals, 1579—Lyly and "Euphues," 1580—Alençon Courtship and "Twelfth Night," 1580—Historic Originals of the Characters of "Twelfth Night"—Buckhurst and Sidney as Sir Toby and Sir Andrew—Oxford as Feste—And as "Speculum Tuscanismi"—Oxford as Actor in his own Comedies—He becomes also Actor-Manager.

OXFORD'S comedies, at this time, were, I imagine, mere interludes, or devices, that occupied, in the playing, little more than an hour or so; and they must have followed in close succession, one upon another, since they contain so many almost contemporaneous incidents of the years 1579 and 1580. A subject that deeply interested Oxford, among many other noblemen, was adventurous, and possibly profitable, expedition into the then unknown world. Martin Frobisher's first journey to the north-west took place in 1576, and we heard Dromio of Syracuse, in *The Comedy of Errors*, IV, iii, inform Antipholus of Syracuse, that "the bark *Expedition* put forth to-night." The third expedition to the new world, also under Frobisher, was in 1578, and Oxford invested therein the large sum of £3,000 which is nearly £30,000 in terms of modern purchasing power.

Unfortunately for him, and for the other investors, of whom Queen Elizabeth was one, the ore brought home from that adventure proved to be worthless; the losers having to content themselves with the empty satisfaction of sending to the Fleet prison Michael Lock, the Treasurer of the Cathay company, as it was called, who apparently knew full well that he had been selling worthless shares to Lord Oxford and the rest.[1] Bearing in mind Lock's name, and remembering also that dictionary meanings of the word " shy " include " disreputable " and " shady," the reader will, perhaps, agree that another unit in the sequence of Shakesperean plays is *The Merchant of Venice* (1579-80), with Shy-Lock as the dangerous lender out of moneys; and will accept my suggestion that the " three thousand ducats," for which Antonio " entered into bond," become interesting, as being the precise sum, in pounds, for which Oxford also engaged himself. It seems to follow, therefore, that Antonio is Oxford, " sad to think upon his merchandize," and a butt, in consequence, for the shafts of his merry friend, Gratiano, who, with reference to this melancholy, asks in the opening scene:

> " Why should a man whose blood is warm within
> Sit like his grandsire cut in alabaster?—

words which, as we have seen, are an allusion to Oxford's grandfather, the 15th Earl, whose figure is " cut in alabaster " in the church of St. Nicholas, at Castle Hedingham, the ancestral home of the de Veres.

[1] Admiral Holland has shrewdly surmised that Oxford-Hamlet's, " I am but mad north-north-west; when the wind is southerly I know a hawk from a handsaw," is a reference to his rash investment in the Cathay Company.

The Shylock-Antonio episodes, however, do not comprise the whole plot of *The Merchant of Venice*. Interwoven with it is the story of Portia, Bassanio, and the suitors, which is simply one more dramatization of the Alençon marriage-negotiations—with Queen Elizabeth for Portia, and Bassanio standing for Alençon or his envoys. Mrs. Clark is probably right in opining that *The Merchant of Venice* was first acted at court, on 2 February, 1580, by the Lord Chamberlain's servants, under the title of *The History of Portio* (Portia) *and Demorantes*—that last word being, perhaps, a mistranscription for "The Merchants." Stephen Gosson, attacking the stage in his *School of Abuse*, 1579, praises a play that he has seen at the Bull, called *The Jew*, and representing "the greediness of worldly chusers and bloody minds of usurers." Probably therefore *The Jew*, *The Merchant*, and *The History of Portio* are all the same play, under different titles; and it is highly significant that Portia's words, concerning her marriage problem:

> "I may neither choose whom I would nor refuse whom I dislike; so is the will of a living daughter curbed by the will of a dead father"—

are an exact echo of the will of Henry VIII, which provided that Elizabeth should not marry without the consent of the Privy Council. A dozen times, it may be, the Queen had murmured, in Oxford's presence, against the harsh terms of that document; and it is wholly characteristic of the Earl, that he, who also knew the burden and the pride of long descent, should weave that royal plaint into his dramatized tale of these wooers, come from the four quarters of the world, in quest of Elizabeth's hand: nor is it by chance, I imagine, that the Lord Great Chamberlain of England, whose special function was that of attendance upon royalty at coronations, has made the suitors choose between three caskets of lead, silver, and gold, standing for the three crowns of iron, silver, and gold, which symbolize the British monarch's triple title and claim to England, Ireland, and France.

Point after point confirms the truth of my arguments. Elizabeth, herself, as Mrs. Clark points out,[1] a disillusioned investor in the Cathay Company, may well have put as much effort, almost, into the prosecution of Lock, as Portia did into that of Shylock; and within some three weeks of what seems to have been the first production of this tragi-comedy, we find the Queen, alone in her chamber, admitting to Cecil, and to the Archbishop of York, concerning the nuptial farce she was playing with Alençon; " Here am I between Scylla and Charybdis," a phrase which, if I am right, she had recently heard used on the stage, by Lancelot Gobbo, quite possibly in the person of Oxford himself:

> " Thus when I shun Scylla your father, I fall into Charybdis your mother; well, you are gone both ways.

Who then is the historic original of young Gobbo? Gobbo, I suggest, personifies simply the Bohemian, or comedic, side of Oxford, who, upon the courtier side, is Antonio, and, perhaps, Gratiano too: the dramatist thus duplicating or triplicating himself here, just as he has done, or will do, in a dozen other plays. Oxford's father had died in 1562; and his widow, Margery Golding, married Charles Tyrrell, who thus

[1] *Op. cit.*, p. 198.

becomes the Earl's step-father. Tyrrell died in 1570, and in 1581 Oxford was accused of necromancy, on the strength of an assertion, by himself, that "Tyrrell appeared to him with a whip, which had made a better show in the hand of a carman than of *Hob-Goblin*." Now remembering that the name of Oxford's mother was Margery, and noting also that the central letters of *Hob-goblin* spell Gobbo, and are applied to Tyrrell, who is Oxford's step-father; and not forgetting, likewise, that Oxford is known to have been in the hands of money-lenders at this time, who are often of Jewry's race—read the dialogue that follows, wherein all the above motives occur, besides that of concealed identity, and then, if you will, graciously admit that though you " have your eyes " you, in common with a vast majority, have, until now " failed of the knowing " that Lancelot Gobbo is none other than " Shakespeare " himself. This is the dialogue, from *The Merchant of Venice*, II, ii.

Launce. Do you not know me, father?
Gobbo. Alack, sir, I am sand-blind; I know you not.
Launce. Nay, indeed, if you had your eyes, you might fail of the knowing me: it is a wise father that knows his own child. Well, old man, I will tell you news of your son: give me your blessing: truth will come to light; murder cannot be hid long; a man's son may; but, at the length, truth will out.
Gobbo. Pray you, sir, stand up: I am sure you are not Launcelot, my boy.
Launce. Pray you, let's have no more fooling about it, but give me your blessing. I am Launcelot, your boy that was, your son that is, your child that shall be.

> *Gobbo.* I cannot think you are my son.
> *Launce.* I know not what I shall think of that: but I am Launcelot the Jew's man; and I am sure Margery your wife is my mother.

The thing could hardly be stated more plainly. Oxford was, indeed, the Jew's man, and Lock's also; and Margery was, in actual fact, the mother of a courtier-dramatist, hidden then, for hundreds of years to come from the eyes of a sand-blind public, but destined, some three and a half centuries afterward, to be discovered. "At the length truth will out," since neither murder, nor even the name of a man's son, can be for ever concealed.

In 1579, at the time of his tennis-court quarrel with Sidney, of which more anon, Lord Oxford, we know, on Fulke Greville's authority, was "superlative in the Prince's favour," at full zenith of his career, as chiefest courtier, and favoured darling of the Queen. But that such deeds of carpet-knighthood as verbal coruscating, court dancing, flirtation, and playing "forehorse to a smock," in no sense fulfilled the young Earl's swelling ambitions, our quotations from Bertram, in *All's Well that Ends Well*, have already abundantly proved. So long ago as 1577, it may be remembered, there was current in London the rumour that de Vere was "not to continue a courtier," but had bought a house in Watling Street, and purposed retiring thereto. Only let not the reader imagine that scholarly or literary leisures were yet, for many years to come, his ideal of national service. Military command abroad, or upon the seas, was unquestionably his strongest wish; but, failing such employment, that restless mind, and ardent fancy, would find fullest and most congenial relief from the fatuities of court-routine, in the composition of court-comedies, at once satirically daring, and lyrically lovely, of which the vivacity, the wit, the word-play, the swelling eloquence, and the compelling human interest, intensely amused, when it did not bitterly exasperate, the Queen and all her entourage. Burleigh, perhaps, with a handful of his puritan and philistine friends, to whom stages were anathema; and a few of Oxford's keenest rivals, such as Hatton and Philip Sidney, may have burned with indignation at finding their withers so often, and so cruelly, wrung; but the court in general was charmed and delighted.

With our national language and literature still in the flood of its fresh exuberance, while the stage, as means of instruction and entertainment, grew daily in popularity and developed in purpose, these early works of Oxford, though crude and fragmentary in form, when compared with the masterpieces familiar to us to-day, must have been mightily esteemed by those high-spirited lords and ladies of Gloriana's court. Words were valued for their own sakes, far more then than they are to-day; and at Windsor, or Whitehall, there was no more popular pastime than wit-cracking, with the clash of mind upon mind matching that of blade upon blade.

Early in 1579, the year with which we are now concerned, John Lyly dedicated to Lord de la Ware, and published, his *Euphues, the Anatomy of Wit*, containing a wealth of metaphor, word-jugglery, and rhetoric, which captured instantly the educated Elizabethans; and made of Lyly's novel, in a single day, the most widely read book in the country. It did more. *Euphues* fastened upon John Lyly the close attention of Oxford himself, already the leading dramatist in the land;

whereby the second volume (1580) will be dedicated to his new patron,

> "by birth born to the greatest office, and therefore me thought by right to be placed in great authority; for whoso compareth the honour of your Lordship's noble house with the fidelity of your ancestors may well say, which no other can truly gainsay, *Vero nihil verius*."

Lyly is already, in 1579, the Earl's private secretary and the plays that Euphues will write under Lord Oxford's patronage, during the 'eighties, show, in my judgment, a far closer connexion with Shakesperean drama than has yet been realized or brought to light.[1]

Another literary friend and protégé of Oxford's must now take his place in our story. The Queen, herself a scholar, and unfailingly sympathetic towards learning in her land, paid in July 1578, a second visit to Cambridge University, accompanied by the whole court, including the Earl of Oxford. The court-party was met at Audley End, by University men, and heard there an address by Gabriel Harvey, a portion of which made direct personal appeal to Edward de Vere.

> "Thy splendid fame, great Earl, demands even more than in the case of others the services of a poet possessing lofty eloquence. Thy merit doth creep along the ground, nor can it be confined within the limits of a song. It is a wonder which reaches as far as the heavenly orbs.
>
> "O great-hearted one, strong in thy mind and thy fiery will, thou wilt conquer thyself, thou wilt conquer others; thy glory will spread out in

---

[1] See my analysis of the lyrics in a few of Lyly's plays: *The Case for Edward de Vere as "Shakespeare,"* pp. 44–66.

in all directions beyond the Arctic ocean; and England will put thee to the test and prove thee to be a native born Achilles. Do thou but go forward boldly and without hesitation. . . . For a long time past Phœbus Apollo has cultivated thy mind in the arts. English poetical measures have been sung by thee long enough. Let that Courtly Epistle—more polished even than the writings of Castiglione himself—witness how greatly thou dost excel in letters . . . thou hast drunk deep draughts not only of the Muses of France and Italy, but hast learned the manners of many men, and the arts of foreign countries. . . . O thou hero worthy of renown, throw away the insignificant pen, throw away bloodless books, and writings that serve no useful purpose; now must the sword be brought into play, now is the time for thee to sharpen the spear and to handle great engines of war."

The oration was, in part, prophetic. Oxford, indeed, though through fearful suffering, was to effect, at last, that hardest of all conquests, the victory over himself; and his glory was to spread in all directions. Moreover, with the mighty conflict against Spain already gathering towards explosion, there was less incongruity then than is now easily apparent, in this fervid plea, by a man-of-letters, to "Shakespeare" in person, to abandon for " great engines of war," a pen that had written already—though in incomplete form—besides that gracious letter to which Harvey refers, *Love's Labour's Lost, Troilus, The Merchant of Venice*, and I know not how many more; and, within some three years, was to have shaped *Much Ado about Nothing, Measure for Measure*, and *Hamlet* also. Harvey, moreover, also knew well that such martial urgings would be congenial; and—though conscious that all men must abide their fate—Edward de Vere's destiny, even while recognizing, in part, his genius, Gabriel could not foresee, nor know, as we know, that already the events of 1579 are shaping in the Earl's mind the scheme and characters of that most delicious and captivating of all his fantastic comedies, *Twelfth Night*.

The great question at court, in the spring of 1579, was the proposed marriage between the Queen and Alençon, favoured by the Burleigh group, including Oxford; but bitterly opposed by Leicester, and by his nephew and prospective heir, Philip Sidney; Leicester, in consequence falling deep into the Queen's disgrace; and deeper still, even to banishment from court, when Simier revealed to her that her aforetime favourite courtier was secretly married to Lettice widow of the first Earl of Essex. Philip Sidney thus became leader of the opposition to the French match, and principal diplomatic opponent of Oxford, who had already crossed his path, in 1571, when both the young courtiers had sought Anne Cecil for wife.

The incident that set this rivalry once more ablaze was the famous tennis-court quarrel, a trivial enough affair, arising out of a peremptory demand by the Earl, that Sidney should leave the playing court. Epithets, including " Puppy " from Oxford, were freely tossed about, to the immense amusement of the French Commissioners, who " had that day audience in those private galleries whose windows looked into the tennis court," and who " instantly drew all to this tumult," thereby permitting several courtiers to hear Sidney " give my lord a lie."

An idle storm in a tennis-court; yet interesting to us by the echoes of it, still clearly audible in the Shakesperean plays, including the duologue between Touchstone and Jaques—both characters being Oxford—in *As You Like It*, V, iv, concerning the lies, "circumstantial" and "direct," in the "quarrel upon the seventh cause"; and, more particularly, in *Hamlet*, V, i, where the prince complains that "the toe of the peasant comes so near the heel of the courtier he galls his kibe"—words that I read as a direct allusion to the rebuke subsequently administered to Sidney by Elizabeth, when she recalls to him, in the matter of this tennis-court quarrel, the difference in degree between an earl and a gentleman, and the respect owed by inferiors to superiors; concluding with a reminder, that failure by gentlemen to recognize the privileges of the nobility, in this respect, did but encourage the peasants to insult both.

Not in *As You Like It*, however, nor in *Hamlet*, but in a comedy drafted, as I suppose, in 1580, soon after the quarrel, is that falling out, and Sidney's share in it, most happily burlesqued. I mean, of course, the fray, "without perdition of souls," between Viola and Aguecheek, in the third act of *Twelfth Night*. Nor have I the slightest doubt about the historic original of that ridiculous letter of challenge written by Andrew to Viola, and concerning which Fabian, who with Feste is Oxford himself, has just remarked, "If this were played upon a stage now, I could condemn it as an improbable fiction." The clue was given to me by Fabian's chuckling comment, as he fingers the epistle; "More matter for a *May morning*," whereupon I turned up Sidney's bellicose letter, written on 31 *May*, 1578, to his father's secretary, Molyneux, and running, in part thus,

"*You have* played the very knave with me, and so I will make you know *if I have* good proof of it. But that for so much as is past. For that is to come. . . . I will thrust my dagger into you. And trust to it, for I speak in earnest. In the meantime fatewell."

One can imagine with what delight Oxford pounced upon the childish inconsequence, and muddle-headedness of this " clodpole " letter, and with his happy aptitude for burlesqueing characteristics of style, gleefully twisted it into Andrew's absurd challenge, using closely similar words, and concluding upon a " fare thee well "—which is Sidney's own phrase—" thy friend as thou usest him." Oxford, probably, knew from Molyneux himself that Sidney's subsequent letters to that individual are signed : " Your loving friend." It may, I think, be taken as positively certain, that the actual dialogue of all the principal characters in *Twelfth Night* remains substantially true to their styles of conversation in real life.

In this year 1580, the troubles that weighed so heavily upon Queen and country, including fear of Spanish power, Puritan anger at Elizabeth's flippant conduct with Simier, her seeming determination to marry Alençon, his acceptance of the nominal sovereignty of Flanders, the tense embitterment of Catholic against Protestant—all these, for a while, seem, nevertheless, but lightly to touch Oxford, now hard at work upon his comedy of Illyria, wherein, as have seen, Olivia stands for the Queen, Orsino mainly for Alençon—with something of his brother, Henry III, thrown in—Sir Christopher Hatton for Malvolio, Sidney for Aguecheek, Lord Buckhurst for Sir Toby Belch, Fabian and Feste for Oxford himself, and Lady Mary Vere, probably, for Maria.

The key note for *Twelfth Night*, however, is, strangely enough, no merry chime of wedding bells, but rather that doleful tolling from the tower of St. Germain l'Auxerrois, which signalled the massacre of St. Bartholomew; the veiled cloistress of that opening scene being none other than Elizabeth-Olivia herself, mourning for her co-religionists foully slain across the Channel, and urged, by the Duke, to fill her sovereign throne, by alliance with one self-king, himself. The play must have been revised in 1586, as many allusions, topical in that year, seem conclusively to show; but point after point, no less certainly, touches the late 'seventies as when Sir Andrew, remarking to Sir Toby, "I think I have the back trick simply as strong as any man in Illyria," reminds us that, in September 1577, in the person of Sidney, he had publicly turned his back upon his father's old enemy, the Earl of Ormond. More intimate still, however, and contrived probably from actual talk and banter between the Queen, and that couple of rival courtiers, Hatton and Oxford, are such lines as these :

Clown. Sir Toby ... will not pass his word for two pence that you are no fool.
Oliv. How say you to that, Malvolio?
Malv. I marvel your ladyship takes delight in such a barren rascal. I saw him put down the other day with an ordinary fool that has no more brain than a stone. Look you now, he's out of his guard already; unless you laugh and minister occasion to him, he is gagged. ...
Oliv. O, you are sick of self-love, Malvolio, and taste with a distempered appetite. To be generous, guiltless, and of free disposition, is to take those

things for bird-bolts that you deem cannon bullets; there is no slander in an allowed fool, though he do nothing but rail. . . .

Clown. Now Mercury endue thee with leasing, for thou speakest well of fools.

Sir Edmund Chambers, endeavouring to support his assertion that there are but few topical allusions in plays which I maintain to be crammed with them, urges that the Stratford man, had he dared thus to play with great names, and exalted persons, would have been sent straight to the Marshalsea. I wholly agree; but Elizabeth's Lord Great Chamberlain, ward, and privileged corrupter of words, and vicar for the lawless marriage of ink and paper, was, for these sufficient reasons, immune from the penalties of the "ordinary fool," and was granted the special prerogatives of "William Shakespeare." That merry kitchen-scene also, of which the austere George Chapman, rival poet of the sonnets to be, will so deeply disapprove, as dragging Shakespeare's potentially beautiful art into the ditch,[1] reveals equally its topical secret upon every page. When Sir Toby calls Olivia "a Cataian," he means, simply, that Elizabeth was, as we have seen her to be, in common with Oxford himself, an investor in, and loser by, that Cathay Company which had come to grief with the third Frobisher expedition of 1578. Again, when Toby asks, "Am I not consanguineous, am I not of her blood?" he is just informing us that his historic prototype, Thomas Sackville, Lord Buckhurst, possessed a grandmother who was aunt to Queen Elizabeth's mother, Anne Boleyn. When he bellows that toast to "the twelfth day o' December," which brings Malvolio infuriated upon the stage, he is

---

[1] See my *Shakespeare and Chapman as Topical Dramatists*, pp. 133-34

repeating, in a later revision of the play, the exact words of the patent by which, on 12 December, 1590, the Queen granted to Buckhurst the office of Lord Chief Butler of England and of Wales, at the large salary of three hundred marks a year—that office being concerned with the regulations of import duties upon wines. Further, his reference, at the opening of the letter-scene, to Malvolio as the "rascally sheep-biter," is aimed directly at Hatton's nickname of "sheep," and links with Hatton's letter to Queen Elizabeth, wherein he describes himself as "sheep," and refers to Oxford as "the boar."

The signature to the forged letter, "The Fortunate Unhappy," is a translation of Hatton's own posy, "Si Fortunatus Infœlix," and—Malvolio being, I think, a composite of Hatton with the Frenchman Marchaumont then high in the Queen's favour—we can find the origin of the yellow stockings and garter business in the following description, written by the Spanish Ambassador to the King of Spain, after Elizabeth's visit to Drake's ship, *The Pelican*, at Deptford, on 11 April, 1581.[1]

> "Marchaumont also sent with it a purple and gold garter belonging to the Queen, which slipped down and was trailing as she entered Drake's ship (the *Pelican* at Deptford). Marchaumont stooped and picked it up, and the Queen asked for it, promising him that he should have it back when he reached home, as she had nothing else wherewith to keep her stocking up.

When one links together the stocking, garter, and

[1] See my *Shakespeare and Chapman as Topical Dramatists*, pp. 39-45.

picking-up motives of this passage, and considers the inflation likely to be caused in Marchaumont's mind, by royal commission to knight so great a national hero, upon so great an occasion, upon the Queen's behalf; and then compares the similar exaltation of Malvolio as " count," sitting in his state, it becomes, to my thinking, almost certain that Oxford must have accompanied the Queen on board the *Pelican*, and have drawn thence ideas which he subsequently made use of in *Twelfth Night*. In this connexion, moreover, it is well to remind ourselves that Drake himself is sometimes held to be the historic original of the Buccaneer sea-captain, Antonio, in this same comedy, though, personally, I hold that the Antonio of *Twelfth Night*—the virile captain of that " bawbling vessel " encountered by Duke Orsino —was, historically, Drake's rival, Antonio, the Portuguese Pretender, of whom we read[1] that his " proceedings are feared almost as much as Drake's."

Lastly, for the identification of Sir Andrew and Philip Sidney, I will quote Sir Toby:

> " He (Andrew) is knight, dubbed with unhatched rapier and on carpet consideration: but he is devil in a private brawl "—

and will here add the explanation, which is, that in 1583 Queen Elizabeth wished to bestow the Order of the Garter upon the Polish Prince, Casimir, who, unwilling to undertake the long journey from Central Europe, asked his English friend, Philip Sidney, to stand proxy for him upon the occasion. By the rules of the English court, however, no one might stand proxy for the bestowal of one of the higher orders of knighthood,

[1] S. P. Dom., 13 April, 1586.

unless and until he himself were a knight. Elizabeth accordingly knighted Sidney on the spot, to enable him to stand proxy for his friend; and that is the dubbing "on carpet consideration," to which Oxford, through the mouth of Sir Toby, mockingly refers.

All these references to events after 1580–81 were, of course, additions to the first draft of the play; but few readers, I imagine, will be disposed to deny that Oxford crammed this comedy, in common with his others, through and through with topical stuff.

We have heard Gabriel Harvey at Cambridge, in the summer of 1578, eulogizing Oxford, and beseeching him to abandon the pen for the sword—advice which circumstance, rather than desire, prevented the Earl from following. Harvey, however, as a member of that literary Club called the Areopagos, over which Philip Sidney ruled, would naturally hear much criticism of the Earl during Areopagite gatherings; and in 1580, at a time when the construction of the English hexameter was much in question, Harvey contributed to the discussion, in that very form, some unconscionably bad verses, entitled *Speculum Tuscanismi*, which, nevertheless, are very useful stuff, as vividly caricaturing Oxford, at thirty years of age.

"No words but valorous, no works but womanish only.
For life Magnificoes, not a beck but glorious in show,
In deed most frivolous, not a look but Tuscanish always.
His cringing side neck, eyes glancing, fisnamie smirking,
With forefinger kiss, and brave embrace to the footward. . . .
Large bellied Kodpeased doublet, unkodpeased half hose,

Straight to the dock like a shirt, and close to the britch like a diveling.
A little apish hat couched fast to the pate like an oyster,
French Camarick ruffs, deep with a whiteness, starched to the purpose.
Every one A per se A, his terms and braveries in print,
Delicate in speech, quaint in array, conceited at all points,
In courtly guiles a passing singular odd man,
For Gallants a brave Mirror, a Primrose of Honour,
A Diamond for nonce, a fellow peerless in England.
Not the like discourser for Tongue, and head to be found out,
Not the like resolute man for great and serious affairs,
Not the like Lynx to spy out secrets and privities of States,
Eyed like to Argus, eared like to Midas, nos'd like to Naso,
Wing'd like to Mercury, fittest of a thousand for to be employ'd.
This, nay more than this, doth practise of Italy in one year.
None do I name, but some do I know, that a piece of a twelve month
Hath so perfited outly and inly both body and soul,
That none, for sense and senses half matchable with them
A vulture's smelling, Ape's tasting, sight of an Eagle,
A Spider's touching, Hart's hearing, might of a Lion,
Compounds of wisdom, wit, prowess, bounty, behaviour,
All gallant virtues, all qualities of body and soul.
O thrice ten hundred thousand times blessed and happy,
Blessed and happy travail, Travailer most blessed and happy."

That the individual aimed at here must be de Vere is absolutely certain; for whether you take the vanity, the womanishness, the Tuscan influences, the conviction that he is cut out for great and serious affairs, the quaintness of array, the frivolous deed, the eccentricities of manner, or the closing epithet of "blessed Travailer," they are not only Oxford to the life, but are all echoed in the attacks made upon Oxford, as Shakespeare, in the plays of Jonson and Chapman. The affair, it seems, had no sequel of any consequence. Oxford himself, I imagine, wisely taking the business for bird-bolts rather than cannon-balls, just laughed at the joke; yet there is a story extant, of Gabriel Harvey hiding in Leicester's house, for dread of the Earl's avenging wrath; and Tom Nashe, Harvey's opponent in the Martin Marprelate controversy, which was an offshoot of the Oxford-Sidney quarrels, promptly reminded Harvey, in the following words, that it was a dangerous business to anger the Queen's Lord Great Chamberlain.

> He is but a little fellow, but he hath one of the best wits in England. Should he take thee in hand again (as he fleeth from such inferior concentation) I prophecy there would be more gentle readers die of a merry mortality engendered by the eternal jests he would maul thee with, than there have done of the last infection.

Eight weeks in Leicester House is a cheap enough price to pay for the privilege of lampooning "Shakespeare" with impunity, about the very time that he was writing *Twelfth Night*.

February of the following year, 1581, brought another lampoon upon Oxford, this time by Barnabe Riche,

TWELFTH NIGHT

lately returned from war in the Low Countries, and now enjoying the patronage of de Vere's rival, Sir Christopher Hatton. The book in which the attack appeared was *Farewell to the Military Profession*.

> "It was my fortune at my last being in London to walk through the Strand towards Westminster, where I met one came riding towards me on a foot-cloth nag, apparelled in a French ruff, a French cloak, a French hose, and in his hand a great fan of feathers, bearing them up (very womanly) against the side of his face. And for that I had never seen any man wear them before that day, I began to think it impossible that there might be a man found so foolish as to make himself a scorn to the world to wear so womanish a toy; but rather thought it had been some shameless woman that had disguised herself like a man in our hose and our cloaks ... a French hood on his head, a French ruff about his neck, and a pair of French hose on his legs, had been right—à la mode de France; and this had been something suitable to his wit."

Here, with the usual allowance for exaggeration of caricature, is another very vivid sketch of Oxford, at this time, and one in which, perhaps, there is more than at first meets the eye; for I concur with Mrs. E. T. Clark, that we may, quite possibly, have here a portrait of Oxford returning down the Strand, in his actor's costume, from the Blackfriars, or some other private theatre, where he had been playing. Gabriel Harvey, in *Speculum Tuscanismi*, had mentioned "Apes Tasting," as one of the Earl's quaint proclivities; and those apes I take to be actors. That Oxford played in court masques, we know; and that he took part in his own court-plays I regard as positively certain; and shall, in due course, bring further evidence to prove. Mrs. Clark points out[1] that, precisely at this time, and in connexion with the very function that has provided hints and clues for *Twelfth Night*, namely Queen Elizabeth's visit to Drake on board the *Pelican*, the following verses appeared, in honour of the sailor's exploits.

> "Sir Francis, Sir Francis, Sir Francis is come;
> Sir Robert and eke Sir William his son,
> And eke the good Earl of Huntingdon
> Marched gallantly on the road.
>
> Then came the Lord Chamberlain with his white staff
> And all the people began to laugh;
> And then the queen began to speak,
> 'You're welcome home, Sir Francis Drake.'"

Why, very pertinently asks Mrs. Clark, should the crowd laugh at the Lord Chamberlain, who was Thomas Ratcliffe, 3rd Earl of Sussex, a serious and dignified courtier, about fifty-five years old? Why indeed! and I wholly agree with my co-worker upon these themes, that the people were, much more probably, laughing not at the Lord Chamberlain, but at the highly popular Lord *Great* Chamberlain, the Queen's accredited comedian, flippant in word, frivolous in deed, whose presence, at that function, our brief study of *Twelfth Night* seemed strongly to suggest.

Oxford, in my judgment, was already becoming actor-manager, as well as playwright, an important addition to his activities, when it is remembered that our

[1] *Op. cit*, p. 124.

opponents bring up against us, until we are weary of hearing it, the argument that Oxford could not be "Shakespeare" because no man other than a professional actor could, for technical reasons, have written those plays. My answer is that Oxford was, in actual fact, just such a practised actor—and actor-manager to boot—as the circumstances seem to require him to be; and that this year 1580 was precisely the one during which the Earl of Warwick's company was transferred to Lord Oxford's service, probably with de Vere's private secretary, John Lyly, as their manager. Until this time, it would seem, Oxford's plays had been produced. either privately at court, or by the Pauls Boys, or the Lord Chamberlain's company, under the patronage of Oxford's friend, the Earl of Sussex; but henceforth, though we have no record of the appearance of Oxford's players at court before January 1584, it is probable that they played at Blackfriars, or some other small private theatre. On 21 June, 1580, John Hatcher, Vice-Chancellor of Cambridge University, wrote to Burleigh, who was the Chancellor, to acknowledge a recommendation from him, and from Sussex, that Oxford's men should be allowed to "show their cunning in several plays already practised by them before the Queen's Majesty." Oxford's further development, as patron of players, we shall reach with *Hamlet*, in 1583.

The comedy that Oxford seems to have drafted during 1580, was, it will be remembered, almost certainly *Twelfth Night*, a play concerning which Dr. Mackail has recently remarked, that it is followed by the "prodigious change of axis," which occupied two or three years, and produced the tragedies. Dr. Mackail, being an orthodox commentator, cannot, of course, even suggest a reason for such happenings ; but Captain Ward and myself are, fortunately, able to supply the necessary information and reasoning, which are imperatively necessary to any real comprehension of the next three or four Shakesperean plays, the themes and manner of which will be definitely shaped by Lord Oxford's bitter experiences during the years lying immediately ahead, as they already have been by the estrangement from his countess in 1576.

CHAPTER SIX

OXFORD'S BATTLE WITH THE HOWARD-ARUNDEL GROUP:
1581–1582

Oxford and the Roman Catholic Howard-Arundel Group—Oxford charges them with Treasonable Practice—Their counter-Charges—Oxford as the "Deformed"—Arundel's Catalogue of Accusations parodied in Dogberry's list of charges against Conrad and Borachio in "Much Ado About Nothing"—A Consideration of the Charges against Oxford—"Two Gentlemen of Verona," and Oxford's relations with Queen Elizabeth—All potentialities, for Good and Evil, in Edward de Vere—De Vere sent to the Tower—Again in the Tower for seducing Anne Vavasour—Oxford's charges result in royal Proclamation against Roman Catholics—January 12, 1582—"Much Ado About Nothing," a Dramatization of the Oxford and Howard-Arundel Affair—So also is "Measure for Measure," in its relation to Oxford and Anne Cecil.

WHEN Oxford returned from his Italian journey, in 1576, strong leanings had been begotten in him towards Roman Catholicism, a change probably accounted for by his vivid sense of, and respect for, historic continuity, and in part by æsthetic sympathy with the elaborate rituals of Rome, a visit to which city we shall find strongly hinted at in *Measure for Measure*.

Soon after his arrival in England, it seems, he made secret profession of his conversion to the Roman Catholic faith, to his cousins, Lord Henry Howard and Charles Arundel, who, with Francis Southwell, formed a group with which he had long been "inward," although Howard and Arundel were probably the authors of those slanders upon the Countess of Oxford, which became de Vere's excuse, if not his justification, for a long separation from his wife. The Earl's Catholic sympathies, however, were never permitted to compromise his patriotism; and when, shortly before Christmas 1580, he discovered that the Howard group were practising secret treacheries, and had become a menace to their country, he hastened to make formal accusation to Queen Elizabeth, against his former companions, begging forgiveness, at the same time, for what he now recognized to be his own wrong-doing in the matter. Instantly, upon hearing that Oxford had accused him, Howard, accompanied by Arundel and Southwell, fled at midnight to the house of the Spanish Ambassador, Bernardino de Mendoza, who wrote, on Christmas day, to the King of Spain:

> "Coming to my house at midnight, though I had never spoken to them [i.e., Howard, etc.], they told me of the danger in which they found themselves of losing their lives, unless I would hide them. As they were Catholics I entertained them. Milord Harry in gratitude ... has informed and continues to inform me of everything that he hears.

There followed a terrific explosion, with powerful repercussions upon Oxford's own career, and upon the Shakesperean drama of succeeding years. Elizabeth was greatly enraged; and although, says de Castelnau,[1] the French Ambassador, the accused "were able to clear themselves very satisfactorily," of the charge of conspiracy against the State, they remained under grave suspicion, and were placed under restraint by the Queen—Francis Southwell in charge of Walsingham; Howard in charge of the Lord Chancellor, Thomas Bromley;

[1] Letter to the King of France, 11 January, 1581.

and Arundel in the care of Sir Christopher Hatton, one of Lord Oxford's bitterest opponents. In answer to the Earl's interrogatories, they issued, from their places of durance, a series of categorical denials, supported by counter-charges, against their accuser, of so serious a kind that, again according to de Castelnau,

> "Oxford found himself alone in his evidence and accusations. He has lost credit and honour, and has been abandoned by all his friends and by all the ladies of the court.... The Earl of Oxford, finding himself alone and unsupported, threw himself on his knees several times before the queen.

The issue was deeply joined; their liberty and reputations against his—*Measure for Measure* also, and, it may be, Life for Life. Here are a few of the counter-charges brought against Oxford by his cousins, as recorded in the State Papers Domestic for 1581.

> *Howard.* Touching mine accuser: if the botchie and deformities of his mis-shapen life suffice not to discredit and disgrace the warrant of his wreakful word: yet let his practises with some gentlemen to seek my life.

Here the word "deformities" is interesting, when we remember that Ben Jonson, in *Cynthia's Revels*, refers, again and again, to Oxford-Shakespeare as "The Deformed," a "Traveller"; "one so made out of the mixture of shreds of forms that himself is truly deform'd[1]" while Borachio and Conrad, in *Much Ado About Nothing*—who are simply Howard and Arundel,[2] with assistance

---

[1] See my *Oxford-Shakespeare Case Corroborated*, pp 94–99
[2] Conrad is almost an anagram for C. Arundel—El. Cunrad.

from the Watch, let fall much enigmatic dialogue concerning a fashionably arrayed "Deformed" thief, who "wears a lock and goes up and down like a gentleman." *Much Ado About Nothing*, in substance a tragi-comedy, we shall discover to be simply a dramatization of this tragi-comical episode in its writer's own career. Oxford, concludes Howard bitterly:

> "shall have less cause to vaunt, who, flocking in all kinds of vice and shameful treacheries, without one care of God, of honour, or of nature, smileth and triumpheth at our durance.

The Earl sent many interrogatories for the prisoners to answer, including questions concerning certain suppers in Fish Street, concerning talk of the King of Scots beginning "to put on spurs on his heels, and so soon as the matter of Monsieur [i.e., the Alençon marriage negotiations] were assured to be at an end," and also relative to the Duke of Guise, that head of the Catholic party, who "would briche her Majesty for all her wantonness," and so forth.

Arundel replied with categorical and comprehensive denials which, he supposed, must bring his accuser's charges to "castle come down, and dissolve to nothing now," since they are forged "out of his own giddy brain." Then, becoming in his turn the accuser, he charges the Earl with a list of appalling offences, including "horrible enormities," "great beastliness," "detestable vices and impure life," so that "to report at large all the vices of this monstrous Earl were a labour without end." Oxford, he continues, is a perjurer, an impudent and senseless liar, and so great boaster, especially when "in his cups," that Arundel has often "been driven (thereby) to rise from his table laughing." In this matter of the Earl's alleged lies, " the least of which will gain a whetstone," we can here recall *Cynthia's Revels*, II, 1, wherein Mercury says, of Amorphus, the Deformed Traveller, who is Oxford-Shakespeare, " He will lie cheaper than any beggar ... for which he is right properly accommodated to the Whetstone his Page."[1]

The catalogue lengthens.

> " He is a notorious drunkard and very seldom sober ... in his drunken fits he is no man but a beast, dispossessed of all modesty, temperance and reason, and roars as one possessed with a wicked spirit—

words that recall Hamlet's " a beast without discourse of reason," in a tragedy that is to follow within some three years from the date of these charges. Arundel's further complaint, that Oxford is " never restrained from this liberty of *railing*," probably voices a grievance commonly felt by the victims of Oxford's tongue, and pen ; and is a most significant reminder of Olivia-Elizabeth's words concerning Oxford-Feste in *Twelfth Night*, that " there is no slander in an allowed fool, though he do nothing but *rail*," more especially when that allowed fool's railings chance greatly to amuse the Queen's majesty.

From the sordidly detailed accusations that follow, of unnatural and nameless crimes and villainies, I must shield my readers susceptibilities, mentioning only Oxford's alleged " detestable practise of hired murder,"[2]

---

[1] *Ibid*, pp 111-13

[2] Compare the catalogue of these charges—including subornation to murder, " monstrosity," etc., with those made against Leontes (Oxford) in the first three acts of *A Winter's Tale*. See ante pp 121-122

of which two intended victims, according to Arundel, were to be the Earl of Leicester, and Leicester's nephew, Philip Sidney, whom Oxford has already been pricking with the pen. Article 45 concludes as follows.

> *Fifthly.* To show that the world never brought forth such a villainous monster, and for a parting blow to give him his full payment, I will prove against him his most horrible and detestable blasphemy, in denial of the divinity of Christ our saviour, and terming the Trinity as a fable. This heard my Lord Windsor, my Lord Harry, Rawlie, Southwell, and myself. And that Joseph was a wittold. . . .
>
> *To conclude.* He is a beast in all respects, and in him no virtue to be found, and no vice wanting.

Reading these lines, in the full consciousness that we were already deep in the atmosphere of *Much Ado About Nothing*, the words "fifthly" and "to conclude" made instant contact, in my mind, with the duologue, in V, i, between Dogberry and Don Pedro, concerning Conrad and Borachio, whom I had long suspected to be none other than Arundel and Howard.

> *Dogb.* Marry, Sir, they have committed false report; moreover, they have spoken untruths; secondly, they are slanders; sixthly and lastly, they have belied a lady; thirdly they have verified unjust things; and, to conclude, they are lying knaves.
>
> *Don Pedr.* First, I ask thee what they have done; thirdly, I ask thee what's their offence; sixth and lastly, why they are committed; and, to conclude, what you lay to their charge.

"Fifthly .. to conclude" urges Arundel : " Sixthly and lastly ... to conclude," mocks Don Pedro ! Comparing the text of the charges with the text of Shrkespeare's play, does it not become indisputablef Shakespeare's final retort upon those " lying knaves," his accusers, who, in a previous page, have complained of his unshackeled liberty of railing, is good humouredly to " rail " upon them, once more, in his very next play; to have them arrested by an imbecile watch, and informed against by a Dogberry, whom themselves " write down an ass." As also in the case of the Burleigh letters and Polonius, and of Sidney's letter in the character of Andrew Aguecheek, in *Twelfth Night*, we have the exact literary style of Arundel, in formulating his charges, ruthlessly parodied as a *Much Ado About Nothing*. Did ever another individual, in literary or other history, placed in circumstances of such difficulty and danger, take a happier revenge upon his foes ?—a revenge that, ever since, has provided legitimate laughter for millions, upon the stages of the world, and will continue to do so, for centuries yet to come.

Rash and reckless, nevertheless, even at these crises of his life, is Oxford's irrepressible love of mockery; so that when Arundel rebukes him for :

" Railing at Fra(ncis) South(well) for commending the Queen's singing one night at Hampton Court ; protesting by the blood of God, that she had the worst voice, and did everything with the worst grace, that ever any woman did "—

there duly appears in *Much Ado About Nothing*, II, iii, the song, " Sigh no More Ladies," followed by this dialogue.

M

Balth. And an ill singer, my lord.

D. Pedr. Ha, no, no, faith; thou singest well enough for a shift.

Bened. (*Oxford*). An he had been a dog that should have howled thus, they would have hanged him: and I pray God his bad voice bode no mischief. I had as lief have heard the night-raven, come what plague could have come after it.

Is it any wonder that Elizabeth about this time, used to call the irrepressible Edward "Her Turk," or that Oxford, accordingly, plants that very expression straight into *Much Ado About Nothing*, III, 4.

Marg. Well, an you be not turned Turk, there's no more sailing by the star—

a line that loses no significance, when we remember that the wooer of Margaret is Borachio (Howard), and that the star-motive, and that of the perfumed gloves, which follows, link themselves, one with Oxford's coat-of-arms, and the other with his Italian journey!

But now, returning to the serious side of a vitally serious matter, to what extent, if any, were the Howard-Arundel charges true? We cannot, of course, positively say; but this much seems to be indisputable, that had the more terrible ones, especially those of nameless sexual offences, and of attempted assassination by suborned murderers, been proved against Lord Oxford, his career at court would have finally terminated, there and then; and he would have become, thenceforth, a man forbid. Substantially, then, as the sequel, moreover, conclusively proves, and as Oxford, in play after later play, will consistently and resolutely affirm, the worser of the charges are lies; and the verdict must be not guilty. The Earl, in fact, was being slandered by opponents with their backs to the wall, fighting desperately for liberty and life, and utterly reckless concerning the weapons they used in their defence.[1]

This much is indisputable; but, since, for truth's sake, I will be at no pains here to whitewash my hero, I set it down, as reasonably probable, that, behind certain of Howard and Arundel's minor, though still serious, charges, there lay, and in some quarters was recognized to lie, a degree, at least, of truth. It is, of course, indisputable that again and again in the later plays, characters standing for Oxford—and written, if not by Oxford himself, then by playwrights, or adapters, working under " Shakespeare's " name—complain, as, for example, Belisarius does in *Cymbeline*, III, iii, how:

> " in one night
> A storm or robbery, call it what you will,
> Shook down my mellow hangings, nay, my leaves,
> And left me bare to weather . . . .
> My fault being nothing, as I have told you oft,
> But that *two villains*, whose false oaths prevail'd
> Before my perfect honour, swore to Cymbeline . . ."

yet it is no less certain that the Earl, writing of himself, a few years later, in the character of Hamlet, admits that he has done such things " it were better his mother had not borne him "; and, further, that the same de Vere, writing during the mid-nineties, and in his own person, in the Sonnets, acknowledges a " bewailed guilt."

Moreover, have we not already seen Oxford, or one of his group, dramatizing himself, in *A Winter's Tale*,

---

[1] Lucio (Arundel) to the Duke (Oxford) in *Measure for Measure*, V " 'Faith, my lord, I spoke it but according to the trick."

as the villain, Leontes, guilty of crimes similar to those charged against him by Arundel, including, in Pauline's phrase, the poisoning of Camilla's honour :

"To have him kill a king ; poor trespasses,
  More monstrous standing by"

Again, granting that our hero's character endured foul and malicious slander, and that Hamlet's life closes upon an assured hope that it is within Horatio's power, as also within his will, to heal that "wounded name"; yet, nevertheless, there remains the indisputable fact, which the remainder of our story will prove, that Oxford, though he succeeded partially in clearing himself, remains henceforth, and for the remainder of his life, under a cloud of, shall I say, suspicion, which neither repentance nor reform could ever wholly lift. Judged even by the relatively tolerant judgments, and easy social canons of his day, the Earl had sinned, or, in Burleigh's puritan phrase, "had forgotten God," though, when all this is said, there still remains, and probably will remain, now for ever undisclosed, some mystery in his life, the solution of which, I believe, may be found in his personal relations with the Queen, particularly hinted at in *Two Gentlemen of Verona,* and discussed in an appendix at the close of this book.

Meanwhile writing of this year 1581, let it be granted that though the more guilty charges were never proved against him, de Vere, at this period of his life, was a fickle, effeminately capricious, headstrong, and difficult nobleman, unfaithful to his wife, whom he had deserted, given to "antic gestures," sometimes a boaster, a liar, even, in his cups, and a weaver of Traveller's tales, which, with increasingly deep potations, become ever more vividly and humorously expressed. For all such charges against Oxford, including even the " deadly vices," there exists, moreover, some corroborative affirmation, since both Chapman and Jonson who—though professional adversaries and rivals of Oxford—knew their man well, both confirm them, by many allusions in their poems and plays, especially *Cynthia's Revels*, and *A Coronet for his Mistress Philosophy*.[1] Further, this pair add to their charges others, of a kindred sort, such as " insolence," an envy that is " fed with others' famishment,"[2] and a fond addiction to " female humours."

" A bad lot, then, this Shakespeare," my readers will be saying : to which I answer : " Yes, judged by modern standards of behaviour, de Vere was a bad man, in those days of his unregenerate, because unlessoned, youth ; yet no whit worse than thousands of other headstrong and undisciplined young noblemen of his period, whether in England, Italy, or France, with passions no less unbridled, and desires equally unrestrained." De Vere also, be it added, was far more excusable than they, when it is remembered that we deal here with no ordinary son of Adam's race, but with the most acquisitive, assimilative, swiftly impressionable mind; the most fantastically fecund and gloriously creative imagination ever yet, for weal and woe, bestowed upon us mysterious children of men—one who bore already within him, potentially, all the characters of his plays to be, from the wise folly of Falstaff, the quaint philosophies of Lear's clown, and the worldly shrewdness of Feste, to Iago and Macbeth, in their vilest aspects, or to Hamlet and Othello, at their gentlest

---

[1] Chapman herein attacks Oxford again and again. See *post* pp.292-96.
[2] Chapman's *Shadow of Night*.

noblest, or most sublime. Edward de Vere, this " gentleman of all Temperance[1] " can be wise as Ulysses, and as eloquent; fantastic as Armado, fierce as Hotspur, gentle as the Prince of Denmark, when, like the female dove, " his pinions will be drooping." In the one man all men lie dormant; and of these no single one for very long. Do you wonder, then, that in his life, as also in his plays—which do but picture that life, in intimate relation to those who lived it with him—all opposites, from best to worst, are true?

Again—and this point is of first importance—as in the plays, which are the expression of the man, so also in the man himself, however often he may " forget God," and do despite to the godlike that is within him, howsoever close and frequent the contacts that he will make with evil, even in its worst and most vicious forms, he does but thereby, as the outcome and issue of it all, recognize evil the more clearly for what it is; and, with further recognition, the more deeply detest and abhore it.

Such a man as this will make amends. By his own confession, set down in after years, he has " looked upon truth askance and strangely "; yet, all the while his keen vision knew it for the truth, and loved it when known; so that never once, so far as I am aware, within the plays or without them, does he pretend that any other thing save virtue can be ultimately triumphant, or the wages of sin, in any wise, at last be other than death. All the while, even while he was warring against the light, the Angel, Consideration, was whipping out of

---

[1] Escalus of the Duke (Oxford), *Measure for Measure*, III, ii. He has just said that the Duke, " above all other strifes, contended especially to know himself."

him ruthlessly the offending Adam; so that within but few years after this most crucial episode in his career, we shall find his plays dramatizing poignantly his own penitence for past misdeeds, and expressing his deep and abiding remorse over an innocent young life—that of his Countess, Anne Cecil—marred, if not broken, by the cruelties of an unregenerate youth.

De Vere's almost godlike power over the beauties of his English tongue, implies, inevitably, some corresponding harmony of inward soul with sound; and it is, in this connexion, most significant that even his bitterest rivals in letters, pre-eminently Chapman and Jonson, beside mockeries and malicious accusations without end, make reluctant admission that his very foolery is " golden," and that, when he soars into his loveliest lyrical ecstacies, this amazing and incalculable de Vere can " wash the heaven and leave the stars more pure." The woman of the scriptures is, surely, not the only individual of whom it may be written, that much love won much forgiveness; nor is it by accident that, some two years before Oxford's death, we find the author of *The Poetaster* writing of his erstwhile foe, as of a " rectified spirit.[1]"

Meanwhile the trespass exacts the penalty; and although Oxford's fault, as Arundel shrewdly argues, is " qualified that it may not take away the validity of his accusations," such qualification will not protect him against punishment. An angered queen sends her favourite to the Tower; and the indignity, I doubt not, burned deep into his soul; so deep, it may be, as almost for a time to unbalance those so exquisitely adjusted faculties. In these the darkest days of Oxford's life, this England,

---

[1] *Oxford-Shakesperean Case Corroborated*, pp. 160, 161, and *post* p. 343

I imagine, was, at moments, near to losing her Shakespeare. Yet, in the providence of God, it was otherwise ordained. Out of the evil, instead, came good; for although de Vere's irrepressible Elizabethan humour could soon turn every worst to laughter, and twist all mischances into side-splitting fun, the ultimate effect of these disasters was to give us, when they were past and done with, a dramatist of far deeper and loftier range than could otherwise have been possible. The gate of that grim fortress may have closed upon a playwright who had been, until that day, almost wholly comedic at heart: it must open, to let pass the world's lordliest writer of tragedy; one, however, that, even to the last line of his last play, will remain fantastic through and through—a Hamlet, who, while simulating, with " antic disposition," the madness which he had, perhaps, glimpsed ahead, was still, at moments, overhung by the dark shadow, if never by the hollow substance, of insanity.

Exactly how long Oxford's detention in the Tower lasted, we cannot positively say; but it seems that, before being conveyed there, the " submissive and penitent demeanour" of the humbled " monster," before a gathering of assembled lords, together with a piteous lament over the " ill destiny that led him to the displeasing of the most gracious princess that ever was," may have shortened the length of his stay. Certainly it came to an end on 8 June, 1581; and certainly also the committal cannot have been for treason, " or for any criminal cause," as we know by the following letter, from the Privy Council to Sir William Gorges, the Yeoman Porter of the Tower, stating that " he [Gorges] did demand his [Oxford's] upper garment and other things as fees due unto him by his office, and hath thereupon caused certain of his Lordship's stuff to be stayed," and pointing out that he cannot legally to so, because the Earl " was not committed thither upon any cause of treason or any criminal cause." If, however, the Fugger News Letter, quoted by Mrs. E. T. Clark,[1] be correct, there was a second imprisonment, since the letter runs as follows :

> *London, April* 29, 1581.
> " The Earl of Oxford also arrested (i.e. with Howard and Arundel), but soon set at liberty, is again in the Tower for forgetting himself with one of the Queen's Maids of Honour, who is in the Tower likewise.

The Maid of Honour was Anne Vavasour, who will soon come intimately into our story; meanwhile, let us briefly conclude the episode, upon its narrative side, by adding that Oxford was not restored to court favour until two years later, the summer of 1583, and that, in December of the same year, Arundel fled to Paris, whence the English Ambassador, Sir Edward Stafford, writes to Walsingham :

> " Lord Paget with Charles Paget and Charles Arundel suddenly entered my dining chamber before any one was aware of it, and Lord Paget says : " they came away for their conscience, and for fear, having enemies."

The matter of " conscience " we can let pass ; but fear, unquestionably, was a sound plea, since an important result of Oxford's charges had been a proclamation by the Queen, on 12 January, 1582, revoking the leniency

[1] *Op. cit.*, p. 286.

and tolerance which she, who was never blood-thirsty, had hitherto shown to the Jesuits, the " Massing Priests," and other treasonable and seditious persons who were then troubling the realm. From this time onward, the law imposing fines upon Catholics, for non-attendance at Protestant services—which had remained almost a dead-letter, since it received the royal assent at the beginning of Elizabeth's reign—was rigorously enforced; and Jesuits venturing into England were ruthlessly hunted down, persecuted, and put to death. These facts I shall show to be of much import to the Shakesperean side of our story. In June 1584—to have done with Arundel's share in these events—Sir Edward Stafford, in the name of Queen Elizabeth, made formal appeal to the French King, for the surrender of Lord Paget, Charles Arundel, and others of the group, as conspirators against her life. The French King, however, declined to accede; and Arundel, the Conrad of *Much Ado about Nothing*, the Lucio of *Measure for Measure*, and the " suborned informer " of the Sonnets, passed the closing four years of a contemptible life, as a spy in the service of Spain.

Thus well rid of him, let us return to Oxford, whom we left disconsolate in the Tower; and discover, if we can, the effect which these formidable experiences produced upon his dramatic work. On the comic side, with no more than a moan of underlying tragedy permitted to sound through, the upshot, beyond question was that merry play, the very title of which, *Much Ado About Nothing*, epitomizes Oxford's defence, and is surely the happiest revenge ever taken by the slandered upon the slanderer. The Beatrice-Benedick scenes, perhaps, though not certainly, were written about

1572, under the influence of *Il Cortegiano*, with Oxford as Benedick, and one of the court ladies as Beatrice; but the developed play certainly dates from 1582-83, by which time Lady Mary Vere has, I think, become Beatrice, and Oxford, while still Benedick, has his own darker and more saturnine side reflected in Don John; though, so far as names are concerned, Don Pedro and Don John are obviously Philip of Spain, and his bastard brother, Don John of Austria. The villain of the piece probably " remembers " also Lord Henry Howard, who, with Conrad-Arundel, is more directly drawn as Borachio. Even Dogberry and the watch, though perhaps added a little later, must have been topical, since Burleigh, in a letter to Walsingham of 1586, mentions the " dog-berries of Enfield," and reports the stupidity of the watchmen on the London Road appointed to apprehend three young men concerned in the Babington plot, who —the watch—being asked how they should know the conspirators answered, " by intelligence of their favour," and being asked what that meant ;—" Marry," said they, " One hath a hooked nose." One is not surprised to read that some royal catechism followed, concerning the negligence of the justices, in " appointing such silly men " to be watchmen.

Claudio and Hero—the first of whom will reappear, under the same name, in *Measure for Measure*, are again Oxford and his innocent, though slandered, wife, Anne Cecil; but symbolically, as in other instances, the pair stand, at the close of the comedy, for the concealed plays, to which, at last their author is legitimately married. Topical allusions to the year 1582, or thereabouts, teem throughout the acts, a good instance being Don Pedro's line in I, i—

In time the savage bull doth bear the yoke—

which connects up, at once, with Arundel's charges against Oxford, who is repeatedly referred to therein as "Ox," and is taken from the Hekatompathia of 31 March, 1582, and dedicated to the Earl of Oxford. Another instance is Benedick's,

"I look for an earthquake too, then,"

a reference back to the earthquake of 1580, which so terrified the citizens of London.[1]

Much Ado About Nothing, then, was written comparatively soon after the events that gave it birth, in that mood wherein, weary of anguish, and amid more hopeful circumstances, the tortured mind, upon the rebound, "returns to laughter" which is to be most cunningly aimed at the persons of Oxford's accusers; but that tense struggle, in which reputation, liberty, and almost life itself, were at the hazard, and which culminated in those dark hours of durance in the Tower, had yet another dramatic outcome, namely that play which, though, from a certain view-point, with its dungeon-scenes, its block, its headsman, its grim talk of imminent death, and its lurid sexual plot—it is generally classed among the most unpleasant of the Shakesperean plays, is, nevertheless, as Mr. Wilson Knight has sagaciously observed, a supremely beautiful problem-drama, showing that the nobility of man, howsoever inextricably intertwined with baseness, is, nevertheless, a real force, making powerfully, through evil, towards good. For in *Measure for Measure* we have " the profound thought

---

[1] Admiral Holland, I think, first called attention to this. *Much Ado About Nothing* was probably first played at court on 12 February, 1583, under the title, *A Historie of Ariodante and Geneuora*. Mrs. Clark, p. 371.

of the supreme tragedian given careful and exact form,"[1] and also an expert dramatization, upon Elizabethan lines, of the Christian law and ethic,

> "Judge not that ye be not judged. For with what judgment ye judge, ye shall be judged: and with what measure ye meet it shall be measured to you again.

Edward de Vere in the character of Claudio—the same name given, as we have seen, to a part representative of his in *Much Ado About Nothing*—immured in the same gloomy fortress from which, one hundred and twenty years before, in February 1461, John, the 12th Earl of Oxford, and his son, Aubrey, were led out to execution on Tower Hill—meditates upon dissolution—" death is a fearful thing——" and, as dying men will, looks back upon his past life, and especially upon those misdeeds which, in full "measure for measure," are recoiling already upon his own head, as well as upon those of his accusers; and are vindicating fearfully upon him the divine threat, which is also a promise, "With what measure ye meet it shall be measured to you again." To a man of Edward de Vere's moral apprehension, and instinctive spiritual response to truth, no such message could come in vain. His dramatic reaction to such a challenge can be no jest—not even a joke so innately serious as is *Much Ado About Nothing*. It will be a dramatic parable, "exquisitely inwoven" upon the text, "Except your righteousness shall exceed the righteousness of the Scribes and Pharisees, ye shall in no case enter into the Kingdon of Heaven."

[1] *The Wheel of Fire*, pp. 80–106.

Let us now briefly consider *Measure for Measure*, as a topical work, fashioned out of the most bitter experience of Oxford's life; and see whether the results are not sufficient, in themselves, to determine almost its Oxfordian authorship. Historically considered, the play is obviously a dramatization of the stern measures taken against the Catholics, from the year 1581 onwards, following upon Oxford's denunciation of the Howard-Arundel group, at the close of 1580.

That enigmatic central figure of the drama, the Duke, is, of course, Oxford himself, once more doubled in the person of his "cousin," and "deputy," Angelo, the "character" of whose life does, as the text informs us, unfold its history to the observer, as a spirit not "finely touch'd but to fine issues." It is already true of the Duke—and it will become essentially true of Oxford's own destiny—that he is a torch lit by heaven, less for his own light, than for posterity's, and for the illumination of the larger world. Angelo is once more Oxford, unfallen as yet, because not yet tempted, and doomed to succumb pitiably to temptations that lie not far ahead: the Duke, on the other hand, is the perfected Oxford, purged, yet so as by fire, who will return, in disguise, ere the play be ended, Godlike almost, to dispense justice, to heal all discords, and to smooth his subjects' cumbered ways. Lucio, that "inward," or aforetime close friend of the Duke's, is simply Oxford's cousin, Arundel, once his intimate friend, who does actually accuse the Duke of almost precisely the same offences listed by Arundel, in the charges of 1580–81, namely "detected for women," drunkenness, folly, cowardice,

"One of all luxury an ass, a madman"

and " much more much worse " of which the worst, as we have seen, is unprintable. This Lucio, further, is the same man who, a moment ago, has pulled off the Friar's hood, and " discovered " the Duke, or, in words shorn of their symbolism, has revealed that " Friar " spiritually, to himself and to us as well:

Thou art the first knave that e'er madest a Duke.

Returning to Claudio, the charges against him are again identical with historic fact, namely with those for which, as we have seen, Oxford was committed to the Tower; and it was in this very year, 1581, that old laws, long neglected, were, as a result of the Earl's own denunciations, put in force against English Catholics, who could thus complain, in the precise words of Claudio, though in a matter of religious-political rather than merely social conduct, that

>   this new governor
> Awakes me all the enrolled penalties
> Which have, like unscour'd armour, hung by the wall
> So long, that *nineteen zodiacs* have gone round,
> And none of them been worn—"

or, in other words, not since Oxford came into the Earldom, nineteen years before, in 1562, have such penalties against papistry been invoked. Claudio is committed for getting with child Madam Juliet, a lady who is confined in the same prison with him; and Oxford, as we know, according to the Fugger News Letter, " is again in the Tower for forgetting himself with one of the Queen's Maid's of Honour who is in the Tower likewise."

This lady, Anne Vavasour, of whom, at the time of writing, I do not, unfortunately, know very much, descended from an ancient and wealthy Yorkist family, being the daughter of Henry Vavasour of Copmansthorpe near York, who died on 18 February, 1584,[1] and was succeeded by his son Thomas, born in 1561. Remembering that Anne is, in part, an original for Ophelia, it is interesting to know that we shall find this brother of Anne's, in 1585, challenging Oxford to a duel, in words that directly recall the treacherous methods of Laertes with Hamlet. Anne is allied also to another well-known Elizabethan family, namely the Wiltshire branch of the Knyvets, one of whom will soon come intimately into our story; and she is certainly the mistress alluded to by Oxford, when, in Arundel's charge against the Earl (December 1580) he is made to say, while with Arundel in the gallery, " Charles, I have ever loved you, and as you have already given me your word to my mistress, so now I crave it myself "—all this, be it added, " after long speeches in secret between him (Oxford) and my cousin Vavisor who was the means of our meeting."

Oxford and Anne Vavasour, therefore, like Claudio and Juliet in *Measure for Measure*, were lover and mistress, both of them under lock and key, by reason of an illegitimate child. The story, however, does not end there; for it is to this same Anne Vavasour, quite evidently, that the Earl, probably some years before, had written his famous " Echo " song, a part of which I have already quoted, and commented upon, in these pages, and which, long before the full significance of the Oxford-Shakespeare solution had dawned upon me, I had perceived to abound with close analogies both to Ophelia and to

---

[1] Inquisition Post Mortem Public Record Office, supplied to me by Capt. B. M. Ward.

Juliet. Those with Ophelia have already been dealt with; those with Juliet may be passed over, until we reach the Verona tragedy, which, contemporaneously almost with *Measure for Measure*, seems now to be germinating in Oxford's mind.

Consider with me, for a moment, certain lines connecting *Measure for Measure*, beyond dispute, with the opening years of the fifteen-eighties. When, for example, Mrs. Overdone laments that "what with the war, what with the sweat, what with the gallows," she is custom-shrunk, she refers to the Papal invasion of Ireland in 1580, and to the sweating sickness, or plague, then raging in London; the gallows being those upon which Campion, and other Jesuit priests, were executed in 1581. When Lucio says to Pompey, the clown of II, i:

> "I shall beat you to your tent, and prove a shrewd Cæsar to you; in plain dealing, Pompey, I shall have you whipt"—

he is presumably referring to the play, *Pompey*, which was produced at court, on 6 January, 1580–81; while the Provost's lines in II, iii, concerning Juliet:

> "a gentlewoman of mine
> Who, falling in the flaws of her own youth
> Hath blistered her report"—

much as Ophelia, judging by her mad-scenes in Hamlet, seems also to have done—links us up naturally with Angelo's speech, which opens the next scene:

> "When I would pray and think, I think and pray
> To several subjects. Heaven hath my empty words
> Whilst my invention, hearing not my tongue,
> Anchors on Isabel."

These lines, I suggest, are pure *Hamlet* in embryo; since, quite obviously, they seem to form the basis from which Claudius' prayer is paraphrased:

" My words fly up, my thoughts remain below.
 Words without thoughts never to heaven go."

Bearing in mind also the resemblance between the names Claudius and Claudio—a point always to be taken note of in Shakespeare—how meaningful, in the world-famous duologues between Isabella and her brother, become these words from III, i.

Claud. O heaven, it cannot be.
Isabe. Yes, he would give't thee, from this *rank offence*—

because again the italicized words are paraphrased by Claudius, in that same prayer:

O my offence is rank, it smells to heaven.

Immediately afterwards, just as Hamlet-Oxford, in his prison that is Denmark, soliloquizes upon death, so also we find Claudio-Oxford, in a prison—the Tower—beside a girl whose life he has shamed, monologuing also upon death, and dialoguing, concerning our mortal end, with his austerely chaste sister.

Claud. Death is a fearful thing.
Isabe. And shamed life a hateful.
Claud. Ay, but to die, and go we know not where.

Thus, in play after play, does the dramatist weave the deepest and most vitally passionate experiences of his chequered career into drama far more enduring than is mortal man.

As for Mariana, lamenting in her lonely moated grange—which may have been one of Oxford's own country manors, such as "Wivenhoe"—those vain seals of her now rejected love, her identity is no whit less clear than that of the other principal characters of this astonishingly revealing play. She is Anne Cecil, long deserted by her husband, Angelo, who, in the Duke's words:

" Left her in tears and dried not one of them with his comfort;
Swallowed his vows whole—pretending in her discoveries of dishonour "—

the last half-line informing us openly that Oxford's wrath over his wife's dishonour in 1576, was nothing, at bottom, but an excuse for his desertion of her. Angelo, also, is equally frank concerning his reasons for leaving Mariana. They are these, set forth in that poignant last act, which, though the despair of professional actors, is intensely interesting to all who can pierce beneath the surface of the play. The Deputy confesses to the Duke:—

" My lord, I must confess I know this woman,
And five years since there was some speech of marriage
Betwixt myself and her; which was broke off,
Partly for that her promised proportions
Came short of composition; but in chief,
For that her reputation was disvalued
In levity: since which time of five years
I never spake with her, saw her, nor heard from her,
Upon my faith and honour."

" I am affianced this man's wife as strongly
As words could make up vows. . . .

Nothing could be more significant, nor more closely fitting to the ascertained facts of Oxford's life. The crisis, forming the theme of this play, develops in the year 1581; and when Angelo admits that, five years before, there had been talk, between himself and Mariana, concerning a marriage which was broken off, he is plainly referring, just as the Duke does, to the breach between Oxford and his countess, who, though actually married, had separated five years before, in 1576, precisely on the ground of accusations brought against her fidelity by this same Howard group represented by Lucio in the play. Let the reader not fail to observe the deep historic interest of these episodes, as throwing light upon doubtful points in Oxford's career, or to note the illuminating interplay of actuality and the drama. Many inquirers, for example, have wondered why the Earl who, in this respect, was reticent of his reasons, left his admittedly innocent wife. Angelo, however, supplies those reasons—first that her " promised proportions came short of composition "—meaning, I take it, that Burleigh never paid to his wife so large a dowry, or allowance, as had been stipulated between himself and de Vere—and, secondly, that de Vere's pride was deeply wounded by the levity concerning her among the courtiers, who as he found upon his return from abroad were laughing at him for a cuckold. The sequel exactly corroborates all this, since Mariana's words:

> I crave no other nor no better man. . . .
> They say best men are moulded out of faults;
> And for the most, become much more the better
> For being a little bad: so may my husband—

fit in smoothly with the tenor of Burleigh's and Anne Cecil's letters to Oxford, all protesting Anne's unbroken devotion to and desire to love and serve her husband: and those same above-quoted lines accord also both with the whole theme of the play, and with the main course of Oxford's subsequent life, which though "a little bad," was, as we have seen, and shall see, "moulded," by these very events and by the self revelation they afforded him, "out of faults," to a more worthy and self-respecting course. As for the substitution of one woman, under cover of darkness, for another in Angelo's bed, have we not seen precisely the same situation used before, not only in the play of *All's Well that Ends Well*, wherein Bertram and Helena are again Oxford and Anne, but also as a trick reputed to have been played, by a stratagem of Burleigh's, and with Anne's participation, upon Oxford himself?

The cause of the Duke's withdrawal, as a "secret which must be locked within the teeth and the lips," will be fully discussed, in later pages, as also will the whole "business he hath helmed upon a warranted need," when we come to trace the connexion between Shakesperean drama and national patriotic propaganda, after the outbreak of the Spanish war, when Oxford, under the guise of "William Shake-speare," is secretly salaried by the Privy Council, as England's national dramatist.

Two more plays, meanwhile are looming not far ahead, namely *Romeo and Juliet*, and, quite obviously, *Hamlet*—Ophelia and the Prince of Denmark being plainly forecast in the letters that, during December 1582, Anne-Mariana, in her misery of abandonment, wrote to her husband, the Earl.

"My lord, In what misery I may account mysel to be, that neither can see any end thereof nor yet any hope to diminish it. And now of late having had some hope in my own conceit that your Lordship would have renewed some part of your favour that you began to show me this summer, when you made me assurred of your good meaning, though you seemed fearful how to show it by open actions. Now after long silence of hearing anything from you, at the length I am informed—but how truly I know not and yet how uncomfortably I do feel some—that your Lordship is entered into misliking of me without any cause in deed or thought. And therefore, my good Lord, I beseech you in the name of that God that knoweth all my thoughts and my love towards you notwithstanding your evil usage of me, let me know the truth of your meaning towards me; upon what cause you are moved to continue me in this misery, and what you would have me do in my power to recover your constant favour, so as your Lordship may not be led still to detain me in calamity without some probable cause, whereof, I appeal to God, I am utterly innocent. From my father's house at Westminster, the 7th December, 1581."

On the 12th, the Countess wrote again, after receiving an answer from her husband:

"My very good Lord, I most heartily thank you for your letter, and am most sorry to perceive how you are unquieted with the uncertainty of the world, whereof I myself am not without some Taste. But seeing you will me to assure myself of anything that I may as your wife challenge of you, I will the more patiently abide the adversity which otherwise

I feel, and—if God would so permit it and that it might be good for you—I would bear the greater part of my adverse fortune, and make it my comfort to bear part with you. As for my father, I do assure you, what soever hath been reported of him, I know no man can wish better to you than he doth, and yet the practises in court I fear do seek to make contrary shows."

From our viewpoint there is deep significance behind these words. Compare, for example, the pathetic and plaintive epistles of this lady " most deject and wretched," and the circumstances in which they are written, with the Hamlet-Ophelia duologues, and compare, especially, these lines relative to the reports circulating in the court, as to her father, Burleigh's, behaviour, with the lines of *Hamlet*, III, i.

>   *Haml.* Where's your father?
>   *Ophe.* At home, my lord.
>   *Haml.* Let the doors be shut upon him that he may play the fool nowhere but in 's own house.

Lastly and to conclude, as Dogberry would have it, let me revert to *Measure for Measure*, and remind my readers that the Duke's own words, in III, ii, concerning himself:

> " Let him be but testimonied in his own bringings forth (i.e. the plays) and he shall appear to the envious a scholar, a statesman, and a soldier"—

match exactly those put into the mouth of Ophelia concerning Hamlet:

> The courtier's soldiers scholar's eye, tongue, sword.

It is also perhaps worthy of remark that the Duke's couplet in V, i—

> "He who the sword of heaven will bear
> Should be as holy as severe—"

is peculiarly apposite to one who, as Lord Great Chamberlain of England, had so frequently borne the sword-of-state before his earthly Queen.

CHAPTER SEVEN

"ROMEO AND JULIET" AND "HAMLET": 1582–1583

Anne Vavasour the original of Juliet, in both "Measure for Measure," and "Romeo and Juliet,"—Feud between Oxford and Tom Knyvet—The street brawling in "Romeo and Juliet" is that between the retainers of the Knyvet and Oxford households c 1582—The Brawls described—Tom Knyvet as historic Original of Tybalt—Duel between Oxford and Knyvet—Connexion between Oxford's "Echo" song and "Romeo and Juliet"—"As You Like It," an allegorical dramatization of Alençon's activities 1581-82—The Earl of Oxford's Players—Plays of John Lyly—Oxford in 1583 appoints John Lyly as his Secretary-Actor-Manager—Oxford's apparent official connexion with court drama—Early version of "Troilus and Cressida"—Oxford restored to the Queen's favour in 1583—Returns to Court and drafts "Hamlet"—Topical Allusions in "Hamlet"—"Cardanus Comfort" quoted in "Hamlet"—Polonius's speeches a burlesque of Burleigh's own literary style.

BETWEEN the events recorded in the last chapter, and the first drafting of *Hamlet*, which I ascribe to 1583–84 there intervenes, I think, in addition to *King John*, which I shall pass over, a lyrical tragedy of a deeply intimate kind reflecting not only its author's abiding love for, and cherished memories of, Italy, but also the now definitely tragical, and morally purified, conception of life, which conversions in the school of bitter experience are bringing about. Dramatically considered, *Romeo and Juliet* is yet another version of the Howard-Arundel quarrel; though it is linked, principally, with neither of these in person, but with their cousin, or more distant relative, Thomas Knyvet, Gentleman of the Chamber, and apparently a personal favourite of the Queen.[1] Exactly how, or when, the feud between Oxford and Kynvet arose, we cannot say, but it links itself naturally with the concerns of the Howard-Arundel group, and particularly with a lady whose acquaintance we have already made, the Queen's pretty Maid of Honour, Anne Vavasour, who was a niece of Knyvet's, and will be remembered as the historic original of Juliet in *Measure for Measure*, with Oxford standing for her Claudio. A further examination of the circumstances generally, and of Oxford's "Echo" song, in particular will, I hope, make it clear that the Juliet of the Verona tragedy is another portrait of Anne Vavasour, lyrically idealized, th s time, and composite, to some extent, with Oxford's wife, Anne Cecil.

Oxford, it will be remembered, had, apparently, been twice in the Tower during the first six months of 1581 —once as a result of the Howard-Arunde charges, with *Much Ado About Nothing* and *Measure for Measure* as resulting plays, and a second time in punishment for his guilty relation with Anne Vavasour, which, regularized by marriage in the play, forms the personal love-theme of the tragedy. So far all is crys al clear: but whence it will be rightly asked, did Oxford draw his topical ideas for the street brawling between Montagues and Capulets, and the sword-fighting, with the deaths of Tybalt and Mercutio, about which the drama's plot

---

[1] Thomas Kynvet born probably *c.* 1543 was the head of the Wiltshire Branch of the Knyvet family, knighted in 1604. He died in 1622 and has an elaborate monument in Stanwell Church near Staines. His sister, Margaret, married Henry Vavasour of Copmansthorpe, York the father of Anne Vavasour (Juliet). This Sir Thomas Knyvet' Tybalt, must not be confounded with his contemporary relative of the same name, who was of the Norfolk branch of the family, and was never at court,

ROMEO AND JULIET AND HAMLET

develops? The answer is again quite simple. Feuillerat when he wrote in his *John Lyly* that "the streets of London were filled with the quarrelling clamours of these new Montagues and Capulets," was nearer to the truth than he realized;[1] for although my last visit to Italy had made it perfectly clear to me that the exotic Italian atmosphere of *Romeo and Juliet* could hardly have been created, except by one who had trod in person the streets of Verona and other ancient Italian towns—it seemed undeniable, nevertheless, that the topical aspects of the world's noblest lyrical tragedy were drawn, in common with those of his other greatest plays, from the vital experiences of his own life; the street brawling which opens the tragedy being, in fact, a dramatization of the encounters between Oxford's men, and those of Thomas Knyvet, of which several occurred during the first two years of the fifteen-'eighties.

One day, in the spring of 1582, Gerard Ashby, an apprentice butcher, walking through Blackfriars, learned from the Thames boatmen that a fight between the Oxford-Knyvet factions was imminent, in the marsh near the river. Such a brawl being a pastime most congenial to a sturdy apprentice of Queen Elizabeth's day, Ashby secured a pike from a neighbouring armoury, and hastened to take part in the fray. Knyvet's men, apparently, considerably out-numbered Oxford's, who were only two; and Ashby, let us hope, strengthened the weaker side. Meanwhile a third Oxford retainer, named Gastrell, arrived, and despite the protests of his opponents—"Gastrell, we don't want to fight you here"—boldly attacked two or three of Knyvet's men, and was promptly wounded. The Oxford faction, in short, had

---

[1] Mrs. Clark's *Shakespeare's Plays in the Order of their Writing*, p. 299.

much the worst of the fighting, and burned for occasion of revenge. They had not long to wait; for on 28 June, a house-warming took place, at the home of a certain Jones—note how close we are getting to the ball in Capulet's house—at which Lord Howard, Arundel, Knyvet (Tybalt), Townshend, and others attended. Towards the close of the dinner, one of Townshend's servants appeared, and reported to his master with much mystery, a conversation he had overheard at the house of Oxford's brother-in-law, Lord Willoughby, where an attack had been planned, for that very evening, upon Knyvet and his friends. Townshend repeated aloud to all the company these whispered news, whereupon the group, with Knyvet at their head, sallied forth in search of the enemy. Near Blackfriars they were suddenly attacked by armed men, who withdrew when they found that their plans had been forestalled; the result, of course, being further threats of vengeance on both sides, and, in July, another brawl in which Knyvet himself slew one of Oxford's men, just as Tybalt does Mercutio in the play. During the fighting, Gastrell, a participant, it will be remembered, in the earlier fray by the river, provoked, and slew, a certain Long Tom, who seems to have passed from Oxford's service to that of Knyvet. The affair came, in due course, to the ears of Elizabeth, whom this street-brawling in her capital city, between rival factions of her own courtiers, naturally and greatly enraged: and I wholly agree with Mrs. Clark[1]—that the Prince's stern and threatening rebuke to the Montagues and Capulets, in the opening scene of *Romeo and Juliet*, may well be fashioned upon the actual

---

[1] Mrs. Clark's *Shakespeare's Plays in the Order of their Writing*, p. 304.

words used to the Oxford-Knyvet factions, by Queen Elizabeth herself.

" Rebellious subjects, enemies to peace,
  Profaners of this neighbour-stained steel—
  Will they not hear ? What, ho ! you men, you beasts,
  That quench the fire of your pernicious rage
  With purple fountains issuing from your veins,
  On pain of torture, from those bloody hands
  Throw your mistempered weapons to the ground,
  And hear the sentence of your moved prince.
  Three civil brawls, bred of an airy word,
  By thee, old Capulet, and Montague,
  Have thrice disturbed the quiet of our streets,
  ... If ever you disturb our streets again,
  Your lives shall pay the forfeit of the peace."

Is it surprising that Elizabeth used to call Oxford her " Turk ? " What she called Knyvet, who was probably no whit less impulsive and headstrong, history does not relate ; but that Knyvet stands for Tybalt I take to be positively certain, having regard to the general circumstances of the case, his relationship to Anne Vavasour——Juliet being cousin to Tybalt[1]—and to the fact, pointed out by Mrs. Clark, that the epithets applied to him by Mercutio—" king of cats," " prince of cats," " ratcatcher "—are all ways of calling Tom Knyvet a Tomcat, by which name he may, possibly, have been known among the Oxford faction. The word Tybalt, moreover, the same authoress reminds us, is made up of the first

---

[1] Lecturing on this subject at the Fortune Theatre, London, on July 12, 1931, I ventured a public forecast that, Anne being historically Juliet, and Knyvet Tybalt, this pair, who are " cousins " in the play, would be found to be related in real life Four days later Capt. Ward discovered that Knyvet and Anne Vavasour were uncle and niece. Again and again we find that the plays confirm history, and history the plays.

consonant of Thomas, and the first vowel of Knyvet, added to the last vowel of Thomas and the last consonant of Knyvet; and it is worth remembering, in this connexion, that Queen Elizabeth spelled the name with a *b*—Kneabet.

Even Romeo's duel with Tybalt is topical; for in March 1582, took place:

> "a fray between my Lord of Oxford and Master Thomas Knyvet of the Privy Chamber, who are both hurt, but my Lord of Oxford more dangerously—"

the subject of the quarrel, precisely as in the play, being Bessie Bavisar, otherwise Anne Vavasour, whom we have already identified as the Juliet of *Measure for Measure*, in a love-affair with Claudio, who is Oxford in that play, as also in *Much Ado About Nothing*. Concerning this duel, it is interesting to note that Oxford, more than twenty years later, will write in the Sonnets (66 and 37) of himself as having been "made lame," and of "strength by limping away disabled," from which I infer that the Earl was permanently lamed in the duel with Knyvet, and probably walked with a limp for the remainder of his life.

The love-motives of *Romeo and Juliet* are somewhat complex, and the two women of the play—of whom the first never appears upon the stage—may be, in part, composite portraits; but I have no doubt at all that Rosaline, the haste, cold, and obdurate dame, so proof against Cupid, is Queen Elizabeth herself, to whom the duologue in I, i, between Romeo and Benvolio, accurately applies. That talk, moreover is very reminiscent of the song to Silvia, who is also Queen Elizabeth, in that other Verona play *Two Gentlemen of Verona*, wherein the lady is sung of as holy, wise, and fair, while here she is fair, wise, and a saint.

>   *Rome.*   she'll not be hit
> With Cupid's arrow; she hath Dian's wit,
> And in strong proof of chastity well arm'd,
> From love's weak childish bow she lives unharm'd.
>   *Ben.* Then she hath sworn that she will still live chaste?
>   *Rome.* She hath, and in that sparing makes huge
>   waste;
> For beauty starved with her severity,
> Cuts beauty off from all posterity,
> She is too fair, too wise, wisely too fair,
> To merit bliss by making me despair;
> She hath forsworn to love; and in that vow
> Do I live dead, that live to tell it now.

I think it most probable—and in an appendix, based once more upon *Two Gentlemen of Verona*, I give reasons for believing—that Elizabeth was, at one time, as much in love with Oxford as she was capable of being with any man, and had been so, even to intimacy; but I would infer from these opening scenes of *Romeo and Juliet* in their relation to this period of Oxford's life, that the Howard-Arundel scandals, and the affair with Anne Vavasour, had brought to a close a liaison, which —though the play would make it seem otherwise—had always been stronger upon her side than on his.

That Oxford, during this year 1582, was still deeply incensed against the royal mistress, who had sent him twice to the Tower, is apparent in the opening of the balcony-scene, the very first lines of which recall the effects of Knyvet's sword; the pains of which, it may be, had not left the Earl's body when he wrote the words:

> *Rome.* He jests at scars that never felt a wound.
>   [*Juliet appears above at a window.*]
> But, soft, what light through yonder window breaks?
> It is the east, and Juliet is the sun!
> Arise, fair sun, and kill the envious moon,
> Who is already sick and pale with grief,
> That thou her maid art far more fair than she.
> Be not her maid, since she is envious.
> Her vestal livery is but sick and green,
> And none but fools do wear it; cast it off.

The references here are unmistakable: for when it is remembered that the Tudor livery was green and white, the envious moon, or Diana as she was so frequently called, whose "vestal livery is sick and green," can be none other than Queen Elizabeth, notoriously aggrieved, as she almost invariably was, by the marriage of her pretty Maids of Honour; while the sun is Juliet, in the historic personages of the two Annes, Vavasour and Cecil, both of whom were among the Queen's Maids, as also was Elizabeth Trentham, Oxford's second wife, in whose honour, I imagine, the play was rewritten in 1591, eleven years after the earthquake of 1580.[1]

The continuation of the balcony-scene, with all its pretty word-play between the lovers, concerning the new baptizing of Romeo and the doffing of his star-crossed name, introduces the secret identity motive, which is to become yet more markedly developed in the later plays:

"Henceforth I never will be Romeo"—

---

[1] *Romeo and Juliet*, I, iii, *Nurse.* Since the earthquake, now 11 years.

ROMEO AND JULIET AND HAMLET

and with Juliet's lines :

> "Bondage is hoarse and may not speak aloud ;
> Else would I tear the cave where Echo lies,
> And make her airy tongue more hoarse than mine,
> With repetition of my Romeo's name,
> Romeo !"

This exquisite dialogue links up, at once, with Oxford's own "Echo" song, already quoted in connexion with *Hamlet*, and—since it was admittedly written to Anne Vavasour—relating her definitely with Juliet, especially in the closing stanza :

> "May I his favour match with love, if he my love will try ? Ay.
> May I requite his birth with faith ? Then faithful will I die ? I.
>   And I, that knew this lady well,
>   Said, Lord how great a miracle,
>   To hear how Echo told the truth,
>   As true as Phœbus oracle.

The parallels could hardly be more close ; for in the two previous stanzas you have the Ever-Vere echoes again and again repeated, and followed by the words : "O hollow caves tell true," that are almost echoed by Juliet's "cave where echo lies." Further, since "E.O.," the signature of many of Oxford's early poems, is simply the echo of Romeo, do not the Earl's assertion that "Echo told the truth" (*Ver*itas) and his request that "hollow caves tell true," in the preceding stanza, take on a significance as deep as do these lines, in the next scene of *Romeo and Juliet* :

> *Benv.* Here comes Romeo, here comes Romeo
> *Mere.* Without his roe, like a dried herring.

O

Here again, eliminating the *M*, "Romeo without his roe" gives EO once more! Ultra-fantastic, almost to absurdity, is the verbal word-play hereabouts; jest after jest being, in Mercutio's phrase, "after the wearing, solely singular" or, as Romeo words it, "single soled, solely singular for the singleness," which partly explains why Gabriel Harvey had commented, two years before, upon Oxford—and also in connexion with Italy—as "a passing singular odd man." Trivial all this, to modern ears; yet the Euphuists of that day, among whom, be it remembered, Oxford was a prominent figure, held all such verbal antics to be a perfectly legitimate form of art, so pleasing, indeed, as to bring from Mercutio the delighted commendation:

> Now art thou *what thou art, by art* as well as by nature—

meaning, of course, that love-making between man and woman is "natural," but that skill in word-play is an acquired art. Mercutio's own contribution hereabouts:

> *Merc.* Without his roe, like a dried herring...
> O here's a wit of cheveril, that stretches from an inch narrow to an ell broad—

is, perhaps, the most daring and complicated pun in all Shakespeare; and has to be construed as follows: The letters CH are "an inch narrow," meaning that the word "inch" is here narrowed down to a mere CH, by the elimination of the letters IN; while the "il," or "ell," is as easily manipulated into an "ell broad": wherefore the word "cheveril" must be read, "Inch E. Ver ell": meaning, simply, that Edward de Vere's wit is equal to all occasions, and will stretch effortlessly, like soft leather, from an inch to an ell; a phrase reminding us of the still current proverb, concerning the man who, given an inch, will take an ell.[1]

Comedies and tragedies, in their shorter early forms, are now streaming from Oxford's pen; the theme which, outside his own immediate personal experience, most deeply interests him being the relations of our English court with the Valois-Medici princes in Paris. On 21 November, 1581, the Queen, at Whitehall palace, made a public pledge that she would marry the Duke of Alençon, a royal comedy which, as we have seen, had already provided the central theme of *Twelfth Night*, with Orsino and Olivia standing for Alençon and Queen Elizabeth, and Feste for Oxford, as her privileged or allowed fool. That comedy, still, after its wistful fashion, the most entrancing entertainment in the world, was, I imagine, extremely popular, from the day of its first performance at court; and its success soon set Oxford at work upon a kindred romantic allegory of which the title, *As You Like It*, is very close to the second title of *Twelfth Night*, namely, *What You Will*. This comedy of Arden, though, like its fellow, obviously based, in part, upon an old story—in this case the fourteenth-century tale of Gamelyn, wherein also a young victor at wrestling, and a retainer named Adam, run away to the woods together—is, as Mrs. Clark has shown us, an historical allegory depicting the activities of the Duke of Alençon during 1581–82, with King Henry II of France Henri de Valois), who had died in 1559, as the dead Sir Rowland de Bois, while Oliver and Orlando, whose names are borrowed from the old French *Chanson de Roland*, stand for Henri de Valois'

[1] Admiral Holland first interpreted this interesting line.

two sons, Henry III of France, and Francis of Alençon—Duke Frederic being probably Philip II of Spain. Rowland de Bois makes a fair anagram for Henri de Valois; the Forest of Arden is the Ardennes, upon the Franco-Netherland border, where the old Duke (Orange) is in banishment. Capt. Ward pertinently suggests that Rosalind and Celia personify the Netherlands; their flight from Duke Frederick, to seek the old Duke in the Ardennes, being an allegorical reference to the revolt led by Orange against the Spaniards, while the victory of Orlando over Charles the wrestler typifies Alençon's victory over Parma at Cambrai, in August 1581; most significant, in this connexion, being the fact, first noted by Mrs. Clark,[1] that Rosalind's wish for Orlando's success against Charles—" Now Hercules be thy speed, young man"—provides a direct hint concerning the identity of the original, whose name was François Hercule de Valois.

Le Beau, the courtier, is probably a composite of de Bex and de Beaumont, this last being one of the titles of Marchaumont, whom we have already recognized as a part original of Malvolio. Fascinating are the links which close scrutiny enables one to detect between play and play; for, as Hume tells us in his *Courtships of Queen Elizabeth*, Alençon, sending de Bex to the Queen with a request for more help in the campaign, attributes his victory at Cambrai to possession of that " bele jartière," otherwise Elizabeth's purple and gold garter, which Marchaumont had requisitioned for his royal master's use, when it slipped from the Queen's leg, on the occasion of her visit to Drake on board *The Pelican*, at Deptford—the very incident which, as I have argued

---

[1] Mrs. Clark's *Shakespeare's Plays in the Order of the Writing*, p. 356.

ROMEO AND JULIET AND HAMLET

elsewhere,[1] supplied Oxford with ideas for Malvolio's part, including the cross-gartered yellow stockings. The bitter strife between Orlando and Oliver, at the opening of the play, voiced in Oliver's words to Charles, before the wrestling match:

> "I'll tell thee, Charles, it is the stubbornest young fellow of France: full of ambition, an envious emulator of every man's good parts, a secret and villainous contriver against me his natural brother"—

expresses exactly the relations then existing between Alençon and his brother Henri, the French king.

With the story that centres round Jaques and Touchstone—both of whom are Oxford—comprising, together with Audrey, William, and Martext, the five characters grouped together, outside the French allegory—we will concern ourselves later, when we reach the year 1589, which probably saw the insertion of that part of the play. For the moment, the important point to notice is, that all these characters are also outside Lodge's *Rosalind*, from which *As You Like It* is generally supposed to be taken; though I agree wholly with Capt. Ward that, much more probably, Lodge wrote his story, under Oxford's instructions, from the text of the old court masque of 1581, handed to him, for that purpose, by Oxford. The curious title-page of *Rosalind*, with its reference to "Euphues' Golden Legacie," becomes additionally interesting, when we remember that Euphues, otherwise Lyly, who had dedicated his book to Oxford in 1580, remained in the Earl's service, as secretary, actor manager, and so forth, right through the fifteen-'eighties, and probably into the early 'nineties.

[1] *Shakespeare and Chapman as Topical Dramatists*, pp. 40-42.

The griefs brought upon Oxford by the quarrel with the Howard-Arundel faction, instead of diverting his interest from the drama, seem rather to have stimulated it, by providing him with burning themes, drawn from vivid personal experience, and affording him also opportunity to take dramatic revenge upon opponents who were out of reach of physical reprisals. We have seen, in turn *Much Ado About Nothing*, *Measure for Measure*, and *Romeo and Juliet*, each tense with de Vere's own loves and hates, scorns and reprisals, all three leading up to that culmination of autobiographical drama, known as *Hamlet*, now already, for some years past, teeming in his mind.

The three plays first above named however were not, I imagine, first played—as, for example, *Twelfth Night* may have been—by courtiers in the palace, but by professional players, with whom, henceforth, a indeed Hamlet himself will make clear, the Earl is more and more to be identified. Early in 1580, while still high in the Queen's favour, he had taken over the Earl of Warwick's company; but during 1583 the majority of Oxford's adult players seem to have been absorbed into the new Queen's company, which had been formed at about the time of the Earl of Sussex's death: and de Vere's dramatic connexions, thenceforth, seem rather to be with the Paul's Boys and Children of the Chapel Royal, generally known as the "Oxford Boys," until 1586,[1] when, for reasons which will appear later, the Earl's name is used no more, and the actors appear simply as the Paul's Boys.[2] The first recorded performance

---

[1] *History of Sudbury*, Borough Accounts, 1585. "Paide to the Lord of Oxenforde's Players ye 17 April 89." Kindly sent me by L. H. Haydon Whitehead.

[2] Mrs. Clark, *Shakespeare's Plays in the Order of the Writing*, p. 429.

of these Earl of Oxford's Players, as the warrant for payment styles them, is at the Court, at Whitehall, on 1 January, 1583–84, with Lyly's play *Campaspe*, acted before the Queen's Majesty. On March 3 following, again before the Queen at court, was played another comedy by Lyly, *Sapho and Phao*, which, as Mr. Bond, Lyly's standard editor, admits, and as I have conclusively shown elsewhere,[1] is yet another allegorical comedy of the Alençon marriage, someways analogous to *Twelfth Night*, and thus linking up Oxford's work with that of his secretary. What had happened may have been, approximately, as follows.

In 1580 Richard Farrant and William Hunnis, Masters of the Children of Windsor, and of the Chapel Royal, conceived the idea of transforming into a rehearsal-theatre for the choir boys a room in the old Blackfriars Convent, a building which, since 1550, had housed the Office of the Revels. Farrant died during the same year, but Hunnis carried on, and in 1583 had transferred his lease to Henry Evans, who passed it on to Oxford, who transferred it again to his secretary and actor-manager, John Lyly, who, as Capt. Ward no doubt rightly surmises, was also lent by Oxford, unofficially, as stage manager and coach to the Queen's company also, when that organization took over some of the Earl's leading adult actors—an hypothesis much strengthened by certain entries in the Exchequer Account Books for 1586–87 and 1590–91.[2]

Again and again the opponents of the Oxford theory of Shakesperean authorship have demanded the production of "documentary evidence," before they are called upon even to consider our case, brushing impatiently

[1] *Case for Edward de Vere as Shakespeare*, pp. 49, 50.
[2] Capt. B. M. Ward in *Review of English Studies*, January 1929, p. 57.

aside our quite legitimate retort, that since Oxford's authorship of the plays was, from the first, and was increasingly to become, a secret government business, the request for specific documentary evidence must be, necessarily, absurd. Yet here we are, during these mid-fifteen-'eighties, exactly as might be expected, again and again upon the very verge of final documentary proof of Oxford's official connexion with the national and court drama of his day! We have seen Lyly presenting Oxford's Boys before the Queen—remember Hamlet's, "Do the boys carry it away?"—in a comedy with the identical theme of *Twelfth Night*, and during the next season, 27 December, 1584, we find the same company of players presenting at Court *Agamemnon and Ulysses*, a drama which even Stratfordian writers such as Murry, have supposed to be by Oxford himself, and which, with Mr. Looney and Mrs. Clark, I take to be the play afterwards worked into the satire known to us as *Troilus and Cressida*. When we remember also that *Sapho and Phao* is set partly in Sicily, where Lyly had never been, but where Oxford had; and further that Lyly, so far as we know, did not write a single play after leaving Oxford's service; when it is yet further considered, that his plays were published anonymously, and that the songs, which, demonstrably, have close connexion with the lyrics of Shakesperean plays, were evidently inserted later—since they do not appear in print until the edition of 1632, by the same firm that published the second Folio of Shakespeare—the inference seems to be inescapable, that Oxford and Lyly, to some extent, collaborated as dramatists, to write an allegorical comedy, around the marriage negotiations of that same royal lady; and that the Earl, working through Lyly, was quasi-officially connected with that same Queen's own company of players; facts and inference which, if substantiated, would at once explain why the actor-manager of Blackfriars closed, at the same time, his connexion with Oxford and his active career as a dramatist.

But, whatever the exact truth of the matter may be, this much is certain, that, during the years 1582–83, Oxford, as patron, manager, playwright, and probably, on occasion, as actor too, was deeply immersed in theatrical affairs, into which his vivid imagination, by plunging him *con amore*, permitted hours of welcome mental relief from consciousness of the stern fact that he was no longer in the good graces of the Queen. During the summer of 1583, however, a reconciliation was brought about; partly through the agency of Raleigh, whom Burleigh, after failing in a similar appeal to Oxford's enemy Hatton, had persuaded to use his influence with Her Majesty. Raleigh, now for a year past, in high favour at court, had written to Burleigh, on 12 May, 1583, a letter in which he tells how "ministering some occasion touching the Earl of Oxford," he had approached the Queen upon de Vere's behalf, and was told that the lady "purposed to have a new repartition," between the Earl and the Howard faction.[1]

"I [Raleigh] answered that being assured Her Majesty would never permit anything to be prosecuted to the Earl's danger ... and that therefore it were to small purpose after so long absence [from court] and so many disgraces to call his honour and name in question.[1]

The Queen replied that her procedure was merely intended as a warning to de Vere, and Raleigh continues:

[1] *Strype Annals*, IV, p. 591.

> "The more to witness how desirous I am of your Lordship's favour and good opinion, I am content to lay the serpent before the fire as much as in me lieth; that, having recovered strength, myself may be most in danger of his poison and sting.

The meaning of this cryptic phrase, following Mrs. Clark, I take to be, that Raleigh—who was to be portrayed in years to come, by some Shakesperean hand, as "Coriolanus"—knew all about the satiric dramatizations already suffered by Burleigh, and which were likely to be practised upon all and sundry, who, whether in the way of friendship or of friction, crossed the path of the playwright—Lord Great Chamberlain.

Raleigh's intercession, however, was successful, as we know from the letter written on 2 June, by Roger Manners, to the Earl of Rutland:

> "Her Majesty came yesterday to Greenwich from the Lord Treasurers. . . . The day she came away, which was yesterday, the Earl of Oxford came to her presence, and after some bitter words and speeches, in the end all sins are forgiven, and he may repair to the court at his pleasure. Master Raleigh was a great mean herein, whereat Pondus is angry for that he could not do so much."

Oxford, then, is free at last to return to court, and does so, bringing with him his wife, to whom, after nearly six years of almost unbroken alienation, wholly undeserved by her, he had again been reconciled; whereupon most of these incidents, including even the name "Pondus," which I take to be another spelling of Polonius, are transferred directly to the biographical drama which the Earl is now drafting, with himself as

Hamlet, his wife as Ophelia, and his father-in-law as Polonius, who, in the early Quarto, is "Corambis," which I take to be a play upon Burleigh's motto, "*Cor unum via una*, and to signify that, in Oxford's opinion, neither the old man's "heart" nor his "way" was so single as the motto would have the world believe, but was more truly described by the word "double." Further, I have no doubt at all that the events foreshadowed in Manners' words: "The Earl of Oxford came to her presence, and after some bitter words and speeches in the end all was forgiven and he may repair to the court at his pleasure"—describes an interview that is directly dramatized, when in *Hamlet*, I, ii, the King, with his Queen beside him, says:

> "We beseech you, bend you to remain
> Here in the cheer and comfort of our eye,
> Our chiefest courtier, cousin, and our son."

That the play, *Hamlet*, drafted 1583–84, is, in part, an allegorical interpretation of the Darnley murder, with the Queen and Claudius standing for Mary Queen of Scots and Bothwell, I have argued elsewhere;[1] but, for our present purpose, the tragedy is simply an autobiographical and topical tale, of which the characters fall naturally into their places, with Thomas, or Robert, Cecil as Laertes, with something from Tom Vavasour added; Sir Horatio and Sir Francis Vere, Oxford's favourite cousins, as Horatio and Francisco; John, 16th Earl of Oxford, who died in 1562, as the ghost; and, as Queen Gertrude and King Claudius, de Vere's mother, Margery, Countess of Oxford—with a little of Queen Elizabeth in addition—and her second husband, Charles Tyrrell.

[1] *The Case for Edward de Vere as Shakespeare*, pp. 332–4.

The number of autobiographical and topical allusions to Oxford is so large that I can select only a few of them here; since they range over many years of his life, beginning, paradoxically, at the end of the play, when Hamlet, remembering, as I believe, happy childhood days, and the delight he took in his father's company of actors at Hedingham Castle, tells Horatio how " He [Yorick] hath borne me on his back a thousand times "— this Hedingham castle being the home to which his mother, the widowed Countess of Oxford, had brought a " usurper," Charles Tyrrell, as second husband, just as Gertrude brings Claudius to the castle of Elsinore. The play's wide autobiographical range accounts, therefore, naturally, for the otherwise inexplicable fact, that Hamlet is about twenty years old at the opening of the tragedy, but is nearer thirty at its close.

Right from the start, then, the topical allusions come in streams. It was in 1583, the date of this play's conception, when the war with Spain was already imminent, that the strenuous activities in ship-building, following upon the appointment of a Royal Commission on the Navy, are alluded to in Marcellus' lines :

> " Why this same strict and most observant watch
> So nightly toils the subject of the land,
> And why such daily cast of brazen cannon,
> And foreign mart for implements of war;
> Why such impress of shipwrights "—

while in the next scene, I, ii, Laertes' appeal for " leave and favour to return to France," reminds us that Burleigh's son, Thomas Cecil, was in France about that time. Prince Hamlet's reappearance at court in the remainder of the

[1]First quoted by Admiral Holland, *Shakespeare Through Oxford Glasses*.

ROMEO AND JULIET AND HAMLET

scene fits closely, as we have seen, with Oxford's return to the Queen's favour, and to court, at that same time. Even the setting of the play in Denmark—and the de Veres, remember, were, in part, Danes by origin—is immediately topical, for it was in July 1582, that Oxford's brother-in-law and friend, Lord Willoughby d'Eresby, a part original of Petruchio, was commissioned by the Queen to Denmark, to invest King Frederick II with the Order of the Garter; and it was from his "relation" of that episode, with its tale of feasting at the Castle of Elsinore, and "a whole volley of all the great shot of the castle discharged," that we owe, I submit, in almost identical phrase, the king's words:

"No jocund health that Denmark drinks to-day,
But the great cannon to the clouds shall tell,
And the king's rouse the heaven shall bruit again,
Re-speaking earthly thunder."

Further, the famous passage in III, iv, where Hamlet, in his mother the Queen's presence, compares her late husband with her present one:

"Look here upon this picture and on this—
The counterfeit presentment of two brothers"—

actually describes the great silken tapestry, which, hanging from the ceiling, and with a passage through the centre, divided into two parts the great Hall of the Kronberg Palace at Elsinore, and bore upon it portraits of the Kings of Denmark. This is the "arras," through which Hamlet kills Polonius, and of which the remains are still to be seen in one of the Copenhagen Museums.[1] "Shakespeare" had not seen that arras; but he had

---

[1] Prof. Connes, *The Shakespeare Mystery*, p. 209.

obtained a first-hand description of it, from his friend and brother-in-law, Lord Willoughby.

Now returning to the early scenes of the tragedy, we will pick up a few more clues, and compare, let us say, Hamlet's " frailty thy name is woman," with the line in Oxford's poem upon " Woman's Changeableness."

" But when I see how frail these creatures are "—

and set Horatio's eloquent prophecy :

" In the most high and palmy state of Rome "—

with its theme of stars, sickness, and of disasters to come, against the plague, deaths, and comet of 1582, and with the even more threatening portents—to be fulfilled three years later—of prolonged war with the mighty power of Spain.

Even the philosophy of the plays, including the soliloquy upon death, links up directly with a work *Cardanus Comfort*, associated, by long tradition, with " Shakespeare,"[1] which was, as we have seen, translated from the Italian by Oxford's friend, Thomas Bedingfield, and published by Oxford himself, in 1573, against Bedingfield's expressed wish, but with the accompaniment of one of the most charming letters ever written by an English nobleman ; and one, moreover, packed with ideas that are subsequently used in *Much Ado About Nothing* and in The Sonnets. When, for example, we hear the sounding word-music of those opening lines concerning excessive grief, that :

" fault to nature,
To reason most absurd, whose common theme
Is death of fathers "—

[1] *Shakespeare's Tragic Heroes*, Lily Campbell.

who will deny that the Earl had in mind such passages as this, from his favourite book of philosophy, *Cardanus Comfort*:

> "This booke shalbe thoght lesse needefull in no parte, than in comfortynge the sorow which chaunceth by the death of parentes . . . another man moderately mourneth for his death . . . .

Further, when Hamlet soliloquizes:

> "O God a beast that wants discourse of reason
> Would have mourned longer"—

the line from *Cardanus Comfort* lurking at the back of his mind is surely this:

> "Beastes therefore be able for one only arte by memory not perceyving reason at any time.

Turn where you will, almost, the pages of *Hamlet*, and similar links are discernible. Those " few precepts," which Polonius bids Laertes " character," are, in part, from the *Euphues* of Lyly, who was Oxford's secretary during this year 1583, and in part from Burleigh's own opinions, as expounded, for example, by Hume, in his book, *The Great Lord Burleigh*.

> "That gentleman who sells an acre of land sells an ounce of credit, for gentility is nothing else but ancient riches. Suffer not thy sons to cross the Alps, for they shall learn nothing there but pride, blasphemy, and atheism. . . . Neither train them up in wars, for he that sets up to live by that profession can hardly be an honest man or a good Christian. Beware of being surety for thy best friends; he that payeth another mans debts seeketh his own decay. Be sure to keep some great man thy friend, but trouble him not with trifles; . . . . Towards

thy superiors be humble, yet generous; with thine equals familiar, yet respectful.

All this is pure Polonius; and the speech to Laertes,—as I have already shown to be the case with other speeches by the same individual—is true therefore to the historic man, and is written by Oxford into a burlesque presentment of the Lord Treasurer—facts which at once explain why certain actors, playing Polonius,[1] have wished to omit the advice of Laertes, as being "out of character." Here let the reference to the gentleman who, by disposing of an acre of land, "sells an ounce of credit," remind us of Hamlet's apology to Rosencrantz and Guildenstern, in II, ii, for being "most dreadfully attended." This statement also is historically true; for Oxford, between 1580 and 1585, made thirty-two distinct sales of land, out of the fifty-six effected during his whole lifetime; and it is a melancholy business to record, that the nobleman who, some twenty-two years before, had come clattering into London town, at the head of a retinue of eighty servants, can now, in the year 1584, command no more than four dependants "in all his house."

How pertinent also to this same period of Oxford's life is Hamlet's personal familiarity with the players; his references to the "tragedians of the city"—Oxford's own adult troupe—to the "aery of children, little eyases," who are his own company of "Oxford boys": and when the Prince asks: "Who maintains 'em," the questioner knew the answer well enough; since a part of the proceeds of those very sales of land, above recounted, went, beyond question, to the subsistence of

---

[1] The late H. B. Irving disapproved of the speech, for that reason.

the players, among whom Hamlet-Oxford's own acting and declamation could win for him, in Horatio's phrase, "Half a share in a fellowship." Is it matter for wonder that Oxford, the playwright-actor, consorting thus, upon terms of easy familiarity with the players, and filling, by his art, the Blackfriars Theatre with drama, such as England had never known before, had become, in the words of Claudius, beloved of "the general gender," and of that "distracted multitude," which, "dipping all his faults in their affection"—even while the disgraced de Vere conceives *Measure for Measure* in his prison, The Tower—"convert his gyves to graces"? thus arousing, against their favourite, even the envy of the Queen, and also of certain great nobles, especially Leicester, whom Oxford had been accused, by Arundel, of attempting to murder. Deeply it must have galled these proud Elizabethan courtiers, to see, in instance after instance, themselves, with obvious malice, or without, and under an easily penetrable disguise, pilloried and held up to public laughter, in these "abstracts and brief chronicles of the time," as Hamlet, with literal truth to historic fact, openly describes his plays. Burleigh-Polonius, himself now being victimized to all posterity, is equally explicit; since "tragical-comical-historical," as Col. B. R. Ward reminds me, is an exact description of the drama in which England's Lord Treasurer is ridiculed by England's Lord Great Chamberlain; and which, accordingly, it would seem, Oxford's own company of actors was playing. In vain, however, Burleigh protests to his royal mistress against the intolerable daring of his irreverent son-in-law, and against her fixed determination to shield her turbulent yet fascinating Turk. Thus Polonius, III, iv.

> "Tell him his pranks have been too broad to bear with,
> And that your grace hath screen'd and stood between
> Much heat and him."

Oxford, assured both of royal protection and of popular support, pushed by the urge of his genius, laughs at all opposition. In the same scene, II, ii,—wherein he turns this from his favourite Cardanus, who will

> "allow of those philosophers as wise who thought that all things consisted in opinion. . . . If in this life there be anything good or evil . . . the same resteth only in . . . virtue of the mind—

into "There is nothing either good or bad but thinking makes it so"—he proceeds deliberately, and with delighted malice, to parody, in the speeches of Polonius, the literary style of Burleigh's talk with, and letters to, himself; precisely as, in *Twelfth Night*, he had already parodied the styles of Hatton, as Malvolio, and of Buckhurts and Sidney, as Sir Toby and Sir Andrew.

Should any reader feel disposed to challenge my assertion, let him read, very carefully, Burleigh's letter to Oxford, of 23 April, 1576, and compare its humourless prolixities of style, with the speeches of Polonius, in II, ii. The following extracts should suffice to prove my case.

> "Most sovereign lady . . . I find in the latter end of my years a necessary occasion to be an intercessor for another next to myself, in a *cause* godly, honest and just; and therefore, having had proof of your *Majesty's* former favours in *causes* not so important, I doubt not but to find the like influence of your grace in a *cause* so near touching myself as your *Majesty* will conceive it doth. . . .

"*To* enter *to* trouble your *Majesty* with the circumstances of my *cause*, I mean not for sundry respects but chiefly for two; the one is that I am *very loth to be more cumbersome to your Majesty than need shall compel me*; the other is for that I hope in God's goodness, and for reverence borne to your *Majesty*, that success thereof may have a better end than the beginning threateneth. But *your Majesty may think my suit will be very long where I am so long ere I begin it*; and *truly*, most gracious sovereign lady, *it is true* that the nature of my *cause* is such as I have no pleasure to enter into it, but had rather seek means to shut it up for them to lay it open, not for lack of the soundness thereof on my part, but for the wickedness of others from whom the groundwork proceedeth. . . . and of my daughter your *Majesty's* most humble young servant, as of one that is towards your *Majesty* in dutiful love and fear, yea, in fervent admiration of your graces to contend with any her equals, and in the *cause* betwixt my Lord of Oxford and her, whether it be for respect of misliking in me, or misdeeming of hers wherof I cannot yet know the certainty, I do avow in the presence of *God and of his angels* whom I do call as ministers of his ire, if in this I do utter any untruth . . . and therefore, if contrary to my desert, I should otherwise be judged or suspected, I should receive great injury. For my daughter, though *nature* will make me . . . to speak favourably, yet now I have taken *God and His angels* to be witnesses of my writing, *I renounce nature*, and protest simply to your Majesty. I did never see in her behaviour in word or deed, nor ever could perceive by any other means, but that she hath always used herself *honestly*, chastely, and lovingly towards him . . . when some doubts were cast of his acceptance of her, that innocency seemed to make her so bold as she never cast any care of things past, but wholly reposed herself with assurance to be well used by him ... *she went to him and there missed of her expectation...*

Now listen heedfully to Polonius, also addressing his Queen concerning Hamlet.

> My liege and madam to expostulate
> What majesty should be, what duty is,
> Why day is day, night night, and time is time,
> Were nothing but to waste night, day and time.
> Therefore since *brevity* is the soul of wit,
> *And tediousness the limbs and outward flourishes,*
> *I will be brief.* Your noble son is mad.
> Mad call I it; for to define true madness,
> What is't but to be nothing else but mad?
> But let that go.
>   *Queen.* More matter, with less art.
>   *Polon.* Madam, I swear I use *no art* at all.
> That he is mad, *'tis true: 'tis true, 'tis pity,*
> *And pity 'tis 'tis true:* a foolish figure;
> But farewell it, for I will use *no art.*
> Mad let us grant him then; and now remains
> That we find out the *cause* of this *effect,*
> Or rather say, the *cause* of this *defect,*
> For this *effect defective* comes by *cause.*

The resemblances here are so "gross and palpable" that the speeches of Polonius above quoted must almost certainly have been written by Oxford with Burleigh's letter of 1576 in front of him; the one being almost a paraphrase of the other with the tricks of style only a little exaggerated in the play.

ROMEO AND JULIET AND HAMLET

BURLEIGH	POLONIUS (PONDUS)
In a *cause* godly, honest and just; and therefore, having had proof of your Majesty's former favours in *causes* . . . I doubt not but to *find* the like influence of your grace in a *cause* so near touching myself.	That we *find* out the *cause* of this effect, Or rather say, the *cause* of this defect, For this effect defective comes by *cause*.
I am very loth to be more cumbersome to your *Majesty* than need shall compel me . . . . But your Majesty may think my suit will be *very long* where I am *so long* ere I begin it.	to expostulate what *Majesty* should be . . . since *brevity* is the soul of wit, And *tediousness* the limbs and outward flourishes, I will be *brief*. . . .
truly, most gracious sovereign lady, *it is true that* the nature of my *cause*.	That he is mad, *'tis true*: *'tis true*, 'tis pity, And pity 'tis *'tis true* . . . and now remains *That we find* out the *cause*.

Polonius is here being made to utter " a brief abstract and chronicle " of his own letter of six years before—a conclusion supported by the further fact that, alike in the play and the letter, Burleigh turns from Hamlet to Ophelia discussing her " honesty " and telling how " she went to him (Oxford-Hamlet) and there missed of her expectation "—phrases that recall vividly the scene between Hamlet and Ophelia, wherein, most pathetically, Polonius' daughter challenged by Hamlet concerning her " honesty "—precisely as Anne Cecil's " honesty " was challenged in 1576—does indeed after " coming to him " " miss of her *expectation* " from the prince who had once been her lover, though in actual history her husband, just as he had also been, and, again, in actual history was no more :—

The *expectancy* and rose of the fair state.

This letter I may add is not the only one written during that critical year 1576, of which Oxford made use in Hamlet; for on 3 January he writes to Burleigh:

"I am to content myself according to the English proverb that it is my hap to serve while the grass doth grow.

words which in the play come out pat, as follows :

Ham. Sir, I lack advancement . . . but *while the grass grows*—the proverb is something musty.

To the tragedy's poignant close I will return towards the end of our story; but I have here set down nough, I hope, to show the historic truth, and living humanity, of this enthralling work, as also the personal affinities of its Prince of Denmark to the man whom I am proving to be "Shakespeare." Hamlet is, probably, on the whole, the most intimately biographical play in the whole range of Shakesperean drama.

CHAPTER EIGHT

CROWDED YEARS: 1584-1588

"Henry IV" exemplifies Failure of Rebellion—Nicholas Dawtrey the Original of Falstaff—Oxford sent to the War in the Low Countries, 1585—He is suddenly recalled and replaced by Sidney—Sidney as Ned Poins in "Henry IV," Part II—"William Visor" of Wincot—How William of Stratford may first have made contact with Oxford's Players—"Merry Wives of Windsor"—Oxford and the War in Flanders—Probable Reasons for Oxford's Recall—Already known as one of the leading Writers of Comedy—He is granted (1586) £1,000 a year from the Exchequer—Probably heads a School of Dramatic War Propagandists, in view of long Struggle against Spain—Oxford a Commissioner at Trial of Mary Queen of Scots—"A Winter's Tale"—Oxford's Oath of Secrecy—Autolycus and the Clown are Oxford and William of Stratford—Lady Susan Vere born May 26, 1587—Death of Lady Oxford—Anne Cecil as Desdemona—Oxford captains English vessel against the Armada—Prominent in Armada Celebrations, 1588.

OXFORD'S return to court, in the summer of 1583, was a matter for chastened jubilation, which is reflected, I think, in the joyously patriotic play that followed, namely the two parts of *Henry IV*. For the court, as such, de Vere, it would seem, had long ceased to care greatly; though with his keen hereditary sense of the majesty of Kings, he still revered Whitehall and Windsor, as the home of that "mortal breathing shrine," the person of the Queen, before whom all who looked for advancement must bend. Apart from her, and from the amusement of such dramatic material as it supplied him with, the atmosphere of the palaces was already boring a man the current of whose life was daily turning, more and more inevitably, towards those "lewd companions," of literature and the stage, against whom Burleigh would raise, upon occasion, a feebly protesting voice. The Earl's hours of ease, at this time, were to be enjoyed, not, for the most part, in royal palaces; but at the "Boar's Head," and such like haunts of "riot and dishonour," where, in the company of men and women who make up all the Falstaff crew, he would drown his bygone troubles behind jesting and laughter, and occasional healths to his placated mistress.

There was method, however, in this Boar's Head madness, and in its outcome, the play which provides our stage with its richest comedy part, as also with its most telling satire upon war. When, some twenty years before this time, Thomas Bedingfield, whose version of *Cardanus Comfort* we have seen Oxford using in *Hamlet*, had brought de Vere, a contrite truant, back from that stealthy dash to Flanders, the culprit, upon his return, it may be remembered, had supplied the Queen and court with a crude play, *The Famous Victories of Henry V*, wherein, personifying himself as the reformed Prince Hal, he made, to his royal mistress, an implied dramatic promise of amendment, which we may suppose to have been graciously accepted, since there now emanate from the "Boar's Head" two plays, covering historically the same period as did *The Famous Victories of Henry V*, and again presenting to the Queen, in allegory, Oxford himself as the mad-cap prince, in process of regeneration, and of transformation into a wise and circumspect king. For that purpose, the Earl borrowed from the older play the Gadshill robbery, in which Oxford's men had been implicated in 1573, also the burlesque of father and son by Falstaff and the prince, and the impressment of that rag-tag company of recruits. Very possibly, indeed, the first idea of *Henry IV* arose, as the play quite definitely hints, out of some convivial evening at the " Boar's Head," and a sudden inspiration—" Let us have a play extempore, and the argument shall be thy (Falstaff's) running away."[1] They had it, accordingly ; and the impromptu charade became that masterpiece *Henry IV*, with the added deeply serious theme, which Oxford's recent experiences had burned into his always patriotic mind, namely the Throgmorton plot contrived against his Queen and country, wherein, along with the Earl of Arundel, there was implicated, once more, Lord Henry Howard, that sinister figure, already linked, all too ominously, with the themes of *Much Ado About Nothing* and *Measure for Measure*.

Unofficially, then, already, and before long officially, de Vere—while still " the privileged vicar for the lawless marriage of ink and paper," as personified by Falstaff—is becoming the poet and dramatist of our realm's national security. With Mrs. Clark and Capt. Ward, I wholly agree that the primary object of *Henry IV* was to show the inevitable failure of rebellion against the crown, whether that rebellion be raised by Hotspur, as in *Henry IV*, part I, or by York, Hastings and Mowbray, as in the second part. King Henry's line epitomizes the theme :

Thus ever did rebellion find rebuke.

Concerning the historic original of Falstaff, there is a general consensus of informed opinion in identifying him with Capt. Nicholas Dawtrey, a hanger-on of the court, and quasi-military adventurer, of immense

---
[1] Prince Hal. *1. King Henry IV*, II, iv.

physical corpulence, who, in 1583 and 1584, took part in hunting down the rebel Earl of Desmond in Ireland. About this Dawtrey, a typical figure of his day, Oxford builds up his matchless portrait of a proletarian national soldier, of the " Old Bill " type, both of whom, one imagines, failing the doubtful security of a " better 'ole," were equally capable of shamming dead, if need be, upon Shrewsbury, or any other field. The Sir Nicholas Gawsey of the play is, probably, a compound of Sir Nicholas Dawtrey, and Sir Robert Gausell, whom Holinshed mentions in his account of the Shrewsbury fight.

Meanwhile, the dreadful prospect, and menace, of a struggle to the death with Spain, hung brooding darkly over England. In 1584, William the Silent had been assassinated; and with the Dutch defence in greater danger than ever of collapse, Sturmius, the leader of protestant thought in the Rhineland, and long an agent in Elizabeth's pay, wrote to the English Queen, urging her to dispatch an expedition into the Low Countries, under the command of " some faithful and zealous personage such as the Earl of Oxford, the Earl of Leicester, or Philip Sidney."

Elizabeth recognized the need, as much as she grudged the money; but, at last, afer prolonged negotiation, the matter was arranged; and on 25 June, 1585, Oxford, who was neither the first nor the last literary genius to conceive himself a competent man of action, and born administrator of difficult affairs, wrote to Burleigh craving his father-in-law's help, to secure him a command, and requesting a loan of £200, " till her Majesty performeth her promise."

Whether that promise was one of cash, or of captaincy,

I cannot say. It was probably the former; but, in any event, the Earl was appointed, with Col. John Norris, to a joint command. On 18 August, Antwerp, to the immense joy of Philip II, surrendered to Parma, and on the 29th Lord Oxford left for the Netherlands. Immediately afterwards, Leicester, his most powerful rival at court, set afoot a scheme for his supersession, which, after the lapse of some weeks, and following upon a sequence of events at which we can only guess—since no despatches to or from Oxford exist—fell out exactly as Leicester hoped.

Early in October, "The Earl of Oxford sent his money, apparel, wine and venison to England," in a ship that was captured by the Spaniards off Dunkirk, on board which was found a letter from Lord Burleigh to the Earl, appointing him to the command of the Horse. Too late! for on 21 October, Davison writes cryptically to Captain Henry Norris, that "The Earl of Oxford has returned this night into England, upon what humour I know not." During November, Sir Philip Sidney, with rank of General of the Horse, took over the Governorship of Flushing, in a campaign that was to bring him to his death; and the next day after Oxford had left Holland for England, the Queen signed the Earl of Leicester's commission, as Lieutenant-General of the English forces in the Low Countries. De Vere's rivals had triumphed; and the Earl's pride, one supposes, was bitterly hurt. Posterity, however, need not regret these happenings, since Shakespeare, like any other, must follow his destiny; and there can be no possible doubt that this sudden, and somewhat mysterious, recall, however reluctantly received and obeyed, left him free to do so in the way that was best for himself and for the world, as a worker with the pen, and not with the sword. In the light of events that are to follow, it is most probable that Elizabeth herself, and her Council, thought likewise; but, be the truth what it may, the three plays that next follow from the Earl's pen—*Henry IV, Part II*, *The Merry Wives of Windsor*, and *Othello*, bear a strong impress of that Flanders campaign—Philip Sidney himself appearing, in the two first-named, as Ned Poins and Slender respectively; Ned Poins being, in fact, almost an anagram for P. Sidnei, which is Philip's own spelling of his name.

That Ned Poins is Sidney was first pointed out by Mrs. Clark[1] who argues convincingly that Prince Henry's (Oxford's) words in II, ii:—

> "but that the tennis court keeper knows better than I; for it is a low ebb of linen with thee when thou keepest not racket there; as thou hast done a great while, because the rest of thy low countries have made a shift to eat up thy holland"—

are an obvious allusion to the tennis-court quarrel between Oxford and Sidney in 1579 while the jest about the "low countries" devouring "holland" refers to Sidney's appointment as Governor of Flushing.

Henry IV, Part II, with its sudden large rise in the number of double endings, after the third act, presents what Mr. J. M. Robertson calls "another evaded problem" in Shakespeare; and Mrs. Clark suggests that Oxford crossed to Flanders before his play was finished, leaving it to be completed by other hands: but whoever wrote the latter portions of the comedy, we find, in he first scene of Act V—which, as regards position, is a

---

[1] Mrs. Clark's *Shakespeare's Plays in the Order of their Writing*, p. 534.

favourite one for the insertion of significant word-cipher—mysterious lines which usher in that enigmatic mystery-motive already looming upon the horizon of our story—the problem of William of Stratford, and his connexion with the genuine Shakesperean drama. These lines, spoken in the house of Justice Shallow, in Gloucestershire, run as follows.

> *Davy.* I beseech you, sir, to countenance William Visor of Woncot against Clement Perkes o' the hill.
> *Shall.* There is many complaints, Davy, against this Visor: that Visor is an arrant knave, on my knowledge.
> *Davy.* I grant your worship that he is a knave, sir; but yet God forbid, sir, but a knave should have some countenance, at his friend's request. An honest man, sir, is able to speak for himself, when a knave is not . . . I beseeech your worship, let him be countenanced.
> *Shall.* Go to; I say he shall have no wrong. Look about, Davy.

What means this most cryptic passage, wherein one Davy pleads for "countenance" to be granted to one "William Visor of Woncot," whom he admits, upon Shallow's accusation, to be, nevertheless, an arrant knave? Now a visor means a mask, used for the purpose of concealing identity; and Woncot, though apparently in Gloucestershire, is not far, in sound, from Wilmecote, close to Stratford-on-Avon, a town that is almost within hail of Gloucestershire. The dialogue, therefore, appears to resolve itself into an appeal by Davy, on behalf of one William who, with a concealed identity, and dwelling at Woncot (Wilmcote), is an arrant knave, and the subject of complaints; but who, being debarred, by reason of his knavery, from speaking effectively for himself, must remain "silent." Shallow, himself standing for justice, and associated, in this play, with another Justice, significantly named "*Silence*," advises Davy to "look about," and assures him that his protégé "shall have no wrong." Very mysterious, is it not? and none the less so when it is remembered that William of Stratford's (Sogliardo's) brother, Sordido, is also bitterly attacked, as a knavish profiteer in corn, by Jonson, in the opening act of *Every Man Out Of His Humour*; and that there was inserted, at some time or other, into the next, and last, of the Falstaff plays, *The Merry Wives of Windsor*, a scene, IV, i, which, in common with the episodes above written of, has nothing to do with the play, wherein is introduced, as a boy, this time, another William who is catechized by Sir Hugh Evans concerning his attainments in the Latin tongue, and emerges none too well from the ordeal. It is worth while also to compare this talk, concerning the "countenancing" of William Visor of Woncot, with the dialogue in *Love's Labour's Lost*, V, ii, a scene packed with cipher-talk between Rosalind, and Biron—who is Oxford-Shakespeare—and who have just doffed both visor and disguise.

> *Rosa.* Which of the vizards was it that you wore?
> *Biro.* Where? when? what regard? why demand you this?
> *Rosa.* There then, that vizard; that superfluous case,
>   That hid the worse and show'd the better face.

Is not our story already effectively hiding the worse,

and showing the better, face—a face born, not in a cottage, but in a castle?

Exactly how the relations between de Vere and William Shaksper of Stratford were joined, our present knowledge forbids us definitely to say, though a solution may be found in the circumstances, now under examination, of the connexion of the Trussell family with the Stratford district of Warwickshire—Elizabeth Trussell, wife to the 15th Earl of Oxford, being Edward de Vere's grandmother. Mrs. Clark's book, however, supplies us with an interesting and suggestive aid towards the solution of the mystery, by informing us that in 1584, about one year in advance of the first drafting of these Falstaff plays, Sir Thomas Lucy, of the deer-poaching story, identified, by tradition, with this same Justice Shallow, was patron of a company of players, who acted at Coventry, where Oxford's players also had worked during every year from 1581 to 1585 inclusive: Mrs. Clark's plausible inference being, that William of Stratford, who was twenty years old in 1584, was "poached," by Oxford from Sir Thomas Lucy's company —a surmise which, if it be sound, helps to elucidate this mysterious plea for the countenancing of William Visor of Woncot, who cannot speak for himself, and also throws light upon Slender's, or Lucy's, assurance that " he shall have no wrong." Here, if the reasoning be good, are Oxford, Lucy, and William all brought together, though in an atmosphere of mystery and of silence. It is possible, however, that, as we shall see later, Oxford may have first met William during a temporary residence of the Earl in Warwickshire, upon a property that may have come to him through the Trussells'.

The Merry Wives of Windsor may not have been written in its present form, until 1601–02; but there seems to have existed an earlier Oxford play drafted probably at Windsor during the mid-fifteen-'eighties, and dramatizing the love-affairs of Oxford and Sidney, as rivals for the hand of Anne Cecil, in 1571. Sidney was practically engaged, for a time, to the lady who was unfortunate enough to become the wife of de Vere, and who is Anne Page of the play, in which Sidney is Slender, and Fenton, the noble-born courtier, who writes verses, dances, riots, and " smells all April and May,"[1] is, of course, Oxford himself; Sidney and Oxford having been adversaries since 1570, in love, letters, court-intrigue, politics, and war. The comedy, I need hardly say, with its book of riddles, and its long succession of puns upon Ford, Ox, Brook, Beck, and other parts of, or allusions to Oxford's names, is, in these respects, of much significance throughout; the most revealing line, perhaps, being:

Ford. Aye, and an *ox* too—the *proofs are extant*.

To my opponents, who are accustomed to make merry over my interpretation of such a line, I recommend a delightful excursion, one summer's day, to the beautiful church, beside the beautiful town of Long Melford, in the heart of the Oxford country of Essex and Suffolk; where they may see, and ponder over, the picture, in stained glass, memorizing the de Vere family, wherein an Ox is seen crossing a Ford.[2] Both parties, I assure them, will thus derive pleasure from my revenge.

[1] De Vere's birthday was 12 April, 1550.
[2] Arundel in his charges of 1580 frequently called Oxford "Ox."

Throughout these years, from 1583 to 1586, while the sunshine of the Queen's favour draws from Oxford those flowers of philosophic comedy, that we connect with the name of Falstaff, the cloud-wrack of his own misdeeds—and the shadows they cast upon a mind always, at bottom, exquisitely sensitive to the right— is still periodically darkening his life. Poignant memories are alive in him, of past behaviours to two women, both of whom had given him their love—and both of whom he has wronged—one his own Countess, by unmerited scorn and neglect; the other Anne Vavasour, by a seduction which brought both her and himself to the Tower. On 19 January, 1585, Anne's brother, Thomas Vavasour, sent to the Earl of Oxford a vigorously worded " lewd " letter by way of challenge.

" If thy body had been as deformed as thy mind is dishonourable, my house had been yet unspotted, and thyself remained with thy cowardice unknown. I speak this that I fear thou art so much wedded to the shadow of thine, that nothing can have force to awake thy base and sleepy spirits. Is not the revenge already taken of thy wildness sufficient, but wilt thou yet use unworthy instruments to provoke my unwilling mind ? Or dost thou fear thyself, and therefore hast sent thy forlorn kindred, whom as thou hast left nothing to inherit so dost thou thrust them violently into thy shameful quarrels ? If it be so (as I too much doubt) then stay at home thyself and send my abusers; but if there be yet any spark of honour left in thee, or iota of regard of thy decayed reputation, use not thy birth for an excuse, for I am a gentleman, but meet me thyself alone, and thy lackey to hold the horse. For the weapons I leave them to thy choice for that

I challenge and the place to be appointed by us both at our meeting, which I think may conveniently be at Nevington (Newington), or elsewhere. Thyself shall send me word by this bearer, by whom I expect an answer. Tho. Vavasor."

The sequel to this outburst is unknown, but Oxford who had already fought, and been severely wounded by Anne Vavasour's uncle, Thomas Knyvet (Tybalt) in a first duel over that lady, was not likely, three years later, to accept another challenge from another member of the family, who also, to judge by the ferocious style, was like Tybalt a " king of cats." This letter, however, is strongly reminiscent of Laertes, in his angry mood—in Juliet there is a hint of Annie Cecil (Ophelia) as well as of the other Anne.

The second great tragedy of this period, *Othello*, first drafted, it would seem, about the year 1585, probably takes its skeleton form from Cinthio's novel, of which a French translation had appeared in 1584; but it is actually, as we shall see later, like *Hamlet*, a composite of vital experiences in Oxford's own life, woven into events in which a prominent part is played by King Philip of Spain, the monarch whose menace to England. in these mid-eighties, was becoming every year more deadly.[1] Miss Winstanley holds that Othello the Moor stands, symbolically, either for the King, or the power of Spain, just as Desdemona symbolically personates Venice, her marriage with Othello typifying the Venetian-Spanish alliance, a result of which was the battle of Lepanto, in 1571, when those two combined navies destroyed the Turkish fleet. Historically viewed, Desdemona is another member of that dark Valois-Medici

[1] " *Othello,*" *as the Tragedy of Italy.*

house, whose fascinations, and devilments, pervade Oxford's comedies and tragedies alike, namely Catherine de' Medici's daughter, Elizabeth of Valois, whom Philip II did actually slay in 1568, not by strangulation, but by poison. Iago has for historic original Antonio Perez, who was in the pay of the Essex group, and came to England in 1604; Emilia being his aforetime mistress: Princess Eboli, who, like Desdemona in the play, was stifled to death by Philip: and lest any reader should be thinking that Miss Winstanley and myself are allowing our imaginations to run riot, in supposing that Oxford would dare, or that Elizabeth would permit, the presentation of anti-Spanish plays upon the stages of England, let him read the following extract from a letter written, by the Venetian ambassador in Spain, to the Doge and Senate of Venice, on 20 July, 1586:

> "But what has enraged him (the King of Spain) more than all else, and has caused him to show a resentment such as he has never before displayed in all his life, is the account of the masquerades and comedies which the Queen of England orders to be acted at his expense."[1]

Thus we know that masquerades and comedies were being staged in England in 1586, by royal order, against the King of Spain; and to these lighter satires, we may now add a great tragedy, *Othello*.

Othello, however, I repeat, is not all Spanish-Venetian; for I wholly agree with Mrs. Clark[1] that, taking but a single example, Othello's words to Desdemona:

"A liberal hand: the hearts of old gave hands;
But our new heraldry is hands not hearts"—

[1] Mrs. Clark, *Shakespeare's Plays in the Order of their Writing*, p. 575.

probably hints at Alençon's vow to protect Antwerp, of which the escutcheon bore two hands as a device—a vow broken by the treacherous attack upon, and massacre in, the city during January 1583, known as the French Fury and hinted at by Desdemona's line, IV, ii:

> "I understand a fury in your words,
> But not the words."

Yet the fundamental links between Flemish history and the play *Othello* are found in the British campaign in Flanders in 1585, in which we have seen Oxford entrusted with a command and recalled, with mysterious suddenness, after his appointment as General of the Horse. That Oxford blamed Burleigh as being the individual primarily responsible for that recall, we do not certainly know; but such an inference is strongly suggested by Desdemona's words to Othello after that general's recall:

> "Alas the heavy day! Why do you weep?
> Am I the motive of these tears, my lord?
> If haply you my father did suspect
> An instrument of this your calling back,
> Lay not your blame on me"—[1]

for if Anne Cecil be topically Desdemona, then Brabantio becomes Burleigh powerful in London, as Brabantio was in Venice:

> "In his effect a voice potential
> As double as the Duke's."

Further, Iago uses, of Othello, the typically Oxfordian phrase, "He is that he is," recalling Oxford's words to Burleigh in 1584: "I am that I am;" also Othello, like

[1] Mrs. Clark, *Shakespeare's Plays in the Order of their Writing*, p. 402.

Oxford, is of noble birth, fetching his

> " life and being
> From men of royal seige."

Finally, Oxford's successor in Flanders, is Leicester whose name I take to be clumsily Italianized in I, iii:

> *Duke.* 'Tis certain then for Cyprus,
> Marcus Luccicos, is not he in town?

The Spaniards were derisively known in England as "Moors," because that eastern nation had, for so long, occupied their country: thus in *Othello*, beneath the Moorish disguise, we have once more portrayed a nobler aspect of Oxford, depicted with his " occupation gone," stricken with remorse, and seeking to atone, towards both himself and his Countess—wounded, alike, by the same slanderous tongues—with a confession, in which he dramatizes, with heart-rending poignancy, those outrages that cunning deceivers, and his own intolerance, have prompted towards an innocent wife, whose only fault, probably, was that, Ophelia-like, she had been weakly complaisant towards her father's behest, to keep a close eye on, and speak more than she should concerning, the doings of her wayward husband.

Thus considered, the tragedy of *Othello*, like that of *Hamlet*, is seen to be another dramatization, by Oxford, of the unforgettable domestic tragedy of his life, the supposed infidelity of his Lady Anne; a theme first staged, from that viewpoint, not in *Hamlet*, but, as we have seen, in *Troilus and Cressida*, during the late 'seventies. In the light of this interpretation, one can compare

Troilus' distracted words:

> O Cressid! O false Cressid! false, false, false!
> Let all untruths stand by thy stained name....
> Farewell, revolted fair—

with Hamlet's, "Frailty, thy name is woman!" and with Othello's:

> But yet the pity of it, Iago!—O Iago, the pity of it, Iago!

and wholly concur, for once, with Coleridge, that, as was, beyond question, the historic fact, jealousy had never been the prime source of Othello's passion.

> "I take it," writes Coleridge, "to be rather an agony that the creature whom he had believed angelic, with whom he had garnered up his heart, and whom he could not help still loving, should be proved impure and worthless. It was the struggle *not* to love her. It was a moral indignation and regret that virtue should so fall—O, the pity of it. Iago!"

Compare the above words with Hamlet's nobly moral indignation over Ophelia—who, like Desdemona, closes her life upon a song—and also over Queen Gertrude's lapse; and who can fail to perceive the psychological unity of these two mighty tragedies, thus autobiographically linked into one poignant dramatic lament over those shattered ideals of perfect womanhood that every romantic poet holds, and guards to the last moment, within the secret citadels of his soul.

Iago, it must follow, is topically either Howard or Arundel; and it is significant that the latter, in common with the historical and Spanish prototype, Perez, was certainly in the pay of the King of Spain. I believe, nevertheless, that de Vere, in his passionate self-condemnation, pictures himself also as a part original of Iago; for had he not, long before, said to Cressida (Anne), in his own character of Troilus (IV, iv):

> In each grace of these
> There lurks a still and *dumb discursive devil*
> *That tempts most cunningly* . . .
> And *sometimes we are devils to ourselves*
> When we will tempt the frailty of our power.

Who will deny that we have here Oxford's own forecast of the potential Iago in himself—as well as in his enemy—that fatal willingness to believe, wherewith the imaginative mind—such as his pre-eminently was—"tempts the frailty of its own powers," and, succumbing, pays the fearful price of a ruined felicity.

Emilia, in common with the Emilia of *A Winter's Tale*, is, topically considered, Oxford's sister, Lady Mary Vere, already dramatized, more prominently yet, as Katharina in *The Taming of the Shrew*.[1]

"Othello's occupation's gone"; and yet, in a sense, it has rather come; for the issue of these events of the past five years—besides giving indirectly to posterity *Hamlet*, *Othello*, and *King Henry IV*—is the establishment of Edward de Vere, officially, and for the remainder of his life, in an occupation far better suited to his supreme literary capacities than could be any command in Flanders —namely, as our accredited national dramatist, secretly appointed, and secretly salaried, to work for England through the despised medium of the stage.

---

[1] "Lady Mary Vere" makes a rough anagram for Emilia, "Amylyar de Vere." We have seen that *A Winter's Tale* is a dramatization of the same episode.

That the underlying reason for Oxford's recall from Flanders was a decision, by the Queen and her Privy Council, that the Earl could serve his country to far better advantage as general of our stage in England, than as leader of our Horse in Flanders, I take to be a certain thing. The powers responsible for the well-being of this country, during those crucial years—when the menace of Spain loomed ever darker upon the horizon, and when patriotic ears could almost hear the clang and boom of the shipwrights' hammers, building the armada—were beginning to discern the potential value of the theatre, as an educative and encouraging factor, in days when those great platform-stages were our only newspapers and debating chambers. In organizing, therefore, a group of playwrights who could be entrusted with this important national task, there were two men to whom the Queen might naturally look; namely Oxford, and his cousin by marriage, Bacon. Oxford's fame, as a writer, must already have been borne upon the wings of rumour far outside the precincts of the court; for during the year 1586, at which we have arrived, William Webbe wrote, in his *Discourse of English Poetry*:

> "I may not omit the deserved commendations of many honourable and noble Lords and Gentlemen in Her Majesty's court, which, in the rare devices of poetry have been, and yet are, most skilful; among whom the Right Honourable Earl of Oxford may challenge to himself the title of the most excellent among the rest."

What Webbe knew, others knew: the poet-dramatist of them all was Oxford; and it was probably with mingled feelings of anger, shame, thwarted pride, and unacknowledged relief, that de Vere, at this time, received directly, from the Queen or her Ministers, a behest to place himself at the head of this movement, and to range under his command, not regiments of horse, but a company of playwrights, who also, in their respective fashions, should serve their country's need.

And, the workman being worthy of his hire, what of the more commercial side of the commission? Oxford, it is certain, desperately needed money at the time; and was in no such financial position, as, apart from other reasons, might have justified a refusal. Forced sales of lands, which had come down to him weighted with a heritage of debt, is a game that cannot continue indefinitely; and at the outset of the Flanders campaign we have seen the Earl attempting to borrow £200 from Burleigh, "till her Majesty performeth her promise." What that promise may have been, we do not know; but in June 1586, some eight months after de Vere's recall from Flanders by the Queen, there came some "performance," in the shape of a Privy Seal Warrant, authorizing "our right trustie and right well beloved Cousin the Earle of Oxford," to receive £1,000 a year from the Exchequer, as from the previous March; another remarkable fact, in this connexion, being that the wording of the warrant is the same as is commonly, and indeed only, used in secret service payments—the Exchequer officials being expressly forbidden to call for any account of its expenditure by the recipient. We know, moreover, that the payment was granted for some state service, because it was excluded from the ordinary annuities, but included in part XIII of the Exchequer Account, which, consist of *payments to the heads of various State Departments.* Further, this amount, which was paid unfailingly until Oxford's death in 1604 —that is, throughout a time of extraordinary expenditure exactly coincident with the duration of the Spanish war— is altogether unprecedented among other recipients of less than royal rank, and was not extended to de Vere's son—Henry, the 18th Earl, receiving only the £200 a year, which was about a normal allowance to distinguished, but impecunious, noblemen.

The inevitable conclusions seem to be that we have, in this commissioning of Oxford, some official organization of work which, unofficially, the Queen had already begun, when she had ordered, or connived at, the writing and acting of masks and comedies against the Spanish king, and the grouping together, under Oxford's leadership, of the " University wits," Marlowe, Kyd, Greene, Peele, Lyly, Munday, Lodge, and Nashe, generally supposed to have been Shakespeare's masters but now to be recognized as his pupils. Most or all of these were probably paid by the Earl to produce the long series of plays, mainly historical, which now, at this time, begin to appear; all or most of them somewhat military and anti-Catholic in tone, and supporting the Lancastrian party, with which both Elizabeth and Oxford were by ancestry closely identified; and hotly attacking the Yorkists, as, for example, in the case of *King Richard III*, who is made a monster in that play, whereas he was historically, no whit worse than the average Plantagenet ruler of his time. Remarkably close are the analogies between this great Anglo-Spanish war, and the World War of 1914–18. Quadrupling of national budget, trebling the price of wheat, scarcity and want, penal taxation, and all costs everywhere soaring—such phenomena were common to both upheavals; and the popular soldier-hero, who was neither of these—Jack Falstaff of the one war, and Old Bill of the other—shamming dead at Shrewsbury, or shell-sheltered in his "better 'ole," can likewise join hands across the centuries.

That all parties, concerned in this ingenious and eventful arrangement, joined in an oath of secrecy, never to reveal what they were doing, nor to disclose the identities of the doers, the Shakesperean plays and supporting allusions in the satires of Ben Jonson, seem to make perfectly clear: and these facts and inferences clarify also such mysterious words as those used by Bacon—who was probably a member of the group, in some editorial capacity—when he requests King James to be "good to concealed poets," and asserts that he has, though in despised weed, "procured the good of all men." The Shakesperean Sonnets also, in their turn, reveal the secret; when their author numbers among the woes that make him cry aloud for death, his enforced subservience to an authority, that has "tongue-tied" his art. Oaths, nevertheless, as we shall see, may be kept, and yet broken, too!

This year 1586, however, was not passed by Oxford, wholly in writing, nor in organizing the writing of plays. As inheritor of one of the most ancient and powerful earldoms in England, and as a patrician, who, nevertheless, possessed personal acquaintance with, and was deeply interested in, the fortunes of that sombre, fantastic Valois group, it is not surprising to find Oxford appointed one of the Commissioners[1] who

---

[1] Cf Kent (Oxford) in *King Lear*, appointed by Lear " o' the commission " that tries Goneril, who was Catherine de' Medici, mother-in-law of the Scottish Queen.

assembled at Westminster, on 27 September, for the trial of Mary Queen of Scots. During the proceedings there was probably circulated among the Commissioners, and passed therefore into de Vere's own hands, as one of the *pièces de conviction*, that contemporary plan of the Darnley murder, still to be seen in the Museum of the Record Office, which, with the dagger floating in the air above the corpses, and that heavily barred and studded gate below, gave Oxford, as I like to think, his first ideas for the scene wherein Macbeth grasps at the inviting weapon—" Is this a dagger that I see before me ? "—and also supplied a hint for that grimly humoresque episode, wherein the importunate knockings disgruntle the old porter of hell-gate, who had let in some of all kinds, " that tread the primrose path to the everlasting bonfire."

What would we not give to know Oxford's secret thoughts and imaginings, while, fascinated, he watched and listened to the doomed Queen, inextricably caught in the meshes of past follies, and of present murder-plotting friends ; or to know by what process of soaring imagination, still with the constant purpose before him, to serve thereby his own country and Queen, Bothwell and Mary, first as Lord and Lady Macbeth, and then as King and Queen of Scotland, become, for all time, examples, for all the world, of those who, wrought upon by vaulting ambitions, have struck anointed kings, and not flourished after. That the pages of Buchanan's *Detection* also helped Oxford considerably, there can be no doubt whatever ; and it may, I think, be taken as certain, that the murder of Mary's uncle, another sinister member of that ill-starred House of Guise, at the Castle of Blois, towards Christmas 1588, assisted subsequently to colour the world's loftiest achievement in the art of dramatic blank verse.[1]

Oxford, then, in this year 1586, is definitely established, under oath of secrecy, as head of a national group of poet dramatists, whose plays are " carried with this method, to teach their subjects obedience to their king "[2]—a task in which his privilege in being thus called to serve his country, as can no other man or woman in the land, and to build, for all eternity, " a monument to his own fame ere he die," is qualified by the fact that such glory must be won with work, not done beside the descendants of kings, nor among men of his own rank and standing, but, instead, by such " public means as public manners breeds "—a task that must indelibly stain those aristocratic hands—which, like his father's before him, have borne golden canopies over crowned heads—" To what they worked in like a dyer's hand."[3] And the unkindest cut of destiny, in these fantastic happenings, is perhaps this, that the years of toil, past and to come, for Queen and country, as well as for art and literature, which also he deeply loves, are to bring him no absolute certainty, even, of future fame, since the royal words has gone forth : " Silence, no man must know."

But can it be so, in fact ; since already, before yet the ink is dry upon that first receipt for secret payment, every writer in London knows that *ipse* is he ? Can no way be found, whereby this subtlest and most resourceful, among all these super-subtle Elizabethan minds, like

---

[1] Oxford, I think, drew his first ideas for *Macbeth*, as a royal tragedy, from that analogous domestic tragedy, *Arden of Feversham*, of which he, or one of his school, was probably the author.
[2] Thomas Heywood, *Apology for Actors*.
[3] Sonnet 111.

the juggling fiends of his own *Macbeth*, can:

> "palter with us in a double sense,
> That keep the word of promise to our ears"—

even while they break it, for the enlightenment of generations yet to come? Assuredly such a way must be discoverable—and already, into the play that de Vere is now shaping, which is *A Winter's Tale*, and into those that he has already written, abjuring henceforth all "russet yeas and honest kersey noes," he will interweave scene after scene of his dramas with "three-piled hyperboles, spruce affectations, and figures pedantical,"[1] all revealing, in their respective fashions, the secret; since, as himself has already said before, in the character of Biron, it is better far to "lose our oaths to find ourselves," than to "lose ourselves to keep our oaths." Further, the loveliness of the plays being symbolized, again and again, by the beauty of a woman, is there not logic in the King's line, in the same comedy:

> "Rebuke me not for that which you provoke;
> The virtue of your eye must break my oath"—

and such will ever be the potency of Princess's beauty over Prince's word, whatever pretence the lady may make of detestation for

> "a breaking cause to be
> Of heavenly oaths vowed with integrity."[2]

The *Winter's Tale*, which, as Admiral Holland and Mrs. Clark have made clear, Oxford now sets about writing, contains many unmistakable allusions to

---

[1] Biron (Oxford) in *Love's Labour's Lost*, V, ii.
[2] *Love's Labour's Lost*, V, ii.

CROWDED YEARS

events of the mid-fifteen-'eighties; though how much of the Earl's own work the comedy contains is a question very difficult to answer; the crucial point, so far as our present story is concerned, being that, in the enigmatic cipher-scene, III, iii, which is inserted between the third and fourth acts, we have the mysteriously banished Antigonus cast upon an alien shore, in possession of a nameless baby princess—historically the Lady Elizabeth Vere—and appointed by Fate, "against thy better disposition," to be the baby's "thrower out," according to his oath. A moment later, after a second plaint against compulsion, to be "by oath enjoined to this," Antigonus rushes from the stage, pursued, and subsequently "half-eaten," though not wholly devoured, by "a bear," which turns out, upon further examination, to be none other than "Authority," otherwise the imperious will of the Queen, and her Privy Council, who have exacted this oath from unwilling Antigonus, and are finding, in return, his secret salary.

After Antigonus, there comes upon the scene, Autolycus, the charming rogue, who has worn three-pile in his day, and who, whether he likes it or not—and Oxford did not always like it—is a courtier, with the air of the court in "these enfoldings," with the measure of the court in his gait, with "court contempt" in his glance, and with "court odours" emanating from his person, to the noses of the passers-by: who, further, in the clown's phrase, is "the more noble in being fantastical," which last Edward de Vere pre-eminently was. That clown, indeed, promptly detects the quality of Autolycus, "by the picking on's teeth"; and Jonson also, before many years have passed, will similarly describe him, walking the centre aisle of Pauls, "with a pick-tooth in his mouth."[1] Bertram, in *All's Well that Ends Well*, whom we have seen to be Oxford again, would also " pick his teeth and sing " (II, ii.)

A mysterious man, this Autolycus, the tattered, fantastical, scented picker-of-teeth, and picker-up of unconsidered trifles, who is contemptuous without rudeness, and familiar without vulgarity, and who, though a rogue and a cut-purse, conveys the odour of, and possesses the entry to, Kings' courts, while he walks through this play, haloed with an alluring mystery which makes half its abiding charm—a mystery that, as is the way of Eve's daughters, the world over, the maids would fain worm from him, how they may, even in the rural intimacies of a sheep-shearing song. Listen to them :

> *Auto.* Get you hence, for I must go
> Where it fits not you to know.
> *Dor.* Whither ? *Mop.* O, whither ? *Dor.* Whither ?
> *Mops.* It becomes thy oath full well,
> Thou to me thy secrets tell.
> *Dorc.* Me too, let me go thither.
> *Auto.* Neither. *Dor.* What, neither ? *Auto.* Neither.

And so on, until the Clown suggests that " We'll have this song out anon by ourselves."

But they do not ; nor, in fact, was this mysterious ditty ever to be " had out " until some three hundred and fifty years later, let Dorcas, and Mopsa too, charm,

---

[1] Amorphus (Oxford) : *Cynthia's Revels*, II, i.

both of them, never so wisely. Silence must be still the word; for while "the dash of his former life be yet upon him," no preferment, as Autolycus plaintively admits, could come of any premature admission.

"Had I been the finder out of this secret, it would not have relished among my other discredits."

The only "relishing," indeed, in such an event, would have been exercised upon the body of Oxford, who, at claws and teeth of the outraged and hungry bear, Authority, would not have been half-eaten, as Antigonus was; but must have been swallowed up and engulfed *in toto*.

But who, now, are these two plain fellows, the old shepherd, and his young son aged, it seems, about two-or-three-and-twenty, the couple who have discovered, along with some fortunate "fairy gold," this "very pretty bairn," whose warm getting, they opine, has been accomplished by some back-stair and behind-door work? They are given, it is true, no names affording very definite clues, except that the youth is denominated a "clown," which is the identical name first given, by Touchstone-Oxford, in *As You Like It*, V, i, to William before his appearance.[1] Here, moreover, as also in *As You Like It*, the young man's age seems to be meaningful, since two-or-three-and-twenty years, added to 1564, gives 1586 or 1587, which are just the dates of drafting *A Winter's Tale*. When, further, it is remembered that this is the pair which, between them, have put what is left of Antigonus "i' the ground," or, in

[1] Oxford-Touchstone's words concerning William, as being "Here in the forest", suggest to me that the Earl was actually staying or living in the Forest of Arden about 1589, and may have first met William there at that time.

other words, have hidden so much of his identity as has not already been devoured by that "stubborn bear Authority"; though William is not here openly named, there can be little doubt or question concerning identity. The old shepherd and his son are the Stratford man and his father: the first of them, like the forest-bred clown of *As You Like It*, unlettered, and though powerless to do it "without counters," willing enough to toil upon the figures of his task.

> "Let me see: every 'leven wether tods; every tod yields pound and odd shilling; fifteen hundred shorn, what comes the wool to?"

He cannot know; but we know that in 1599 John Shakespeare, William's father, sued John Walford, for £21 debt, for twenty-one tods of wool,[1] at about the time, therefore, that Ben Jonson, in *Every Man Out Of His Humour*, was bitterly mocking at Sogliardo's (William's) new coat-of-arms, which, in 1598, made him a gentleman—a gentleman being the identical degree of social advancement to which, as a reward for their discovery, the Shepherd and Clown may aspire at the end of this play:

> *Auto.* I know you are now, sir, a gentleman born.
> *Clow.* Aye, and have been so any time these four hours.

Further, the appalling catalogue of penalties jocularly hurled, by Autolycus, at the "ram-tender" and "sheep-whistling rogue," who dares to have his adopted "daughter come into grace"—all this stoning, flaying, wasp-

---

[1] Common Pleas, 40, 1626 (353, d.) Discovered by Prof. J. L. Hotson and announced in *The Times* of 22 November, 1930.

nesting, and fly-blowing, which proclaim the threatener's " great authority," are exactly parallelled by the " one hundred and fifty deaths " wherewith Touchstone, in the forest, menaces William, should he not cease forthwith to frequent the company, not of a daughter, but of one Audrey (de Vere) who has become Touchstone-Oxford's " wife."

From this time onward in the course of the Earl's career, although, as Feste-Oxford himself says, in effect in *Twelfth Night*, III, i, he is " loth to prove reason with words, because words are very rascals since bonds disgraced them "—meaning, of course, thereby, that he is reluctant to prove his identity by mere word-play, now that his art is bound and " tongue-tied by authority " —he does, nevertheless, contrive, or, shall I say, condescend, by using his good wit for the turning inside out of his cheveril-glove sentences,[1] to din, again and again, into the consciousness of readers and spectators, who are in possession of the clues, the truth concerning his identity, especially towards the close of the plays. Thus, near the end of *Twelfth Night*, Oxford—who in the earlier scenes of the comedy was Feste, Olivia's " corrupter of words "—has become, in the last scene, Olivia-Elizabeth's steward—originally Christopher Hatton— by name Malvolio, " imprisoned," and gulled, but now, at last, upon Olivia's own promise, made to him in the play, become

> " both the plaintiff and the judge
> Of his own cause."

Thus he is enabled, by the process of time's whirligig, in play after play, with a series of usually kindly, though

---

[1] For this Vere pun, see *ante*, p. 194

occasionally ruthless, burlesques and satires, to be revenged upon " the whole pack "[1] of courtiers and others, who had incurred his enmity or displeasure.

The years 1587–88 were probably too much disturbed, and anxious, to leave Oxford much time for doing more than revise old plays; and even though his relations with Anne were, henceforth, as we may fairly conclude, from this time onward, much less strained than before, his affairs, domestic and financial, remained all in disorder; and judging by a pathetic letter from Lord Burleigh to Walsingham, dated 5 May, 1587, both father and son-in-law shared a cordial detestation, reflected in Polonius and Hamlet, and would gladly be quit of one another, if they might. Thus the Lord Treasurer :

> "I was so vexed yesternight very late by some grievous sight of my poor daughter's affliction whom her husband had in the afternoon so troubled with words of reproach of me to her—as though I had no care of him as I had to please others (naming Sir Walter Ralegh and my Lord of Cumberland whose books I had speedily solicited to pass)—as she spent all the evening in dolour and weeping. And though I did as much as I could comfort her with hope; yet she, being as she is great with child, and continually afflicted to behold the misery of her husband and of his children to whom he will not leave a farthing of land; for this purpose I cannot forbear to renew this pitiful cause. . . .
>
> " No enemy that I have can envy me this match ; for thereby neither honour nor land nor goods shall come to their children ; for whom being three already to be kept and a fourth like to follow, I am only at charge even with sundry families in

---

[1] *Malv.* I'll be reveng'd on the whole pack of you.

sundry places for their sustenance. But if their father was of that good nature as to be thankful for the same, I would be less grieved with the burden."

Oxford, it may not be denied, must have been as bad a husband and father as any in literary history; yet Burleigh, undoubtedly, was, himself, in part to blame; since, as our analysis of *Troilus and Cressida* has amply confirmed, it is most probable that his own ambitions and covetousness first contrived this unhappy marriage—"a wife hath caught him"—the misery of which now returns upon *Pandarus*, in the shapes of a bitterly hostile son-in-law, a daughter all in "dolour and weeping" over her own ill-fortune, and that of her children, born and unborn; all equally unprovided for by a reckless and improvident man-of-genius, who cared little with what families, in what households, or at whose expense, his children were farmed out, provided that, freed from family responsibilities, he may follow the strange destiny that keeps him still among his lewd penmen and players; and fulfil, at once with loathing and with love, the great national task, to which, under oath of secrecy, and for the ultimate glory of English letters, he is deeply sworn.

With love and loathing, I wrote; for all this while, paradoxical though it may seem—even in a life-story that is crammed with paradox—de Vere is hankering still after preferment at that court which he despised; a part of his quarrel with Burleigh being, that his father-in-law, as he believed, was deliberately barring the way to such preferment—a conclusion which provoked from the aged statesman the vigorous protest that "Your Lordship mistaketh my power," and that, although he (Burleigh) had indeed "propounded ways to prefer you to services," these had come to nothing, by reason of certain "hinderers," who had made allegations "to impeach your Lordship from such preferments." That these hinderers numbered among them Lord Henry Howard, the Borachio of *Much Ado About Nothing*, and, in part, perhaps, the Iago of *Othello*, with Leicester, and Sir Christopher Hatton, who is, in part, Malvolio of *Twelfth Night*, may be taken as more than likely.

On 26 May, 1587, there was born into this world the girl child, with whom, to the sound of dolours and weeping, the Countess of Oxford had been "great." That baby, Lady Susan Vere, lives to marry Philip Herbert, Earl of Montgomery, one of the "Incomparable Paire" to whom, in 1623, the First Folio edition of Shakespeare's plays is to be dedicated. This lady will act at court, in masques written by Ben Jonson, who is to indite to her an epigram which, with "comparison of former age," and other verbal similarities, strongly recalls the lines written, also by Ben Jonson, within that same Folio, and containing precisely similar words and ideas touching

"Of all, that insolent Greece, or haughtie Rome
Sent forth."

Thus upon this eventful story do coming events cast shadows before; though the immediate shadow now falling upon our tale is not backward from the future, but a present one, in the release, by death, of the Countess of Oxford from her fears, her sorrows, and all her shattered hopes. Anne Cecil died of fever, in the Royal Palace of Greenwich, on 5 June, 1588, and was "interred in Westminster Abbey on 25 June, attended by many persons of great quality and honour."[1] Among those

[1] MSS. of William Dethicke, Garter King-at-Arms. *Bibliographica Brit.*, Vol. VI, part I, p. 4031.

persons of great quality and honour, however, Lord Oxford's name does not appear; for a reason, or reasons, that we cannot positively state. It may be that a sense of estrangement, or even of shameful remorse over duties shirked, and responsibilities unfulfilled, kept him away; it may be, on the other hand, that stern call of duty prevented him. Lady Oxford, as I have said, was buried on 25 June; and already, by that date, the event was imminent which was to determine, for the time being, our national destiny—England's battle, against the Spanish Armada, for the sea supremacy of the world. During mid-July, the mighty fleet, serenely confident of victory, was crossing the Bay of Biscay; on July 23 Sir Francis Drake was engaging its ships off Portland, and on the 28th the Armada anchored in Calais harbour. Next day the decisive, and to them disastrous, battle was fought.

As long before this as 1581, de Vere had been negotiating for the purchase of a ship, the *Edward Bonaventure*; and Camden tells us that, for the Armada fight, he fitted out, at his own expense, a ship—the *Edward Bonaventure* or some other—upon the deck of which, in James Lear's ballad of the battle, strongly suggesting the eye-witness, we are given a vivid picture of Edward de Vere, standing, in full armour, with the boar upon his crest " foaming for inward ire."

" De Vere whose fame and loyalty hath pearst
  The Tuscan clime, and through the Belgike lands
  By winged Fame for valour is rehearst,
  Like warlike Mars upon the hatches stands,
    His tuskèd Boar gan foam for inward ire,
    While Pallas filled his breast with warlike fire."

It is pleasant to know that " Shakespeare " took an

active part in repelling the Spanish Armada from our shores; but though the Earl had some share in the preliminary fighting, between Plymouth and the South Foreland, he missed the decisive battle, as evidenced by Leicester's letter to Walsingham, written from Tilbury Camp on 28 July:

> "My Lord of Oxford ... returned again yesterday by me, with Capt. Huntly as his company. It seemed only his voyage was to have gone to my Lord Admiral; and at his return hither he went yesternight for his armour and furniture. If he come, I would know from you what I should do. I trust he be free to go to the enemy, for he seems most willing to hazard his life in this quarrel."

About the end of July, Oxford was offered, by the Queen, the post of Governor of Harwich, "a place of great trust and of great danger," as Leicester phrased it, in a letter to Walsingham; but the Earl refused it, on the ground that he "thought the place of no service or credit," although, in Leicester's opinion, it "was of good grace to appoint that place to him, having no more experience than he hath." All these events suggest that active work, in connexion with the Lord Admiral's fleet in the west, may have kept de Vere in or near Plymouth, at the time of his wife's death; and it is conceivable that he returned to London too late to attend her funeral, much as Hamlet returns from England, only upon the very eve of Ophelia's burial.

That Lady Oxford shaped the characters of Ophelia, and of Desdemona also, may, I think, be taken as proved; and I firmly believe that the Earl's bitter remorse over the neglect of a wife, whom his own misbehaviours—

CROWDED YEARS

with the assistance, at times, of Howard and Arundel—had robbed of happiness in life, if not, though indirectly, of life itself—is reflected in the tragedy of Desdemona, unwittingly slain by her husband, as also of Ophelia, driven to suicide by the crisis of her love-affair with Hamlet. No less certainly the " banging " of the Turkish fleet, in *Othello*, echoes the destruction of the Spanish Armada, in which, as we have seen, the Earl played an active, if not specially prominent, part.[1]

On Sunday, 24 November, the Queen headed a solemn procession to St. Paul's, " to give God praise for the overthrow of the Spaniard." Behind the Queen's chariot rode the Earl of Essex, as Master of the Horse, leading her palfrey of honour, by a costly silken rein. Before Her Majesty rode the Lord Mayor of London with the Garter King-at-Arms on his left, and, immediately behind him, the Lord Marquess of Winchester, bearing the sword of state before Elizabeth; on his right the Earl of Shrewsbury, Earl Marshal of England; and on his left, bonnet in hand, the Earl of Oxford, as Lord Great Chamberlain.

Before the western façade, the procession halted, and was then reformed, when the Queen, to the chanting of the Litany by the assembled ecclesiastics, walked " through the longest aisle to her travers in the quire," beneath a rich golden canopy, borne over her head by the two senior earls of the realm, Lord Shrewsbury, the Earl Marshal, and the Lord Great Chamberlain, Edward de Vere.

" And afterwards unto Paul's Cross she did directly pass,
  There by the Bishop of Salisbury a sermon preached
    was.

---

[1] Admiral Holland, in *Shakespeare Through Oxford Glasses*, first showed the very close parallel between the sea-battle in *Othello* and the Defeat of the Spanish Armada.

> The Earl of Oxford opening then the windows for her Grace,
> The children of the Hospital she saw before her face."

Ten years later, in 1598, "Shakespeare," writing, in despondent mood, Sonnet 125, thus recalls that memorable day:

> " Were't aught to me I bore the canopy,
>   With my externe the outward honouring?
>   Or laid great bases for eternity,
>   Which prove more brief than waste or ruining"—

lines wherein he wearily asks himself which, in effect, was the greater achievement—to have " honoured the outward," by thus bearing, upon that august occasion, the golden canopy over his sovereign's head, or to have done homage to the inward of his own genius, by laying " great bases for eternity," with immortal dramas, which, as we shall see, seemed to him nevertheless to be, even then, threatened with permanent extinction.

CHAPTER NINE

WITHDRAWAL FROM PUBLIC LIFE: 1589-1596

*Oxford withdraws from Court and from Public Life—His Withdrawal and
" As You Like It "—The " William " scene in that play, and Repudiation of
William of Stratford as Author—Relations between Oxford and " William "—
Adoption by the Earl of Pen-Name, " William Shakespeare "—Oliver Martext
and Marprelate Conspiracy 1590—Oxford's liabilities assessed at £22,000—
Endeavours to commute his official Salary—Spenser and " Our Pleasant Willy
is Dead "—Oxford marries Elizabeth Trentham, 1591—Lives at Stoke
Newington, near the Theatres—" King Lear " and the Earl's Suit for Grant of
Monopolies—Nash's and Greeene's references to " Will Monox " and " Shake-
scene "—Oxford 1592 as actor in his own plays—Attacks on the Earl in
Chapman's Poems, 1593—Name " Shakespeare " first appears in print;
" Venus and Adonis," 1593—Birth of Henry de Vere 1593—Elizabeth de
Vere marries Lord Derby, 26 January, 1595—" A Midsummer Night's Dream,"
probably played on the occasion—Derby's hand in " Love's Labour's Lost "
—The Oxfords take King's Place, Hackney, 1596*

FOR some inscrutable reason, or reasons, sufficient, no doubt, at the time, this year 1589, which we have now reached, brings about the most mysterious event in all this enigmatical life of de Vere, namely his permanent retirement from court. Whether the cause was remorse, and self-judgment over his own partial responsibility, as he judged, for the premature death of his Countess, or whether some temporary access of wild melancholy, deeper than any other that had obsessed hitherto a mind always oscillating swiftly between light-heartedness and despondency; or again, whether we must look to the Martin Marprelate scandals, or to the wrath of powerful courtiers pitilessly burlesqued by

"Shakespeare," or to Oxford's fixed determination to devote the remainder of his life to completing his national work upon plays and poems, we cannot now decide; but my definite impression, unanswerably borne out, as I think, by the texts of the plays, is that, for whatever cause, he withdrew in obedience to the Queen's express command, possibly resulting from a rupture between the pair, of which the secret may be found in *Venus and Adonis*, a poem which, as will be seen when we come to it, reads like a lyricized narrative of Elizabeth's rejected advances to Oxford, and of her resultant anger, as that of a woman scorned.[1]

Whatever the reasons, this fact is certain—that the bearing of the canopy over her Majesty's head, on the occasion of the Armada celebration, marked the close of his public life, as a courtier. Where the Earl lived, even, until his second marriage at the end of 1591, is not known. He may have been at Wivenhoe; he may have been at Hackney; or more probably still, he may have gone to the Forest of Arden, and there have met William: but, though we cannot say where de Vere was, we can say, with some assurance, what he was doing, namely hard at work preparing the long list of plays which, from his own, and other pens of the group that he headed, are going to flood the stages and book-stalls of London, during the whole of the fifteen-'nineties; thus synchronizing with the continuance of the Spanish

---

[1] Lucio, in *Measure for Measure*, says that the reason for the Duke's (Oxford's) withdrawal is "A secret that must be lock'd between teeth and lips"—pointing to an intimately private reason. Achilles (Oxford) in *Troilus*, will not, when challenged, say why he withdrew, but insists that he has "good reasons" for his privacy: whereupon Ulysses adds:

"'Tis known, that you are in love with one of Priam's daughters."

See *post*, pp. 279-285

war, which the Armada catastrophe had by no means brought to an end.

One play, in particular, the Earl's banishment, whether voluntary or enforced, from the court to the country, immediately recalls; and that is the comedy known to us by the name, *As You Like It*, set originally in France, and dramatizing, in some sort, events connected with negotiations for the Alençon marriage. Oxford seems to have first drafted his play about 1581, in the usual short form of his early work, and without the five important symbolic characters, Jaques, Touchstone, Audrey, William, and Martext, who, at bottom, have nothing whatever to do with the original plot, and who, as I suppose, are first written into the play in this year, 1589, when Oxford, as Jaques the Philosopher, and as Touchstone the courtier-clown, metaphorically accompanies Rosalind and Celia into the "Forest," with the banished Duke.

That Jaques and Touchstone stand for the serious and lighter sides of Oxford himself, seems to me an indisputable thesis. When, for instance, Jaques, in II, vi, speaks or sings of

"Leaving his wealth and ease
A stubborn will to please,
Ducdame, ducdame, ducdame—"

he refers simply to himself, who, to please the stubborn will of his governing lady Elizabeth, has left the palace for the forest—"Ducdame" being "a Greek invocation to call fools into a circle," or, in plainer English, the compelling power of Queen Elizabeth to hold foolish courtiers at her court, "that deep and inscrutable" organization, the centre of which, according to Bacon, "is Her Majesty's mind." Abbott, in his *Life of Francis Bacon* writes, though without Shakespeare in mind: "Such a court as this may well be described as . . . a fatal circle."[1]

That "stubborn will," then, turns out, once again, to be identical with the "stubborn bear," authority, that imperious will of Queen Elizabeth, which, as we saw when examining *A Winter's Tale*, imposes upon de Vere-Autolycus an oath of silence, concerning these secret matters, which, while the Earl keeps, at least, the letter of it, he is even now breaking in spirit, by the insertion of name-revealing cipher into the plays; though it does not follow, of course, that these insertions, even while hinting at a specific year, were necessarily added during that year, or were included in the text of performances that may have been given to the court, or at Blackfriars. *As You Like It*, it will be remembered, was not published prior to the Folio of 1623.

Things may be going well with de Vere, or they may be going ill; but whichever it be, the irrepressible humorist will not be restrained for long; and, as always with him, sooner or later, but generally sooner, the worst returns to laughter. How for example he enjoys himself in the Jaques-Touchstone parts, and with what daring skill he keeps his oath, and breaks it, making every word " almost tell his name," as within a few years, he will be doing again in the Sonnets. Yes, that philosopher-cynic of Arden is happy in his own fantastically individual way, laughing," sans intermission, an hour by his dial," at himself, and then calmly proceeding to bring his secret to the verge of revelation:

"O *noble* fool!
A worthy fool! Motley's the only wear . . .
O worthy fool! One that *hath been a courtier* "—

[1] Abbott's *Bacon*, pp. 10 and 67.

WITHDRAWAL FROM PUBLIC LIFE

and a few lines later, after making the secret fathomable to any keen intelligence, he permits the philosopher-poet to be usurped by the jester.

> "Invest me in my motley; give me leave
> To speak my mind, and I will through and through
> Cleanse the foul body of the infected world,
> If they will patiently receive my medicine"—

meaning thereby that, stooping to conquer, by this transmigration from courtier to clown, he will, through the mouth of a motley fool and a despised player, speak healing truths to an infected world, which, but a few moments later, he envisages as nothing else but a stage for men and women to play on.

Jaques, indeed, says Orlando, has but to look down into the reflecting brook, to see himself—a fool, or a cipher. The thing could hardly be put more plainly; but, as Touchstone remarks to Audrey in III, iii, unless a man's verses can be understood, and

> "a man's good wit seconded with the forward child understanding, it strikes a man more dead than a great reckoning in a little room"—

or, in other words, only an imagination pliable and fantastic enough to pierce through my words into their underlying significance can ever bring me back from "death" to life. "The truest poetry," he continues—punning once more upon his name de Vere—is yet no true thing, because it is the most feigning—all of which, though three hundred and fifty years lie between the words and their interpretation, describes exactly Shakespeare's verse, ever feigning, and yet ever true.

Then, straightway, into the opening scene of the

fourth act is inserted a passage wherein Rosalind extracts from Jaques an autobiographical confession concerning his travels, " the rumination of which wraps him in a most humorous sadness," easily accounted for, when we remember that, out of the fifty-six separate sales of the Earl's lands, that were effected between 1572 and 1592—six of them during the period of foreign travel—the years 1587-88 had seen three, the year 1591 was to bring a fourth, while 1590—the year now lying just ahead of him—is to see listed, by the Court of Wards to the Queen and others, a huge catalogue of de Vere's debts, amounting, in our money, to at least a quarter of a million pounds!

With money-matters and affairs, therefore, during 1589, he may be philosophically bored, or exasperatedly uneasy; but in his reputation, as poet and dramatist, he is, quite evidently, interested and concerned; so that when, as seems to have happened about this time, Rumour begins to whisper loud throughout London, that his comedy *As You Like It*, and it may be, other plays of " Shakespeare " also, are being actually written by, and claimed for, a certain William from Stratford, there is promptly slipped into the comedy of Arden, by Oxford's own, or some other hand, the famous scene in which Audrey—whose name is almost an anagram for de Vere[1]—now " married " to Touchstone, is spoken to, by her husband, concerning a youth, " here in the forest," who lays claim to her; to which Audrey replies that she knows the man, who " hath no interest in me in the world." Thereupon enters a " clown," who, in reply to Touchstone's questions, informs us that his name is " William," that he was born in the forest—of Arden or Ardennes—

[1] De Vary.

WITHDRAWAL FROM PUBLIC LIFE 257

twenty-five years ago, thus giving us the date, 1564, plus 25, or 1589, and going on to add still under catechism, that though "so so rich," and enjoying "a pretty wit," he is not "learned"; whereupon Touchstone informs him, in simple imagery that "drink being poured out of a cup into a glass, by filling the one doth empty the other," or, dropping the metaphor, that there cannot be two authors of the plays : "for all your writers (who are Jonson, Chapman, Nash, Greene, and the rest) do consent that *ipse* is he : now you are not *ipse*, for I am he "—*ipse*, let me here add, spelling "Vere" in all the three numerical ciphers, that we know Shakespeare to have used.[1] Then—exactly analogous to the Autolycus and Clown dialogues in *A Winter's Tale*—there follow the fearfully burlesqued threats of one hundred and fifty deaths, that will speedily extinguish any farther attempts, by William, to frequent the "society of this female," who stands for the plays.

Now let us leave dramatic allegory, and ask where, in this year 1589, we can touch historically upon the fact of the matter; first of all suggesting to my readers, that though we cannot say definitely where Oxford was living in the year 1589, he may have been actually living, for a while, in the Forest of Arden, since Touchstone, who is Oxford, says openly to Audrey : "There is a youth *here in the forest*, lays claim to you." Again and again, while writing this book, I have gone to the plays, to confirm or to corroborate history; and knowing, as we do now, that the Oxford family, through the Trussells, were connected with the Stratford district,

---

[1] For the full interpretation of this important scene, see my *Case for Edward de Vere as Shakespeare*, pp. 259–63; and Appendix to my *Oxford-Shakespeare Case Corroborated.*

S

the presence of the 17th Earl in Warwickshire, during the late 'eighties, and meetings with William there, would at once account for the Stratfordian connexion with "Shakespeare," in a more direct way than that surmised in chapter eight, when I showed that both Sir Thomas Lucy's and Lord Oxford's players had been acting close to one another, at Coventry and thereabouts, in the early part of that decade. Further, I have shown clearly that the scene of *As You Like It*, V, i, is definitely located by "Shakespeare" in the Forest of Arden, with exact clues as to both time and place.

If, therefore, we can link the de Veres historically with the Stratford district of Warwickshire, and also with Shaksper's family, my interpretation of these forest-scenes will become yet more plausible than it is; and this, though the matter needs further investigation, I am already in a position to do.

That Edward de Vere was connected with Warwickshire through the Trussells is indisputable; for when, in 1510, the 15th Earl of Oxford married Sir Edward Trussell's daughter, Elizabeth, several manors in that part of the country passed with her to her husband, including those of Bilton in Warwickshire, some eighteen miles north-east from Stratford, and Elmesthorpe in Leicestershire, not far from the Warwickshire border. Edward de Vere subsequently sold both these properties, of the first of which Dugald writes in his *Warwickshire*[1]:

> "By Edward Earl of Oxford was it (i.e. Manor of Bilton) sold unto John Shugborough Esq., then one of the six Clerks in Chancery; which John died seized thereof in '42 Eliz. (1600)."

[1] Edn., 1730, volume I, p. 38.

WITHDRAWAL FROM PUBLIC LIFE

All this is most significant, but it by no means exhausts the connexion of the Trussells with Warwickshire; for Mr. John Trotman, editing, in 1914, *The Triumph Over Death* by Robert Southwell, who also has come into our story, calls attention to the startling resemblances in *The First Rape of Fair Helen*, to Shakespeare's earlier works, and notes also that John Trussell sprang from an ancient and honourable family resident for centuries at Billesley, near Stratford-on-Avon.[1] Now the sister and heir of this John Trussell was none other than Edward de Vere's grandmother, Elizabeth Trussell;[2] so that here we find Edward de Vere, through his Trussell grandmother, definitely connected with and coming into possession of manors and lands in and near Warwickshire, including it would seem, Billesley near Stratford-on-Avon.

The links are being drawn close; but if only we can connect the Trussells, in some way, with William Shaksper of Stratford, they will thereby be drawn closer yet; and that is precisely what we can do, for the Trussells were certainly connected with the Ardens, the very family into which William Shaksper married.

The following interesting letter, written by Mr. S. C. Wilson, appeared in *The Morning Post* of 6 June, 1931.

> " Sir,—An early connexion between the Trussell and the Arden families is brought out by the late Dr. John Smart, of Glasgow, in his book *Shakespeare, Truth and Tradition*, p. 64. He is establishing the relationship of Shakespeare's Arden grandfather with the main Arden family of Warwickshire and

---

[1] Miss Agnes Mott, *Morning Post*, 6 July, 1931.
[2] H. Kennedy-Skipton, *Morning Post*, 10 July, 1931.

writes: 'A direct connexion between the husbandman of Wilmecote and the main branch of the family is established by a common friendship of an interesting and significant kind. When Walter Arden made a settlement upon his wife he formed a body of trustees to whom certain property was conveyed by a legal instrument for the purpose. (Early Chancery Proceedings, Bundle 278, No. 70.) The most prominent among them was Sir Robert Throckmorton, a gentleman of dignified rank in Warwickshire. . . . The same Sir Robert Throckmorton gave his services in a similar capacity to Thomas Arden of Wilmecote. When the latter purchased his estate in Snitterfield, he executed a deed by which several of his friends were associated with him in the transaction; and the first name in the list is that of Sir Robert Throckmorton. The next is that of *Thomas Trussell of Billingsley*, a man of good birth and rank, who was Sheriff of Warwick and Leicester in 1508. It is plain that Thomas Arden of Wilmecote, Shakespeare's ancestor, was accustomed to move in the best society which Warwickshire could afford. . . . He had at Wilmecote a farm called Asbies . . . and houses and gardens in Snitterfield . . . . The property descended at his death to his son, Robert Arden, Shakespeare's grandfather. . . . In due course it would have descended to Shakespeare himself."

All this is very interesting, and is made the more so by these words written by Mrs. C. C. Stopes in *Shakespeare's Environment*, page 13, when discussing the Arden property at Snitterfield, bought by Thomas Arden for his son, Robert, Shaksper's grandfather, in 1501.

"If we might read into the ordinary reading of such arrangements, it might be supposed that the unknown wife of Thomas Arden was a Throckmorton, and the unknown first wife of Robert Arden a Trussell.

The whole question of this connexion of the de Veres, through the Trussells, with Warwickshire, and through the Ardens with Shaksper of Stratford, needs full investigation; but the already ascertained facts fit in so amazingly well with the theme of this book, that I am almost disposed to describe William, of Arden Forest, as one of Edward de Vere's poor relations, whose forbears had seen better times.

Oxford, of course, was already well known as a secret court poet; for the author of *The Arte of English Poesie*, probably Oxford's cousin, Lord Lumley, had written in 1589, that foremost among the band of "courtly makers (poets) Noblemen and Gentlemen of Her Majesty's own servants, who have written excellently well as it would appear, if their doings could be found out, and made public with the rest ... is first that noble gentleman Edward Earl of Oxford." One year later, in 1590, Spenser prefacing the *Faerie Queene* with dedicatory sonnets, addresses one of them to Oxford, and speaks therein of

"the love which thou dost bear
To th' Heliconian imps and they to thee,
They unto thee, and thou to them most dear."

The Heliconian imps are, of course, the Muses, and Spenser's is but one in a stream of dedications, which. during the 'seventies and 'eighties, had been pouring in upon the Earl, from, among others, Munday, Lyly, Watson, Greene, and Angel Day.

Oxford then, by common consent of " all your writers," was recognized as one of those secret poets and dramatists now working at the head of that officially paid group; but the outside public evidently did not know, and were beginning, naturally enough, to father the plays upon William of Stratford, whose surname was very like that of " Shakespeare," with results, upon the texts of *A Winter's Tale* and *As You Like It*, that I have now made sufficiently clear. Further, the wrath of Autolycus, and of Touchstone, so fancifully expressed, together with William's cheerful exit, upon the words, " God rest you merry, Sir," make it perfectly clear that the Earl connived at, if he did not originate, the plot by which the plays came first to be ascribed to the forest-born William.

When did the " Shepherd's " son, of *A Winter's Tale*, leave Stratford for London? The orthodox commentators, I believe, give dates around 1586; but, following Mrs. Clark, I think it possible that the young man, already an actor at twenty years of age, may have been taken from Sir Thomas Lucy's small provincial company, which was playing in 1584 at Coventry, the town in which Oxford's actors had occasionally played from 1581-85—and was thence impressed into their service. Another possible link for acquaintance between William and Oxford; and one that also connects well with the possibility of the Earl's temporary residence in the Stratford district, during the late fifteen-'eighties, is the fact that there was living at Stratford, at this time, a tanner, one Henry Field, whose son, Richard Field, had been a printer in London, working upon his own

WITHDRAWAL FROM PUBLIC LIFE

account since 1587. He must, it seems, have known Lord Oxford, since, in this very year we are considering, 1589, we find him printing, probably with Oxford's financial help, a beautiful edition of one of de Vere's favourite books, Ovid's *Metamorphoses*, which, it will be remembered, Oxford's uncle and aforetime tutor, Arthur Golding, had first translated into English. I think it further probable that, towards the close of the 'eighties, Shaksper of Stratford entered temporarily the Earl of Oxford's service, an idea which first occurred to me when examining Jonson's *Cynthia's Revels*, wherein Cos, the Whetstone, or Liar, whom I take to be the Stratford man, has become Page to Amorphus the Deformed, a Traveller, who, beyond doubt, is Oxford-Shakespeare himself. The dialogue I, i, runs thus:

> *Cos.* Save you, sweet bloods! does any of you want a creature or a dependant?
> *Crit.* (*Jonson*) Beshrew me a fine blunt slave!
> *Amor.* A page of good timber! it will now be my grace to entertain him first, though I cashier him again in private—How art thou call'd?
> *Cos.* Cos, sir, Cos.
> *Crit.* Cos! how happily hath fortune furnish'd him with a whetstone?
> *Amor.* I do entertain you, Cos; conceal your quality till we be private; if your parts be worthy of me, I will countenance you; if not, catechize you—Gentles, shall we go?

All this seems palpably clear. Here is Oxford happily furnished with "a page of good timber," upon whom he can plant the plays he may not acknowledge—a youth who is not, any more than was his master, scrupulous in the letter of veracity, and who is advised by that master to "conceal his quality when in public"—the question whether Amorphus will countenance, cashier, or catechize his page, depending, apparently, upon how well young Cos can live up to his difficult part of dramatic author. That the Earl, however much he may have countenanced the man of Stratford in public, did actually, and severely, catechize and cashier him in private, through the mouths of Autolycus and Touchstone, our preceding investigations have made clear.

Just as we are unable to say precisely when, where, and how William and Oxford met; so also we can only surmise when, how, and why the Earl—who evidently was known, popularly, among writers as "Will"—came to adopt the pen name of "William Shakespeare." It may have been in connexion with the quasi-military purpose of the patriotic plays, intended to stiffen and encourage resistance against Spain; or it is possible that he remembered, and liked, Gabriel Harvey's words, spoken of him in Latin, in the Queen's presence, at Cambridge University in 1578:

> "Thine eyes flash fire, thy countenance shakes a spear; who would not swear that Achilles had come to life again?"

words that become still more significant, if my arguments be accepted identifying, in a later chapter of this book, Oxford and Achilles in *Troilus and Cressida*. Again, it may be that Oxford became "William Shakespeare"[1]

---

[1] As evidence for "Shakespeare" being a pseudonym, it is remarkable that the hyphenated spelling, "Shake-speare," is used in print on eighteen different occasions.

because such a pen-name, by its resemblance to that of the Stratford man, made it easier for him to " countenance " the forest-born William, and so evade awkward situations. At all events, the plot or hoax, or whatever you choose to call it, must, at times, have caused grievous embarrassment to the provincial, thus saddled with " Audrey " ; so that I am not in the least surprised to hear of the tradition, recorded by John Aubrey, that Shakespeare, " if invited to write ... was in paine." Considering also those six laborious signatures, I cannot withold sympathy from William, nor grudge him any portion of such hush-monies as, with a bitter jest or two, may have passed to the rustic, from the Earl.

With *As You Like It* still in mind, it is worth remembering that the mysterious Marprelate Controversy of 1589-90, in which Oxford certainly was involved, probably provides the name of Sir Oliver Martext, who " married " Touchstone to Audrey. Mrs. Clark holds that the stage participation of the Paul's Boys—who were the same company as the Oxford Boys—in the Marprelate controversy, was the offence which led to their dissolution followed, it would seem, by their absorption into Lord Strange's Company. It may be that this Marprelate business, which began with the secret issue, in 1589, of tracts scurrilously libelling the prelates in general, and Archbishop Whitgift in particular, and attacking their alleged abuses of power, may account, in part, for Oxford's withdrawal into private life. Be the causes what they may, the Earl did withdraw ; and I wholly agree with Mrs. Clark in naming Oxford as the man aimed at by Spenser, when in 1590, the year of the first edition of *The Faerie Queen*, he wrote in *Muiopotmos*, or the Fate of the Butterfly :

> "O you the mournfulst Muse of nyne,
> That wont'st the tragick stage for to direct,
> In funerall complaints and wylfull tyne,
> Reveale to me, and all the meanes detect
> Through which said Clarion did at last declyne
> To lowest wretchedness. *And is there then
> Such rancour in the harts of mightie men?*[1]
>
> "Of all the race of silver-winged flies
> Which doo possess the empire of the aire,
> Betwixt the centred earth and azure skies,
> Was none more favourable, nor more faire . . .
> And all that faire or pleasant may be found
> In riotous excesse doth there abound.
>
> "But what on earth can long abide in state,
> Or who can him assure of happie day;
> Sith morning faire may bring fowle evening late,
> And least mishap the most blisse alter may.
>
> "Not thou O Clarion, though fairest thou
> Of all thy kinde, unhappie happie flie,
> Whose cruell fate is woven even now
> Of Jove's own hand to work thy miserie."

Thus Spenser, in liquid verse, laments the passing of Oxford into the shadows; but we need not echo him, since these years of leisure, and probably of despondent loneliness, in "unhappy happy" toil were a means of giving to the world the old Shakesperean court-comedies and histories expanded into their present literary forms;

---

[1] The words in italic type strongly suggest that "rancour" in the hearts of courtiers, satirized by Oxford in the plays, was a principal cause of his withdrawal: and, as it must necessarily be kept secret would fit in with Lucio's remark concerning the Duke's withdrawal. "'Tis a secret that must be lock'd between teeth and lips."

and, besides these, in all probability, provided the Sonnets, *Troilus and Cressida*, and, as culminating achievements, *Macbeth*, and the whole of *King Lear*.

Conventionally and superficially regarded, however, the details of the story are sordid enough. There are extant, for this year, 1589, and for the next, letters to Burleigh requesting a loan of "£300 of ready money to redeem certain leases at Hedingham which were gotten from me very unreasonably," and another dated 18 May, 1591, wherein he begs his father-in-law to obtain the Queen's sanction for him to commute his salary of £1,000 a year for a lump sum of £5,000, concerning which, seeing that he has still thirteen years to live, he would have been proved right in conjecturing, as he did, that "Her Majesty makes no evil bargain." Any desperate shift, almost, it seems, he will acquiesce in, that may enable him to stave off importunate creditors, whose total claims, according to the Court of Wards' decision of this year, was, as we have seen, £22,000, or about a quarter of million of our money! The Earl, moreover, is anxious, henceforth, "to have an equal care over my children," with Burleigh, who, it would seem, had been financially, and, perhaps, in other respects also, their best father until then.

Neither duns, nevertheless, nor disgraces, nor cares, nor creditors can change the essential man; nor will even the Court of Wards Commission make prosy a great poet, or rob the satirist of his sense of humour, even though it is to be levelled, as Oxford's often was, against himself and his servants; so that when, in a somewhat obscure matter concerning Thomas Churchyard, the poet, who had been before, and was now again, in Lord Oxford's service, the Earl receives from Churchyard, and from Mistress Penn, long-winded letters replete with "Lords" and "Lordships," and containing such phrases as (Churchyard), "I will employ all I have to honour his worthiness," and (Penn) "If it had been a thousand times more I would have been glad to pleasure your lordship withal," I can see Oxford reading the lines, with exactly such a smile of ironical boredom upon his expressive face as upon Don Leonato's, listening to Dogberry; and I can picture the Earl reaching down, from a shelf, the manuscript of *Much Ado About Nothing*, and inserting, among the burlesques of Arundel's charges, made against him in 1580, an almost literal transcript of these obsequious eulogies, written of him some ten years later.

"If I were as tedious as a king"—and de Vere, I imagine, was expert in royal tediousness—"I could find in my heart to bestow all of your worship. Yes, an't were a thousand pound more than 'tis." The sole quarto of *Much Ado About Nothing*, let me add, was printed in 1600.

Meanwhile his life withdrawn continues; and once again, in 1591, Edmund Spenser, this time in that section of his *Tears of the Muses* devoted to Thalia, the Muse of Comedy, by repeating his moan, already made in *The Faerie Queene*, that Oxford,

"Our pleasant Willy, ah is dead of late—"

seems to tell us that already, with this first year of the 'nineties, the Earl's name, among those who knew him, was "Will"; the adjective "dead" meaning, as it did also with Romeo-Oxford—"not body's death but body's banishment." The next verse runs:

WITHDRAWAL FROM PUBLIC LIFE

> But that same gentle Spirit, from whose pen
> Large streames of honnie and sweete Nectar flowe,
> Scorning the boldnes of such base-born men,
> Which dare their follies forth so rashly throwe;
> Doth rather choose to sit in idle Cell,
> Than so himselfe to mockerie to sell "—

words that recall vividly one of the early Sonnets (21), now, it seems, beginning to be written, which aims also at a base-born singer—Oxford's junior and rival poet Chapman—whose works will soon be challenging comparison with Shakespeare's own.

> " Let them say more that like of hearsay well;
> I will not praise that purpose not to sell."

Shakespeare will not sell his Sonnets, written for the eyes of private friends; but his ancestral home, and his lands, he needs must dispose of, or, at least, partly alienate, for reasons that these pages have made clear. Castle Hedingham, the lordly home of many Earls of Oxford, his ancestors—and his own home for the first twelve years of his life—now probably uninhabited since his four-day-old son had been buried, in the parish churchyard adjoining, in 1583—had fallen into grievous disrepair. Edward, instead of spending upon its rehabilitation vast sums of money, which he did not possess, and certainly could not borrow, upon other than Shylockian terms, issued a warrant authorizing the pulling down of many of the outhouses, and the dismantling of a portion of the main building. He subsequently transferred the castle to his three daughters, and to Lord Burleigh—a probable reason for this act being readjustments occasioned by his second marriage, which took place towards the end of 1591.

Of his new bride, and of de Vere's subsequent life with her, comparatively little is known. Elizabeth Trentham was the daughter of a Staffordshire landowner, Sir Thomas Trentham: she was, also a court-beauty, and one of the Queen's Maids of Honour. Taking these facts into consideration, and the further facts, that Queen Elizabeth's notoriously practical methods of resenting the marriages of her prettiest Maids of Honour were not, upon this occasion, put into force; that Oxford, as one gathers, was not even royally rebuked —much less sent to the Tower, as Raleigh had been, over Elizabeth Throgmorton, and as Oxford himself had been, over the non-matrimonial affair with Anne Vavasour—we may, I think, take it as proved that Elizabeth's regard for her Turk survived even this open affront.

The newly married couple set up house at Stoke Newington, within two or three miles of the most successful of London's popular playhouses, the Curtain and the Theatre. It was probably in honour of his new Countess that the Earl revised, during this year, *Romeo and Juliet*, which with its reference, by the old nurse, to eleven years that have passed since the earthquake of 1580, gives 1591 as the date of overhauling a play first drafted, it would seem, about 1583. To what extent de Vere confided in that second Juliet, Elizabeth Trentham, concerning his relations with the first, who was Anne Vavasour, is a point that I leave to the nicer judgment of my readers.

Yet another Shakesperean tragedy, and a greater than *Romeo and Juliet*, the events of this month foreshadow; for, as we have already seen, there has been arranged, of late, with Oxford's own consent, and, I surmise, with the concurrence of the Court of Wards, a division in some sort, of his kingdom; partly for the benefit of his three daughters, who, thus linked together, recall at once *King Lear*. That masterpiece of grotesque sublimity is, in my judgment, substantially of much later date than we have yet reached; but Mrs. Clark ascribes the drafting of it to 1589-90, and it is certainly with the early 'nineties that the following dialogue between Kent, the Fool, and Lear, would seem to connect up.

> *Fool (to Kent).* Prithee, tell him, so much (i.e., nothing) the rent of his land comes to: he will not believe a fool. . . .
> *Lear.* Dost thou call me fool, boy?
> *Fool.* All thy other titles thou hast given away, that thou wast born with.
> *Kent.* This is not altogether fool, my lord.
> *Fool.* No faith, lords and great men will not let me; if I had a monopoly out, they would have part on't: and the ladies too, they will not let me have all the fool to myself; they'll be snatching.

Burleigh here is, assuredly, one of the "great men," whose sound advice would not let Oxford be "altogether fool"; and as for the ladies snatching for a share in monopoly, it is precisely at this time, in 1592, that Oxford, with his three daughters in mind, sued to the Queen for a grant to himself of the import monopoly on oils, woods and fruits; the granting or selling of monopoly rights to favoured courtiers being a regular practice of Queen Elizabeth's, at that time.

Throughout London the while, rumour and gossip, we may suppose, are passing swiftly from mouth to mouth, concerning the identity of this mysterious

"Shakespeare," whose shining talents, though they have illumined, as yet, no printed page, are already prominent among play-going themes.

Here come into the story those commoners, or "lewd companions," whose frequentations, by Oxford, Lord Burleigh had been used to lament. Chettle is among them, and Nash and Greene, of which last-named dissolute playwright, now at the end of his tether, Chettle wrote, this year (1592) in *Kind-Hart's Dream*, "He (Greene) was of singular pleasaunce, the verye supporter, and, to no man's disgrace be this intended, the only comedian of a *vulgar* writer in this country"— a somewhat cryptic phrase, of which, nevertheless, the meaning seems fairly clear,[1] namely that while Greene was the best writer of comedy that the *commoners* could provide, there existed a better one among the nobility— to wit, him of whom, six years later, in 1598, Francis Meres was to write:

> "The best for comedy among us be Edward, Earl of Oxford."

Among these bawdy tavern-brawlers, the university wits, eking out with rogueries and chicane such subsistences as their pens, and their cunning might bring them, Oxford evidently deigned to keep more or less familiar company; for during 1592 Nash writes in *Strange News*:

> "I and one of my fellowes Will Monox (hast thou never heard of him and his great dagger?) were in company with him (Greene) a month before he died"—

[1] Mrs. Clark, *op. cit.*, p. 645.

words for which I can find only one interpretation, namely that " Will Monox "—a name unknown hitherto in Elizabethan literature—spells " Willm. Oxon," or William Oxenford; the " great dagger " being the " speare " of " Shake*speare*."[1] In plain English, then Nash and Greene, a month before the latter's death, were in company with " Will. Shakespeare," the Earl of Oxford, a meeting which, however, may not have been altogether harmonious, since, when Greene is upon his death-bed, a short time after, he writes an information to his readers, that he " names nobody," and then, after proceeding in the characteristic Elizabethan fashion, to perpetrate a series of puns, all pointing clearly towards the man he dare not openly name, he writes, against the Earl, this now world-famous passage :

> " Yes trust them not: for there is an upstart Crow, beautified with our feathers, that with his *Tygers hart wrapt in a Players hyde*, supposes he is as well able to bombast out a blanke verse as the best of you : and being an absolute *Johannes fac totum*, is in his owne conceit the onely Shake-scene in a countrey."

Now all this is aimed, in my belief, not, as we are insistently told by the orthodox, at an actor turned poet, but at a poet turned actor. This " Johannes Factotum " who, in his own conceit, can administer the state, general the army, pen a poem, or compose a play—this being thus all-gifted with

> " The courtiers, soldiers, scholar's, eye, tongue, sword "—

---

[1] First observed by Mrs. Clark, *op. cit*

has taken to acting; and, supposing himself as well able " to bombast out a blank verse as the best of you," has decided—now that, as is indisputably the case, the rest of his fortunes have " turned Turk with him "—to claim " a whole share," or " a fellowship, in a cry of players." For years past he has been accustomed to act at court, or even, occasionally, it may be, at the Blackfriars, in comedies or masques written mostly by himself; but now that he has permanently withdrawn from that vicious court circle, of which the Queen is the centre, why not make a bold venture, and play, for example, Hamlet—who, after all, is only himself—at the Curtain, or at its neighbour, the Theatre, where, from his house at Stoke Newington, his pony will take him in twenty minutes!

It is, of course, impossible to say, among all these surmises, precisely what is fact and what may be no more than fancy; but all inferences seem here to indicate that, if only for a short while, the playwright becomes, to some extent, a public player; and the commonalty—actors and authors alike—hardly know what to make of it, or are frankly hostile. At best, my lord is, in some sort, wasting himself, for as Greene phrases it; " It is pity men of such rare wits shold be subject to the pleasure of such rude grooms."

That last phrase concerning " rude grooms " who, nevertheless, have charge of plays, seems to have caught on in theatrical London; for, as I have shown in detail elsewhere,[1] Jonson, in the fifth act of *Every Man Out of His Humour*, makes Puntarvolo, who is Oxford, commit the care of his " dog," the plays, to a " groom "; and as for the upstart crow being " beautified with our

[1] *Oxford-Shakespeare Case Corroborated*, pp. 72-3, 79-80.

feathers," have we not, ten years before this, in 1581, heard Barnabe Rich describing that strangely frenchified individual, whom we took to be Oxford himself, riding perhaps in his stage clothes, from the direction of Blackfriars, down the Strand, towards Westminster—. "in his hand a great fan of feathers bearing them up (very womanly) against the side of his face"? That same perpetually reiterated charge against Oxford, of womanishness, Greene's earlier words concerning the author " wrapt (i.e. concealed) in a player's hide " recall; because the original words thus paraphrased, from *3 Henry VI*, I, iv, are " wrapt in a *woman's* hide."

Deeply though Oxford may immerse himself in the writing or revision of his plays; yet discontent with his position, or want of position, broods ever in his mind:

> " The priest, George Dingley, is again examined before the Lord Keeper, Lord Buckhurst, and Mr. John Fortescue about the things he had heard in Spain. He declared that many of our nobility were believed to be discontented at not being advanced, and would be easily moved to follow the Spaniard who would promise to put them in places of authority if he could possess England. The Earls of Oxford and Cumberland, the Lord Strange and Percy are much talked of as alienated by discontent. Their chief hope is in the Queen's death; wherefore the Spaniard lingers in his attempt at again assaulting England because time will call her away, when they have certain hope of a debate between the two houses of Hertford and Derby, who will seek the throne, each for himself, during which contention the Spaniard thinketh entry into England would be without danger. They greatly rejoiced in the mutterings of the Martinists."

The above passage, cited by Dr. Harrison,[1] is very important, for it seems to show that in 1593, when negotiations are afoot for a marriage between de Vere's daughter and Southampton, and de Vere is writing Sonnets urging the Earl towards the match,[2] he (Oxford) is favourably disposed towards the Essex party, and is probably not much interested in his future son-in-law, Lord Derby, until he discovers that that peer is interested in plays. Later on, as we shall see, when we come to *Richard II*, de Vere definitely turns against the Essex faction.

Meanwhile, by this year 1593, the plot is thickening fast. Greene is dead; but a greater than Greene—that inchoate, splenetic genius, George Chapman, already in 1598 classed by Meres among the best tragic dramatists of his day—and by this time, 1593, hot with a smouldering jealousy of his rival's ever-increasing fame—will carry on the attack commenced, it would seem, by Robert Greene; and in his *Hymns to the Night*, will, as Cynthia's votary, attack the poet of day, in verses of which the barbaric vehemence and crabbed turgidity are unmatched in all the range of our literature. Concerning the identity of the individual aimed at in Chapman's poem, there cannot be the slightest doubt. The man to whom Madam Skill[3]

> " hath so prostitutely shown her secrets, where she will scarce be looked upon by others ... without having drops of their souls like a heavenly familiar."

repeats the *Johannes factotum* idea, and is manifestly de

---

[1] S.P.Dom. CCXLIII, ii. G. B. Harrison's *Elizabethan Chronicle*, p. 167.
[2] " Shakespeare's " Sonnets, 13, 16.
[3] Dedication of Chapman's *Shadow of Night* to Matthew Roydon, 1594. It was written in 1593.

Vere himself, who will retort in the Sonnets, upon which he is already at work, with that jibe at Chapman's

> "affable familiar ghost
> Which nightly gulls him with intelligence."

Throughout these *Hymns to the Night*, the characteristic attacks continue upon Edward de Vere, this "Caledonian boar," this "manless nature," "without the parts of man," contrasted, again and again, with "more perfect characters" which, even though lowborn,

> "prove they be
> No mockers of their first nobility."

At moments, Chapman will turn from the playwright to the plays, and in a few lines, vigorously imitated from his rival poet, he will gibe at the "golden foolery" of that scene in *Richard II*, wherein the effeminate king falls weeping upon the ground; and then, in yet another outburst of imitative and topical mockery, will envisage the palace of Theseus, in Shakespeare's fairy comedy of the Dream,

> "Which cast a shadow like a Pyramis,
> Whose basis in the plain or back part is
> Of that quaint work "—

a characteristically strained and grotesque, though accurate, statement by Chapman, that the palace in which Pyramus performs is, indeed, at the back, or end, of that "quaint work," *A Midsummer Night's Dream*! A moment later, after a passing and reluctant admission, that Vere, though vicious, is a gifted man:

> "Good gifts are often given to men past good,
> And Noblesse stoops sometimes beneath his blood."

—especially when consorting with actors—he goes on to praise not Hamlet, but Horatio:

> "war's quick artisan,
> Fame-thriving Vere, that in these countries wan
> More fame than guerdon."

The reference, of course, is to Oxford's favourite cousin, Horatio de Vere, then fighting in the Low Countries—the same guerdonless Horatio of the Hamlet play,

> "Who no revenue hast but thy good spirits
> To feed and clothe thee."

Thus the "Poetomachia," or battle of the poets, is joining between the respective votaries of the Night and Day, with developments that are highly interesting and important to our story. De Vere, meanwhile, is renewing his suit, "which I made at Greenwich to Her Majesty her last being there," for a grant to himself of a monopoly on oils, woods, and fruits; and is further exasperating the royal lady, by importuning her for yet another favour, the stewardship or Custody of the Forests of Essex, or, if not the Stewardship directly, then, at least, permission "to try my title to the Forest at law." He obtained his lease, I think, at last; but only after brow-beatings, and "many bitter speeches given me," and probably returned in kind.

This year 1593 is a dark one for London, stricken virulently with the plague. The theatres are compulsorily closed, and the actors are idle, or working in the provinces; yet from our viewpoint 1593 is memorable enough; since it gives us, for the first time, in the month of April, the name of "Shakespeare" printed upon the title page of *Venus and Adonis*; the printer being that same Stratford-born Richard Field, who had done the fine edition of Ovid's *Metamorphoses* in 1589, and was to publish *Lucrece* in 1594. Both poems are dedicated to the young Earl of Southampton, probably in graceful acknowledgment of the negotiations then afoot, for a marriage between Southampton and Oxford's eldest daughter, Elizabeth. The relations between the two Earls may possibly have been strengthened by a common discontent with the Queen's behaviour—shared, as we have seen, by other noblemen—in the matter of desired advancement; for there can exist, I think, no doubt at all, among careful readers, that this " first heir of his invention "—by which, it would seem, de Vere means the first of his poems to be printed under his pseudonym[1]—is a veiled attack upon his royal mistress ; the expression, " if the first heire of my invention prove deform'd," linking itself significantly with a phrase that we have seen made play with, again and again, in connexion with Oxford, by Jonson, who applies it to Amorphus-Oxford in *Cynthia's Revels*, wherein Cynthia is Elizabeth, and by Oxford himself in *Much Ado About Nothing*, and also in *Two Gentlemen of Verona*, where it is used by Valentine, who is Oxford, in intimate relation with Silvia, who is Queen Elizabeth once more.

Adonis, and also the Boar, in the poem, are the usual dual presentment of de Vere, to the first of whom the Queen makes shameless and unrequited love. Nothing could be more meaningful than such a stanza as that wherein Venus, " applying this to that," i.e., the poetic dialogue to actual life, asks Adonis :

---

[1] First pointed out by Mr. Looney, *Shakespeare Identified*.

> " 'Where did I leave? No matter where' quoth she.
> 'Leave me, and then the story aptly ends.
> 'The night is spent.' 'Why what of that?' quoth she.
> 'And now 'tis dark, and going I shall fall.'
> 'In night,' quoth she, 'desire sees best of all.' "

The Queen, like the earth, is in love with Adonis, who will none of her, whereupon,

> Cynthia for shame obscures her silver shine,

lamenting that treasonable nature should have stolen "moulds from heaven," for the fashioning of men so divine as he, who, nevertheless, is beyond her reach; for which reason she but loves him the more, despite the strange mingling in him of

> " beauty with infirmities
> And pure perfection with impure defeature;
> Making it subject to the tyranny
> Of mad mischances and much misery."

All this is plain description of Oxford's eccentric and baffling paradoxical genius; while the stanzas 139-40 continue, upon Oxford themes:

> " And now she beats her heart, whereat it groans,
> That all the neighbour caves as seeming troubled,
> Make verbal repetition of her moans;
> Passion on passion deeply is redoubled.
> 'Ay me,' she cries, and twenty times 'Woe, woe.'
> And twenty echoes twenty times cry so.

> " She, marking them begins a wailing note,
> And sings extemporally a woeful ditty;
> How love makes young men thrall and old men dote;
> How love is wise in folly, foolish-witty.
> Her heavy anthem still concludes in woe,
> And still the choir of echoes answer no."

Both these stanzas are crammed with the identical motives of de Vere's own " Echo " song, which we have already examined, and with the cave-where-echo-lies motive of *Romeo and Juliet*, where also the Rosaline is Queen Elizabeth. At the close of 151, we are told how Venus " back retires to rate the boar for murther," upon which follows immediately 152 :

" A thousand spleens bear her a thousand ways ;
  She treads the path that she untreads again ;
  Her more than haste is mated with delays,
  Like the proceedings of a drunken brain,
    Full of respects, yet not at all respecting,
    In hand with all things, nought at all effecting "—

lines that are nothing, if not an accurate epitome of Queen Elizabeth's political methods, seen from the view-point of a disgruntled courtier of her reign, and reproducing exactly her characteristic tricks of treading and untreading, of mating her haste with splenetic or time-gaining delays, and effecting, by herself, nothing of the hundred businesses she has in hand.[1] Then, speaking of the flattery of love, she continues, showing how

" Despair and hope make thee ridiculous,"

by flattering in thoughts of unlikely realization—an idea developed by Oxford in Sonnet 126/87, wherein again, as we have seen before in *Two Gentlemen of Verona*, he dreams of sleeping with the Queen :

" Thus have I had thee as a dream doth flatter,
  In sleep a king, but waking no such matter."

[1] It will be seen that *Venus and Adonis*, like the plays, corroborates, and is corroborated by actual historic fact.

Venus goes on, to speak of death:

"She clepes him king of graves and grave for kings"—

which is very near to Oxford's "a kingdom or a cottage or a grave"; and a little later, in close likeness to Titania (Elizabeth) infatuatedly feeding her Bottom by the hands of her fairies,

"With purple grapes, green figs, and mulberries,"

she, Venus,

"Would bring him mulberries and ripe red cherries,
He fed them with his sight, they him with berries."

The best clue, however, to the whole business, is, I think, the Oxford-boar motive, and the implication that the mischief has been done by that strange, secret, E. Vere beast,

"the boar that bloody beast,
Which knows no pity, but is still *severe* . . .[1]
'Tis not my fault, *the boar* provoked my tongue;
Be wreak'd on him, *invisible commander*;
'Tis he, foul creature, that hath done thee wrong;
I did but act, he's author of thy slander.
　　Grief hath two tongues; and never woman yet
　　Could rule them both without ten women's wit.

There follow, in the remaining stanzas, motive after motive from de Vere's own songs; such as "how much a fool was I," "as falcon to their lure," and so forth; but I have set down enough, I hope, to show, beyond reasonable doubt, that behind all the trouble, from the

[1] s E. Vere may be an intentional Vere pun.

WITHDRAWAL FROM PUBLIC LIFE

Queen's view-point, lurked hidden that "invisible commander," the melancholy boar,

"Whose downward eye still looketh for a grave;"

while, desponding, he meditates upon death—that boar whose extravagancies, obduracies, and infirmities have provoked her to exasperation, even while his fantastic genius delighted the fancy, and his irresistible charms wrung the heart of an exigeant mistress.

Venus and Adonis was written, no doubt, many years before publication, perhaps almost contemporaneously with *A Midsummer's Night Dream* and at about the time of Oxford's withdrawal from court—but it appeared only in 1593, as a secret answer to an incensed Queen, whose amorous advances, of earlier days, had been scorned by her Lord Great Chamberlain.

Another relaxation that Oxford found, during this same year of *Venus and Adonis*, 1593, was the unlocking of his heart in the early Sonnets, a set of verses first inspired, I suspect, by the birth, on 4 February, of his son Henry, destined to become the 18th Earl of Oxford. The child was christened in the Parish Church of Stoke Newington—his Christian name, Henry, unique in the Vere, Cecil, and Trentham families being probably given him as a compliment to the Earl of Southampton, Henry Wriothesley, who followed de Vere as royal ward in Burleigh's household, and who, as we have seen, narrowly escaped possessing him as a father-in-law.

Venus and Adonis, dedicated to Southampton, had appeared in April, and on 7 July, 1594, Oxford writes to Burleigh an enigmatic letter, concerning "sundry abuses whereby both Her Majesty and myself were in my office greatly hindered," but giving no hint at all as to what those abuses might be. I suppose that Oxford is referring to matters connected with the group of playwrights, at whose head, as "invisible commander," he was working, and evidently with some friction and jealousies, as our glances into the writings of Greene and Chapman have already made perfectly clear. The death of Marlow, who, like Oxford, had been in the secret service of the government, and whose assassination, on 1 June, 1593, we now know to have been a case of "putting away," connived at by the government, provides an example of the deeds of violence, that, in a still quasi-barbarous age, could be, and were, perpetrated in that dark underworld of Elizabethan drama, in which de Vere, by a strange stroke of destiny, finds himself so inextricably involved.

Meanwhile, the transformation of the plays into literature was continuing; and on 25 August, 1594, Henslowe's company acted, for the first time, what must have been a revised version of *The Merchant of Venice*, which will account for the distinguishable though faint resemblances between Shylock and Dr. Lopez, the Jewish physician, whose attempt to poison the Queen came to light, and who was executed on 7 June.

Burleigh, no doubt, would have been well content for the marriage between Southampton and his granddaughter, Lady Elizabeth Vere, to have taken place; but it was not so fated—a probable reason being that the lady, who had refused Lord Northumberland also, had fallen in love with another nobleman, William Stanley, second son of the Earl of Derby, and younger brother to Ferdinando, Lord Strange, who succeeded as 5th Earl of Derby, in 1593, and, dying less than seven months after, probably of poison, left the Earldom to William.

The new Earl, who came to the title on 16 April, 1594, was a cultured and travelled man. He had undertaken, in 1582, a long tour through France, where he visited Paris, the Loire district, and other parts of that country, before returning to England in 1587, or a little earlier. His marriage with Elizabeth de Vere took place at Greenwich, on 26 January, 1595, in the presence of the Queen and court, " with great solemnity and triumph," and to an accompaniment of much feasting and revelry; the most interesting, by far, of all the many entertainments provided, being *A Midsummer Night's Dream*, which was almost certainly played, upon that occasion, by the Lord Chamberlain's men.

The "Dream," there is good reason to believe, was not a wholly new play at this time; and Mrs. Clark is probably right in regarding the work, in its original form, as an allegory of the Alençon marriage, designed for production at court, with Theseus and Hippolyta, and, later, Bottom and Titania, standing for Alençon and Elizabeth; it being a reasonable surmise that only a lover with a French prototype would address the Fairies as " Messieurs." All this would date from 1581-84; but such spectacular entertainments, and elaborate water-pageants, continued to be extremely popular in the courts of western Europe throughout the fifteen-'eighties, as witness, for example, those intensely interesting tapestries by Quesnel, of 1585, in the Long Gallery of the Uffizi Palace at Florence—a city visited by Oxford in 1575— and introducing a group of individuals who figure prominently in the Shakesperean plays, including Catherine de' Medici, Henry III, and Henry IV. One of these tapestries depicts a great water-pageant, with a dolphin-ship, and another vessel following it, filled with siren-mermaids making music—a picture that at once recalls the lines of Oberon concerning

"Uttering such dulcet and harmonious breath"—

a phrase, indeed, that may have been actually suggested by some such pageant, first seen by Oxford in France or Italy. These entertainments no doubt, though generally more crude in England than abroad, were often imitated from one another, and bore a strong family likeness.

A Midsummer Night's Dream, in the form in which we have it, refers, beyond question, to the famous entertainment given, in 1591, by Edward Seymour, Earl of Hertford, as propaganda for what is known as the Suffolk, as against the Scottish, succession, in the person of Hertford's son, the daughter of Lady Katharine Grey. A description of this pageant, published in the same year, showing Queen Elizabeth enthroned with her Maids of Honour behind her, and the word "west" written beside them, explains definitively Oberon's reference to the "fair vestal throned by the west."[1] It may well be that the love-affair between Lord Derby and Lady Elizabeth Vere was inspired by a meeting at that function, and that the joint authors of Bottom—who, as caricatured in our version of the play, is almost certainly not Alençon, but James of Scotland—are Oxford and the Earl of Derby, who seems to have collaborated with his father-in-law in writing the "Dream." This surmise is supported by the close resemblances traceable between the Fairy comedy and *Love's Labour's*

---

[1] Professor Abel Lefranc of the Institut de France first proved that *A Midsummer Night's Dream* refers to the fête at Elvetham of 1591. Its political propaganda in favour of the Suffolk Succession was first noted by Miss Edith Rickert.

Lost, in which also Derby, as we shall see, had a hand.¹ Evidently the father and son-in-law are on good terms ; for soon after the wedding, the Earl of Oxford is staying with the newly married couple, at their House in Cannon Row. On 7 August de Vere wrote to Lord Burleigh :

> "On my coming to Byfleet from Cannon Row the Earl of Derby was very earnest that he might assure £1,000 a year for my daughter, and marvelled that Sir Robert Cecil her uncle and I her father were so slack to call upon it ; so I desire something may be done therein."

"I her father" had never yet been found importunately forward in seeing that his children were properly provided for ; and this slackness of 1595, was, I imagine, a lethargy that the Earl—an old man now, when judged by Elizabethan standards—will never learn to throw off. Impecuniosity following upon financial recklessness, had become a habit with him ; but his young wife, relatively, it seems, a rich and prudent woman, purchased in 1596 an old manor at Hackney upon the verges of Clapton, named "King's Place"—Hackney being then a pleasant little country town, close to Stoke Newington, where they had hitherto been living. "King's Place," which was to be the home of the Earl and his Countess for the remainder of Oxford's life, was so called because in 1538 it had passed into possession of King Henry VIII, who had held a court there in 1546. Edward VI had done the same in 1549 ; and Queen Elizabeth in 1583, when the probable occupier was Lord Vaux ; and it was here, apparently, that this Roman Catholic peer offered sanctuary to the Jesuit, Robert Southwell, who was hidden there in "the priest's hole," the existence

¹ See my *Shakespeare, Jonson and Wilkins as Borrowers*, pp. 9-13.

of which is one of the traditions of Brooke House, as the mansion came to be named. For six years, Southwell, closely watched by Walsingham's spies, led a fugitive and hunted life, until 1592, when he was arrested at Harrow, and after torture and imprisonment, a part of which was passed in the Tower of London, he was hanged at Tyburn, on 21 February, 1595, the same year in which there passed from this world his protector at Brooke House, Lord Vaux, who also had suffered fine and imprisonment for his faith. When the Countess of Oxford took possession of the house, she apparently allowed the widow, Lady Catherine Vaux, to reside there for a time.[1]

Here, then within less than half an hour's ride, on horseback, from "The Theatre" and "The Curtain," which were not far outside the Bishop's Gate of old London Wall—to a home which, already historic when he first entered it, still stands, though fallen and changed —came "William Shakespeare," at the age of forty-six; and here, in close retirement, broken only, upon occasion, by a brief visit to his son-in-law or a friend, or by a day's emergence into the public life of London, he will write the majority of the later Sonnets, the Achilles-Hector portions of *Troilus and Cressida*, the whole probably, of *King Lear*: and here also, immured in his study, or pacing the gardens or the great balconied corridor, one hundred and sixty feet long, which looked out upon them, he will, by revision after revision, transform from a melodramatic stage play of revenge, into the work of poetical literature now known the whole world over, the tragedy of that Prince of Denmark, who is himself.

[1] Col. B. R. Ward's *Mystery of Mr. W. H*, p. 15.

Most often, probably, he worked quite alone; but occasionally as, for example, in the year 1599, he would exchange visits with his son-in-law, whom the march of events had also excluded from active political life; since in 1593 there had been discovered a Jesuit plot, designed for the dethroning of Queen Elizabeth, and the proclamation, as King of England, of William Stanley's brother, Ferdinando, who had then recently succeeded to the earldom. Ferdinando and William were descended, through their mother, from Henry VIII's younger sister, Lady Mary Tudor; and though clear of any complicity in this ridiculous scheme, their closeness to the succession rendered them, henceforth, easily suspect. Ferdinando's premature death has been traced, it seems, to these Jesuit conspirators; and it was natural, therefore, that Lord Derby should prefer a life of retirement, occupied, as was also his father-in-law, among the "Country Muses" of poetry and music. In 1599, a year during which the Derbys paid at least two visits to the Oxfords, George Fanner wrote, "The Earl of Derby is busied only in penning comedies for the common players," in whom, as we know from a letter (undated) of Lady Derby's to Sir Robert Cecil, her husband took "delight."

In 1624, Francis Pilkington printed, in his *Second Set of Madrigals and Pastorals*, a "Pavin made for the Orpharion by the right honourable William Earle of Darbie, and by him consented to be in my Bookes placed." That the two Earls, to some extent, collaborated dramatically, and musically, and exchanged ideas, at this time, is, I think, indisputable; for John Farmer, dedicating to Lord Oxford his two Song Books, entitled *Ways of Two Parts in one made upon a Plain Song*, and *The First*

Set of English Madrigals, published respectively in 1591 and 1599, when Farmer was probably in Oxford's service, writes as follows concerning the Earl's skill in music:

> "Hereunto, my good lord, I was the rather emboldened for your Lordships great affection to the noble science (music) hoping for the one you might pardon the other. (1591).
>
> "In this I shall be most encouraged if your Lordship vouchsafe the protection of my first-fruits, for that both of your greatness you best can, and for your judgment in music best may. For without flattery be it spoke, those that know your Lordship know this, that using this science as a recreation, your Lordship have overgone most of them that make it a profession. Right honourable Lord, I hope it shall not be distasteful to number you here among the favourers of music, and the practisers, no more than Kings and Emperors that have been desirous to be in the roll of astronomers, that being but a star fair, the other an angels choir."

But no man who has read, or seen acted, *The Merchant of Venice,* or who has savoured, even a little, the lyrical impulse, and the natural singing qualities of the songs scattered throughout the plays, needs much more evidence than these afford, that "Shakespeare" was a musician. Almost certainly, he was a composer also; for in 1588 Anthony Munday, who had been formerly in the Earl's employ, published in his *Banquet of Dainty Conceits,* two poems of his own, which, he tells us, can be sung to the " Earl of Oxford's March " and The Earl of Oxford's Galliard."[1]

[1] For these tunes see article, "Mr. Bird's Battell," *Musical Times,* January, 1929, by Katharine E. Eggar.

CHAPTER TEN

OXFORD'S LITERARY WAR WITH CHAPMAN AND JONSON: 1596–1598

Literary Feud between Oxford and Chapman during the mid-'nineties—Oxford counter-attacks in the Sonnets, and " Love's Labour's Lost "—William repudiated as Sly in " The Taming of the Shrew "—The Shrew Dialogue based upon actual Marital Tiffs—Jonson's Attacks upon Oxford-Shakespeare as Puntarvolo, and upon William as Sogliardo, in " Every Man Out of His Humour "—The Plot to destroy Oxford's Plays—Oxford " purges " Jonson as Ajax in " Troilus and Cressida "—Oxford as Achilles in " Troilus "—" King Lear " as an historical Allegory of the French Civil Wars—Oxford as Kent in " King Lear "—The " Ashbourne " Portrait of Shakespeare—Actually a Portrait of Oxford at about the age of forty-seven—Chapman's reference in " The Revenge of Bussy " to the rich binding of his Poems by " Shakespeare."

ONE by one, as the mood of the moment sings within him, the Sonnets are being written, and are carefully copied upon royal parchment, which has first been lead-lined and smoothed with pumice-stone, to let the ink flow freely, as Chapman has told us in one of his attacks on Shakespeare in *The Revenge of Bussy d'Ambois*, the companion play to which, *Bussy d'Ambois*, was probably drafted about this time, 1597–98. By the year 1595, in fact, the literary war, destined to be waged for several years, is in full activity between " Shakespeare " and the rival poet of the Sonnets, George Chapman; its initiatory event being, in part, I suspect, the publication of *Venus and Adonis* in 1593. Chapman did not approve of the " first heir " of Shakespeare's invention, which, to him, was artless and mere nature stuff, an unpardonable fault to the more pedantical Elizabethan minds. Thus he condemns *Venus and Adonis*, in *Ovid's Banquet of Sense* (1595):

> " Ladies must be adored that are but fair,
> But apt besides with art to tempt the ear
> In notes of nature, is a goddess part,
> Though oft men's natures notes please more than Art"—

by all of which he means that, though it may well be a goddess's (Elizabeth's) part to tempt a man's ear (Shakespeare's) with notes of nature, as she does in *Venus and Adonis*; yet Shakespeare's poem, though no better than "nature notes," is, yet by some strange mischance, vastly more popular than Chapman's own verses, which are a product of art. But, as we have seen, already in 1594, one year prior to the *Ovid's Banquet of Sense*, Chapman, as Poet of the Night, has been fiercely attacking de Vere, the singer of Phœbus and the Day, otherwise "Shakespeare"; and in that same year, 1595, the splenetic George publishes *A Coronet for his Mistress Philosophy*, in which he returns, with even greater vigour, to the attack upon his rival. The opening line:

> " Muses that sing Love's sensual empery "—

is manifestly another stroke aimed at *Venus and Adonis*, while the equable soul, in stanza 5, who " bears one chanceless mind in all mischances," is again Horatio de Vere, whom Chapman has praised in his earlier poems, and of whom Horatio's cousin, Edward, had written, in *Hamlet* almost identical words:

> " As one in suffering all that suffers nothing,"

The merit of Sir Horatio Vere in fact, seems to be one of the few points upon which the rival poets agree. Vehemently the attack upon Edward is renewed:

> " not the weak disjoint
> Of female humours; nor the Protean rages
> Of pied-faced fashion, that doth shrink and swell,
> Working poor men like waxen images,
> And makes them apish strangers where they dwell,
> Can alter her, titles of primacy,
> Courtship of antic gestures, brainless jests,
> Blood without soul of false nobility,
> Nor any folly that the world infests
> Can alter her who with her constant guises
> To living virtues turn the deadly vices."

Concerning who he aims at here, there can be no possible mistake. From "female humours," down to "false nobility" and "deadly vices"—with a flattering pun for the Catholic Guise thrown in—the quoted stanza is a catalogue of the stock charges against Oxford, the vicious, noble-born protestant, and also against Oxford-Shakespeare, as the concluding stanza unanswerably shows.

> " Muses that Fame's loose feathers beautify,
> And such as scorn to tread the theatre,
> As ignorant: the seed of memory
> Have most inspired and shown their glories there
> To noblest wits, and men of highest doom,
> That for the kingly laurel bent affair
> The theatres of Athens and of Rome,
> Have been the crowns, and not the base impair.
> Far, then, be this foul cloudy-brow'd contempt
> From like plumed birds: and let your sacred rhymes

> From honour's court their servile feet exempt,
> That live by soothing moods and serving times.
> And let my love adorn with modesty eyes,
> Muses that sing love's sensual emperies."

The first line of that stanza supplies, at a glance, a clue to the individual aimed at; for the "loose feathers" metaphor, followed later by "like-plumed birds," is the same that Greene, upon his death-bed, had aimed at "Shakespeare," three years before, when he wrote of the crow "beautified with our feathers"; and if Shakespeare were of lowly birth, and comparatively unlearned, as we have been told for the past three centuries, why should he scorn the ignorance of a theatre the antique memories of which, going back to Athens and Rome, inspired "nobler wits and men of highest doom"? As for those sneers at "honour's court," not that of Whitehall, and for the gibe aimed at those

> "That live by soothing moods and serving times,"

was not Oxford, at this very period of his life, seeking to wheedle the grant of a lucrative monopoly from a lady whose mood must be cunningly nursed for the purpose?

Thus, in poem after poem, chaotically, obscurely, with stifled strength, and struggling vehemence, with uncouth contortions and vitriolic hate, expressed in strangely perverted grammar, does this splenetic poet attack his rival. Not only is Horatio de Vere magnified, to the disadvantage of his cousin, while Oxford's mingled scorn of, and love for, the stage is held up to disparagement and contempt, along with jibes at such plays as *Richard II* and *A Midsummer Night's Dream*, then being revived; but the attack, by 1598, is being turned also upon those " sugared sonnets," now circulating, in this very year, as Meres tells us, among Shakespeare's private friends. Here and there Chapman will yield to his rival a little grudging praise, as when, in *To M. Harriots* (1598), we find him using the same sugary metaphor above quoted from Meres, yet unable to desist from peppering plenty of sour over his reluctant dole of sweet:

> " And though to rhyme and give a verse smooth feet,
> Uttering to vulgar palates passion sweet
> Chance often in such weak capricious spirits
> As in nought else have tolerable merits."

Throughout *To M. Harriots*, in fact, he is aiming straight at the Sonnets; and when, about this time, remembering how, ten years before—by bearing the golden canopy over Elizabeth's head when, in celebration of that Armada victory, his Queen made her triumphant progress down the nave of St. Paul's—the Earl had signally " honoured the outward," de Vere wrote:

> " Were't aught to me I bore the canopy,
> With my extern the outward honouring "—

Chapman must needs remind his readers, and patron, that he himself holds Harriots' name to be

> " in merit far above
> Their tympanies of state that arms of love
> Fortune or blood shall lift to dignity "—

that tympany of state being just a paraphrase for the canopy Oxford had borne—though not, grumbles Chapman, upon reason of desert and merit, but by mere chance of fortune and of blood.

And what does Oxford think of it all? De Vere, with his instinctive consciousness of, and swift reaction to, all that was good and noble in men—even while himself sinning grievously against the light—could not but recognize that, in Chapman, he had met a rival of wider learning, and of deeper metaphysical insight than himself; and in sonnet after sonnet he pays tribute,

" To every hymn[1] that able spirit affords,
In polished form of well refined pen ";

generously and freely admitting that

" the full proud sail of his great verse
Bound for the prize of all too precious you,"

had drawn much wind from the swelling sail of his own saucy and inferior barque.

The reader who would envisage clearly the relative characters of these two greatest poets of their day should set Oxford's open-hearted and magnanimous admissions, made to that sun of their firmament, "precious you," whom I take, in this instance, to be Cynthia, or Queen Elizabeth herself, against the splenetic and vindictively jealous railings of Chapman: yet he must not suppose, nevertheless, that the Earl, sitting cheek by jowl with his rival satirist, neglected opportunity to hit back. Had he done so, the less Shakespeare he, constitutionally unable to resist a joke, and, for years past, the most dreaded mocker in Gloriana's court. Oxford praises Chapman, indeed; but it is carefully qualified praise; and the Earl, one supposes, is at times amusedly doubtful whether, in this austere and humourless rival

---

[1] i.e. *Hymnus ad Cynthian*, etc.

—rancorous also, mournful, disgruntled, and intensely self-conscious—he has to do with an inspired seer, with a befogged pedant, or with both of these together; and I can hear the author of the sonnets splitting his sides, in lighter moments, over these mystically involved fawnings of a compeer gulled nightly by that "affable familiar ghost."

But it is not only in the Sonnets that the Earl hits back. Oxford was furbishing up, at this time, an old play that he had first worked upon, it would seem in the late 'seventies, as a court-comedy or double masque, *A Mask of Amazons and a Mask of Knights*, played before the Queen early in 1579, and had now revised altogether probably with the help as collaborator of his son-in-law, Lord Derby, who had been in France in 1589, when the accession of Henry IV, and the subsequent alliance between that monarch and Queen Elizabeth had suggested the writing of plays of pro-French propaganda for the English stage. In this second or third version, round about 1598, of the early comedy known to us as *Love's Labour's Lost*, "presented before Her Highness this last Christmas newly corrected and augmented by W. Shakespere," the union of the three French factions, Huguenot, Royalist, and Guisian, is symbolized in the persons of the three attendant lords upon the King of Navarre; though the greatest interest of this version, from our view-point, lies, perhaps, in the obvious attacks made by several characters upon Chapman. The Princess of France, Marguerite de Valois—whom Oxford probably met in France in 1575, and of whom according to Arundel (1581), de Vere had declared that she "sent a messenger to desire him (Oxford) to speak with him in her chamber"—declares that her

> "Beauty is bought by judgment of the eye,
> Not uttered by base sale of chapmens tongues"—

while Biron, who is Oxford himself, when, in IV, iii, he says, of that same Princess:

> "O she needs it not.
> To things of sale a seller's praise belongs"—

is simply pointing out that since his sonnets are not for sale, he disdains to use a seller's praise to laud his wares, as Chapman must who, in his poem to Harriots, had written of these same sonnets as

> "bugs form'd in their foul conceits
> Nor made for sale...."[1]

Similarly the king, talking with Biron, a few lines lower down—

> "Black is the badge of hell,
> The hue of dungeons and the school of night"—

aims patently at Chapman's school of darkly mystical poetry of the Night, that forms so strong a contrast with his rival's luminous verse.

Thus the pair hammer at one another, each of them striking and counter-striking through poems and plays written in direct and open rivalry of person and of subject; in plays, also, I add, because a certain unfinished, unnamed play, in respect of which Henslowe, on 4 January, 1598, lent Chapman three pounds, was probably *Bussy d'Ambois*, a French tragedy drawn, in part, from the memoirs of that same Marguerite de

---

[1] Chapman's jibe is: "You, Oxford, are only an amateur, and could not sell your verses if you would." Oxford's retort is: "You, Chapman, are only a tradesman; out to sell yours, if you can."

Valois, and, in its finished form, teeming, as did its successor, *The Revenge of Bussy d'Ambois*, with multitudinous comments, hostile and eulogistic, upon many of the best known Shakesperean plays, and upon Oxford himself as their author[1].

But it is now time to inquire a little into another mysterious personage of our story—William Shakspere of Stratford-on-Avon, who, for a little while past, has been in the background. Oxford, it will be remembered, and with him, no doubt, others who were in the secret, seem to have sworn an oath to conceal the identity of "William Shakespeare"; but de Vere, nevertheless, during the decade 1589–99 was inserting, as we have seen, or was causing to be inserted, into the plays specific repudiations of the spurious William, along with proofs of identity of the genuine one. None among these repudiations, excepting only the "William" scene in *As You Like It*, is more striking than the Induction to *The Taming of the Shrew* which, by all indications, seems to date from the closing years of the 'nineties. This Induction records how a certain Tinker, one Sly, now socially fallen, though descended from a family that "are no rogues," but "came in with Richard Conqueror,"[2] is found dead drunk outside an ale-house, beside a heath, and is discovered there by a Lord returned from hunting. There enters a company of

---

[1] See my *Shakespeare and Chapman as Topical Dramatists*.

[2] E. K. Chambers in *William Shakespeare*, II, p. 212, quotes from John Manningham's Diary, 13 March, 1602. "Upon a time when Burbage played *Richard II*, there was a citizen grew so far in liking with him that before she went from the play she appointed him to come that night unto her by the name of Richard III. Shakespeare overhearing their conclusion went before, was entertained, and at his game ere Burbage came. Then message being brought that Richard III was at the door Shakespeare caused return to be made that William the Conqueror was before Richard III. Shakespeare's name William."

players, one of whom is well remembered by the lord, as having played " a farmer's eldest son," whereupon—the players having accepted an invitation to stay with the lord that night—their host conceives the idea of putting the drunkard to bed, in a rich chamber within the mansion, and, when the toper wakes, making him believe that he is none other than the lord in person, who, for fifteen years, has been in a state of dreaming lunacy, from which he is only now recovered, and during which he was wont to complain that he had been " beaten out of door," and, accordingly, " would rail upon the hostess of the house."

Not only is Sly a Lord, " and nothing but a lord," but he is also married withal, blessed in possession of

" a lady far more beautiful
Than any woman in this waning age."

Lastly, since " melancholy is the nurse of frenzy," and too much sadness has congealed this blue and noble blood, his honour's own players, hearing with joy of his amendment, are come to play before him " a pleasant comedy," which is also, and significantly, described, upon the rise of the curtain, as " household stuff," and as " a kind of history," which in literal truth it is.

Now the explanation and implications of all this seem to me to be crystal clear. The tinker, who, nevertheless, is of quaintly ancient stock, since his forbears " came in with Richard Conqueror," can be, in my opinion, none other than William of Stratford, who, though come down in the world, could trace back certain gentlemen ancestors for a generation or two, and, at this very time was making application to the College of Heralds for a coat-of-arms, which, after failure in 1596, he achieved in 1598—a business bitterly mocked at by Jonson, in *Every Man Out of His Humour*, III, i, wherein Sogliardo is the Stratford man, whose coat-of-arms—" your boar (Oxford's) *without a head rampant to gentility* "—is derided by Puntarvolo, who is Oxford himself, as " the most vile, foolish, absurd, palpable, and ridiculous escutcheon that ever this eye survised "; in which connexion it is remarkable that Carlo's comment upon Sogliardo's escutcheon, " a swine without a head without brain," matches exactly the Lord's remark, as he looks down upon Sly, " O monstrous beast how like a *swine* he lies." Further, Sly, in the Induction, is found, lying on a heath, apparently near Wincot, which orthodox commentators take to be Wilmecote, in Arden, not far from Stratford—all of which fits in perfectly with an assumption that Sly is Shaksper; since Jonson, in *Every Man Out of His Humour*, expressly tells us that Sogliardo was not living in London when his play was written and acted (1598–99) but was " housekeeping in the country," he having, in fact, bought New Place at Stratford, in 1597.[1] The situation here also fits in with the suggestion made earlier in these pages, that Lord Oxford, though permanently installed at Hackney during the late 'nineties, had probably been living for a time in the Arden district of Warwickshire, and had met William there, some ten years before. Knowing, as we do, de Vere's predilection for weaving actual fact into his plays, I should not be in the least surprised to know, that the Earl, in sportive mood, conceived, one day, the idea of inviting Shaksper

---

[1] We are told by Sir E K Chambers that Shakespeare did not live there until 1610 Why, then, did William buy one of the largest houses in Stratford, and not live in it for thirteen years? I suggest that he did live in it, and that Jonson knew that he did.

into his Warwickshire home; of making him thoroughly drunk; and of playing upon him some such trick as that recorded in the play. It is exactly the sort of thing that the impulsive Oxford might have thoroughly enjoyed doing, especially if it were carried out with the help of his own company of players, who, we know, had acted often in Warwickshire.

On the other hand, the Induction may be simply allegorical; though, in either event, the episode is powerfully striking, by reason of its exact consonance with the facts of Oxford's life. Sly is told, that, for fifteen years, he has been a victim of this lunatic disease, during which time, with bitter complaints against his having been "beaten out of doors," he rails "upon the hostess of the house," otherwise upon Queen Elizabeth herself, who, in a sense, had indeed beaten her Lord Great Chamberlain from her court, sending him also to the Tower in 1581, about two years before the first draft of *Hamlet*, in which Oxford himself is portrayed as an eccentric prince. Now if we add those fifteen years to 1581, or to 1583, we get the date 1596–98, which is precisely the period under discussion for *The Taming of the Shrew*. Again it is notable that Sly's remark concerning himself:

"I have no more doublets than backs, no more stockings than legs, nor no more shoes than feet."

is exactly parallelled by Monsieur, when in I, i, of Chapman's *Revenge of Bussy*, set among a stream of references to Hamlet, Monsieur describes Epaminondas as having "no more suits than backs." Also the Induction, with its friendly appeal to the Players, in Hamlet's actual words, " You are Welcome," and with its play-within-a-play motive, strongly recalls the Hamlet drama, which I suspect to have been revised during this year 1598, that saw the death of Burleigh who stands for Polonius. When, therefore, I read such lines as these by the Lord :

> " O that a mighty man of such descent,
>   Of such possessions, and so high esteem,
>   Should be infused with so foul a spirit "—

and

> " Hence comes it that your kindred shuns your house,
>   As beaten hence by your strange lunacy.
>   O noble lord, bethink thee of thy birth,
>   Call home thy ancient thoughts from banishment,[1]
>   And banish hence such abject lowly dreams—"

I read them partly as satire upon the comparatively insignificant Stratford man, who was thus fathering wonderful plays, actually written by a great lord of ancient lineage ; but, in a deeper sense I read the lines as a reminder to himself—a comment, by the true Shakespeare, upon the abject fits of melancholic despondency, which, from the crisis of 1581 onwards, and the days of his disgrace and imprisonment in the Tower, have, at times, clouded his life and being, almost into that quasi-madness which is hinted at in Hamlet, and will be further developed in the study not of young but of senile madness, first drafted, as I believe, in this year 1598, and known to us as *King Lear*. The Lord's line :

> " Thou hast a lady far more beautiful
>   Than any woman in this waning age "—

---
[1] The plays teem with this " banishment " motive.

may be read, first as a deserved compliment to the Earl's lovely countess, Elizabeth Trentham, and, secondly, as another instance of Oxford's trick of marrying himself symbolically, as author, to his plays, precisely as Romeo marries Juliet, or Touchstone Audrey. Sly, of course, also, in popular estimation, is author of, and therefore married—though symbolically, and therefore unconsciously—to the first beauty of the Elizabethan age.

Long before satisfying myself as to what this Induction to *The Taming of the Shrew* might mean, I had noticed resemblances between the expressions in Sonnets 147 and 148, in Sir Denis Bray's order,[1]

" A Maid of Dian's. . . .
 I grant, I never saw a goddess go,
 My mistress, when she walks, treads on the ground,"

" Let me see thee walk . . .

and Petruchio's, II, i:

 Did ever Dian so become a grove
 As Kate this chamber with her princely gait?"—

and had concluded that this passage in the sonnets was suggested by actual tiffs between Oxford and his second wife, and was inserted about 1598, into a revised version of *The Taming of the Shrew*, whose first historic original was Oxford's sister, Lady Mary Vere. Significant therefore, in this connexion, is the statement at the Induction's close, that the comedy is " household stuff . . . a kind of history " ; and I believe myself to have described, with fair approximation to actual truth, the kind of history that it is.

[1] 130 and 153 in Quarto.

Open-minded Shaksperean students are now generally realizing that a vast proportion of Elizabethan drama is either topical or allegorical—Jonson's no less than the rest; and I think it most probable that the ludicrous scene in *Every Man Out of His Humour*, V, i, wherein Puntarvolo-Oxford presents Sogliardo-Shaksper before a court lady, Saviolina—who may be Queen Elizabeth—as a consummate actor, who can so peerlessly imitate other persons,

> "especially a rustic or a clown, madam, that it is not possible for the sharpest sighted wit in the world to discern any sparks of the gentleman in him when he does it"—

is probably the dramatic record of some such other trick as that irrepressible jester, Oxford—his "spleen great, with laughter," the while—would practise, when the mood took him, upon the rustic William and his Queen.[1]

This year 1598 brings us to another phase in our story, which, though hard to elucidate clearly, and known to us only by a series of inferences, must be briefly examined here; I mean the literary plot, or cabal, organized, apparently, about this time, against Oxford, by Chapman and his other rivals. In Sonnet 125, which is 92 in Sir Denis Bray's order, following immediately upon the reminder, written in 1598, that he "bore the canopy" over his Queen's head at the Armada celebration, we find this act of "honour to the outward" at once compared to the laying of "bases for eternity," which I take to be the plays.

[1] For full analysis of above episode in *Every Man Out of His Humour*, see my *Oxford-Shakespeare Case Corroborated*, pp. 73-78.

"Were't aught to me I bore the canopy,
With my extern the outward honouring?
Or laid great bases for eternity,
Which prove more brief than waste or ruining.

The first three lines are simple; but what does that last one mean? My interpretation is, that the Shakesperean plays, which, on their merits, might have endured for ever, are now, during these closing years of the sixteenth century, in grievous danger of extinction. Such a meaning, if correct, fits in exactly, and becomes comprehensible only by comparison with those enigmatic episodes inserted, during this same year 1598, by Jonson into *Every Man Out of His Humour*, V, i, concerning an elaborate scheme for the killing of Puntarvolo's (Oxford's) "dog," which the rash Earl has confided to a "groom," who carries a basket:

Punt. See! here comes one that will carry coals, ergo, will hold my dog.
(*Enter a Groom with a basket*)
My honest friend, may I commit the tuition of this dog to thy prudent care?
Groom. You may, if you please, sir.
Punt. Pray thee let me find thee here at my return...
Fast. Why, but will you leave him with so slight command, and infuse no more charge upon the fellow?
Punt. Charge! no; there were no policy in that; that were to let him know the value of the gem he holds, and so to tempt frail nature against her disposition. No, pray thee let thy honesty be sweet, as it shall be short.
Groom. Yes, sir.

This "groom" upon whom the plays are thus casually fathered—as thoughtlessly, it may be, as they were thrust upon William, in historic fact—I take to be the Stratford man, who does not "know the value of the gem he holds"; the dog, of course, standing symbolically for the plays, a surmise borne out by comparison of this scene with the one in *The Two Gentlemen of Verona*, II, iii, wherein Launce, representing the comedic side of Oxford, also comes on leading a dog, one Crab, that hard-hearted cur, which, Launce tells us openly, is "me"—"I am the dog"—that is to say the author of the comedy.

The scene in *Every Man Out of His Humour* continues, with Macilente standing for Chapman:

Groom. Honesty!... slid, what a mad humorous gentleman is this to leave his dog with me! I could run away with him now, an he were worth anything.
            (*Enter Macilente and Sogliardo*).
Maci. Od's my life, see where Sir Puntarvolo's dog is.
Groom. I would the gentleman would return for his follower here, I'll leave him to his fortunes else.
Maci. 'Twere the only *true* jest in the world to poison him now; ha! by this hand I'll do it, if I could but get him of the fellow. (*Aside*) Signior Sogliardo, walk aside, and think upon some device to entertain the lady with.
Sogl. So I do, sir. (*Walks off in a meditating posture.*)
Maci. How now, mine honest friend! whose dog-keeper art thou?
Groom. Dog-keeper, sir! I hope I scorn that i' faith.
Maci. Why, dost thou not keep a dog?

> *Groom.* Sir, now I do, and now I do not. (*throws off the dog*) . . . make me his dog-keeper (*Exit*).
>
> *Maci.* This is excellent, above expectation! nay, stay, sir; (*seizing the dog*) you'd be travelling; but I'll give you a dram shall shorten your voyage here. (*Gives him poison*). So, sir, I'll be bold to take my leave of you. Now to the Turk's court in the devil's name, for you shall never go o' God's name (*kicks him out*)—Sogliardo, come.
>
> *Sogl.* I have it i' faith now, will sting it. . . .
>
> *Mit.* O, piece of *true* envy.

Upon these intensely meaningful lines I can put no other construction but this—that the " throwing off " of the dog, while Sogliardo-William meditates over some device to entertain the lady (Queen Elizabeth) withal; and the poisoning of the beast by Macilente-Chapman, with the comment—" Now to the Turk's court in the devil's name "—Turk being one of the Queen's pet names for Oxford—simply describes a plot to keep the Shakesperean plays off the common stages[1]—where their popularity was injuring the professionals—and the return of the dramas, to the Queen's court, whence, of course, they originally came, before " pressing forth," as they had done, on to the " broker's stalls," in the form of quartos, and also to "the common stages."

This mysterious plot which, judging by the Earl's despondent sonnet already quoted, Oxford, at one time, thought might be successful, was, no doubt, connected with the " Poetomachia " or War of the Theatres of 1598, to which Oxford's personal contribution is *Troilus and*

[1] The plot would become much easier of accomplishment by the handing over of the plays by Oxford, during his retirement, to a " groom " or " dog-keeper ".

LITERARY WAR

Cressida, wherein he administers the famous purge to Jonson, and includes Chapman in the chastisement. Oxford, of course, writing under oath of secrecy, was precluded from taking any open part in the quarrel, or, I suppose, from openly protesting against secret cabals for the poisoning of his " dog," or against an analogous process, suggested by Carlo in *Every Man Out of His Humour*, V, iv, namely the " flaying of the animal, and the stuffing of the skin with straw, or, alternatively, the getting of " a somewhat less dog " to be " clapp'd into the skin "—a difference which, he assures the exasperated Puntarvolo, " shall never be discern'd." In other words, the play-going public at the common theatres, in Carlo's opinion, would not be cute enough to detect the difference if non-Shakesperean plays were foisted upon them as being written by the master : this last being the trick which was actually put into practice, after Oxford's death.

Troilus and Cressida, in its original form, was, it will be remembered, almost certainly that *History of Agamemnon and Ulysses* played by the Earl of Oxford's company before the Queen at Greenwich on 27 December, 1594; an old play which Oxford now, in 1598, proceeds to rewrite, partly as a counterblast to Chapman's *Homer* which had appeared in 1597, and in part as a criticism— " I will show you all whether these Greek heroes are such fine fellows as Chapman would have you believe." The play's deeper interest, however, lies in the relationships between Ajax and Achilles who are Jonson and Oxford; Achilles' counsellor being Ulysses, whose speeches are among the loftiest in all Shakespeare, and whom I identify, conjecturally, as Oxford's cousin by marriage, Francis Bacon, probably the Editor of the

Shakespeare Folio of 1623, and certainly a member of the Oxford group of writers.

With the position of Oxford, in 1598, the analogies seem to be almost perfect. The "hart" Achilles,

> "Having his ear full of his airy fame
> Grows dainty of his worth."

He has "taken cover," and in his tent (at Hackney) "lies mocking our design," while Ajax (Jonson) bearing his head

> "in full as proud a place
> As broad Achilles, keeps his tent like him,
> Makes factious feasts, rails on our state of war"—

which, I gather is a double allusion, to the war with Spain and also to the literary conflicts between the parties—and sets Thersites (Chapman) "whose gall coins slanders like a mint," to weaken the government by dirty and discreditable comparisons. (Nestor in I, iii.) Thersites next bitterly attacks Ajax-Jonson (II, i), for grumbling and railing at Oxford, of whose greatness he is deeply envious,[1] "as Cerberus is at Proserpina's beauty"; but, at the same time, Chapman warns his friend of the danger of openly attacking Oxford, whose tongue and pen are so formidable in retort:

> "Should'st thou strike him, He would pun thee
> into shivers with his fist as a sailor breaks a biscuit"—

a warning identical in kind with that given by Tom Nashe to Gabriel Harvey, as to what was likely to happen to him, if once Oxford "took him in hand."

---

[1] As Mitis says Macilente-Chapman was of Puntarvolo-Oxford.

"Kingdom'd Acilles," meanwhile, has grown furious, "in commotion rages and batters down himself," and is withal so "plaguey proud" as Ulysses puts it (II, iii), that the "death tokens of the matter hold small hope for his recovery." If Oxford disappears, the only man the people will follow, "when they go from Achilles," is Ajax-Jonson; and debate is joined as to which must go to the other, to seek some understanding or composition. Says Jonson:

"If I do go to him, an a' be proud with me I'll pash him o'er the face"—

but when they do meet (III, iii), the boast is not made good, for Ajax avoids the contest, and there follows between Achilles-Oxford and Ulysses-Bacon—if I have identified him rightly—one of the most loftily written and enthralling duologues in all the range of Elizabethan literature, wherein Ulysses warns his companion against the fast-increasing popularity of his rival:

"Why, even already
They slap the lubber Ajax on the shoulder,"

and in answer to Oxford's question, "What, are my deeds forgot?", we are given the lordly speech of Ulysses to his friend, beginning:

"Time hath, my lord, a wallet on his back."

Here in a passage of majestic wisdom Oxford is reminded, or reminds himself, that withdrawal from further literary activity means oblivion; since—granted that the quality of his rival's present work is behind that of Oxford's own—and who would set Jonson's plays beside Shakespeare's?—the lesser man, planted well in the public eye, will soon achieve popularity, since Time, like a fashionable host, will speed the parting guest, and open wide his arms, and his door, to the new-comer. Oxford, then, cannot live permanently upon his past reputation, nor afford long to let his gold be " o'er dusted."

> " Then marvel not thou great and complete man
> That all the Greeks begin to worship Ajax,
> Since things in motion sooner catch the eye
> Than what not stirs. The cry went once on thee
> And still it might, and yet it may again
> If thou would'st not entomb thyself alive
> And case thy reputation in thy tent."

Not so much of this recluse life in Brooke House, suggests Ulysses—to which Oxford retorts:

> " Of this my privacy I have good reason "—

as indeed we know to have been the fact, though Ulysses will not have it. On his side, he urges,

> " The reasons are more potent and heroical ";

whereupon, with the enigmatic announcement that follows:

> " 'Tis known, Achilles, that you are in love
> With one of Priam's daughters "—

we have introduced, into this play also, that mystery which is continually making itself felt in Oxford's life, and until we have fathomed it, must prevent us, I think, from ever completely understanding his story—I mean this enigmatic connexion with Priam's daughter, whom I take to be the daughter of Henry VIII, known to us as Elizabeth Tudor, Queen of England. Ulysses, indeed, in his next speech admits openly that here is a mystery " in the soul of state "; or, in other words, some dark matter " with whom relation durst never meddle," seeing that it has

> " an operation more divine
> Than breath or pen can give expression to "—

the word divine in this case, meaning simply the divinity of which Shakespeare, beyond question, was always profoundly conscious, as continually hedging a king. One can not argue, of course, that the Lord Great Chamberlain in his forty-ninth year, was suffering from the pangs of unrequited love; but we may, and indeed, I think, must take Ulysses' speech as indicating a common knowledge at court, that the Earl's past relations with his royal mistress provide a clue to the mystery.[1]

Oxford's answer shows that Ulysses did not plead in vain.

> " I see my reputation is at stake,
> My fame is shrewdly gored "—

and

> " My mind is troubled like a fountain stirred,
> And I myself see not the bottom of it "

So aloof and dispassionate is Ulysses' advice to Oxford, in this play, that, having regard to the apparent links between *Troilus and Cressida* and *The Tempest*—— wherein Ajax-Jonson reappears as Caliban—and also to the possibility that *The Tempest* may have been written by Bacon, I sometimes wonder whether Bacon himself did not have a hand in writing this later version of the

[1] See Appendix A

play—although the preface to the Quarto of 1609, with its open reference to the "grand possessor's wills," and its obvious E. Ver puns:

"A nEver writer to an E.Ver reader"—

and so forth, together with the significant fact that *Troilus and Cressida* was published in the same year (1609) as *King Lear* and the Sonnets, just after Lady Oxford had finally left Brooke House, are facts generally pointing to Oxford, as having had a predominant share in the play, even though he did not himself pen the Ulysses' speeches.

This play, *Troilus and Cressida*, and another, *Richard II*, link themselves up, in a most interesting fashion, with the history of the sixteenth century's closing years.

Of the first-named work, Dr. G. B. Harrison has written[1] very shrewdly, identifying Achilles, not, as I have done, with Oxford, but with Essex, a very just comparison, and one in no way stultifying my own views, since dual allegories of this kind—one dealing with Oxford's private life, and the other with contemporary political events—I have shown, again and again, to be Oxford's habitual dramatic method. Dr. Harrison concludes:

"The reasonable inference is that *Troilus and Cressida*, in its present form, was performed privately before an anti-Essex audience, either in the summer of 1598, or else about two years later when Essex and his followers were brewing treason."

The sequence of events seems to have been, approximately, this. In 1593, when Southampton was considering

[1] *Times Literary Supplement*, 20 November, 1930.

a marriage with Elizabeth Vere, Oxford dedicated to him an anti-Elizabeth poem, *Venus and Adonis*, and also wrote sonnets, urging the match upon the young man; de Vere, at that time, being in sympathy with the disaffected Essex party. By 1597, as I surmise, all the leading English statesmen, including Robert Cecil, Raleigh, and Essex, deeply dissatisfied with the rule of the ageing Queen, were on the verge of combining in a plot against her; and it was precisely at this time, 1597, that Oxford, probably with Bacon behind him, published *Richard II*, a transparently disloyal play. But, for reasons at which we can only guess, but which I suppose to be mutual distrust, or failure to agree upon a common policy, the threatened combine drifted apart, the scheme collapsed, and Cecil, Raleigh, and Essex separated, never to come together again. Oxford naturally followed his brother-in-law, Robert Cecil, the dramatic sequel being *Troilus and Cressida*.[1]

Richard II, a play probably written about 1587—though its lyrical style suggests an earlier draft—was perhaps rewritten about ten years later, when the deposition scenes were added. The following passage by Sir E. K. Chambers is pertinent:

> "There are many indications of an analogy present to the Elizabethan political imagination, between the reign of Richard II and that of Elizabeth herself. A letter of Sir Francis Knollys on 9 January, 1578, excuses himself for giving unwelcome counsel to the Queen, He will not 'play the parts of King Richard the Second's men,' will not be a courtly and unstatesmanlike flatterer. Clearly the phrase was familiar—Henry Lord Hunsdon similarly

---

[1] Capt. Ward first suggested to me this line of thought.

wrote at some date before 1588, 'I never was one of Richard II's men.'—More cryptic is a letter from Raleigh to Robert Cecil on 6 July, 1597, 'I acquaynted my L. Generall (Essex) with your letter to mee and your kind acceptance of your enterteynemente, he was also wonderful merry att ye consait of Richard the 2. I hope it shall never alter, and whereof I shalbe most gladd of as the trew way to all our good, quiett and advancement, and most of all for her sake whose affaires shall thereby fynd better progression! All these allusions are, of course, in perfect loyalty, the utterances of devoted, if critical, officials.[1]

From Sir Edmund Chambers's last conclusion I wholly dissent; for reasons that my preceding remarks will have made quite clear to all careful readers.

That the speeches I quoted from *Troilus and Cressida*, in common with dozens of others in Shakesperean drama, were based upon actual talks between the individuals concerned, I hold to be most probable, as also that further talks produced immediate dramatic result, in what is perhaps the most sublime as it is certainly the most titanic tragedy that has yet glorified our literature —a tragedy the subject of which is precisely that of the conversation in *Troilus and Cressida*, which may have begot it—that of a prince withdrawn in

" fast intent
To shake all cares and business from our age,"

and so " unburthen'd crawl toward death." Oxford, as I suppose, argued thus. " My contemplated withdrawal from the active life of a dramatist is objected to. I

[1] *William Shakespeare*, I, 353.

will not, therefore, withdraw immediately; but will write a tragedy of the king who sought in vain to divest himself of care by putting off care.' He did so; and that tragedy he called *King Lear*.

Lear, as the subject of a drama, was then, of course, no new theme to Oxford; for although he certainly did not write the earlier Lear play of 1592—which following Capt. Ward, I take to be a simple and hopeful allegory of the mounting cause of Protestantism in France, after Henry IV's military triumph at Ivry—that play was, I think, written under the Earl's own direction, by the secret-service writers of his own department, as propaganda for the Protestant, or Suffolk, succession in England, on behalf of which Oxford had long worked, and of which *A Midsummer Night's Dream* affords another example. *Lear* the tragedy, however, is a tremendous, threefold allegory, dealing with those two great triumphs of the counter reformation—the murder of Darnley, the Massacre of St. Bartholomew—both of which are also part themes of *Macbeth*—and, in later revision, the accession of James Stuart to the English throne. Historically considered, Lear himself is, in part, Coligny, Admiral of France, murdered at St. Bartholomew; psychologically considered, however, he is, at least as much, the King Lear, or King Earl who also, like Achilles in the *Troilus and Cressida* play we have just been examining, " rages in commotion," " batters down himself," and is so " plaguey proud " that " the death tokens of it cry 'No recovery.'"

Oxford, like Lear, has three daughters, married or becoming marriageable at this time; and actually, during those very years, has been making application for a grant to himself of monopolies, to which the Fool calls attention. Further—and a consoling thought it is to all lovers of de Vere—the human sympathies of the aged king, as misfortune deepens, and disasters hurl themselves pitilessly upon him, are perfected through suffering into a nobler sense of his kingship with all mortal things—a change that finds sublime expression in the majestic invocation to the storm, and in the passage beginning:

" Poor naked wretches, wherso'er ye be."

Never discarding, even in this last of his plays, that atmosphere of the fantastic, and of the humorous-grotesque, in which his spirit habitually moved, and which finds intensely vivid expression in the wise folly and philosophical madness, real or assumed, of three of his principal characters—he learns, amid it all, to renounce, at last, that " plaguey pride " of birth and being ; and, as old age closes upon him, more and more to identify his spirit with those cosmic forces of our world that make for spiritual harmony and peace.

Many lines in this tragedy, however, may well have been added later, during a last revision towards the end of his life. Meanwhile the character in the play standing most directly for Oxford, is not the king, but Kent, who tells us that he is forty-eight years of age, thus providing, among the other clues, the date 1598 for the first draft of the tragedy. Kent, " banished," and serving the King, though in disguise, is Oxford, also " banished " from court, and working secretly for a national purpose.

> *Kent.* If but as well I other accents borrow,
> That can my speech defuse, my good intent
> May carry through itself to that full issue
> For which I *razed my likeness*. . . . (I, iv.)

> " some dear cause
> Will in *concealment* wrap me up awhile (IV, iii.)
> My boon I make it, that you *know me not*
> Till time and I think meet. (IV, vii.)

Time has thought meet to set some three-and-a-quarter centuries between the work, and its recognition as Oxford's; but, surely, now that de Vere, in some measure at least, is "known aright" no reader, as I hope, will grieve, "lending me this acquaintance." (IV, 3.)

What manner of man, in outward physical appearance, was this so strange and gifted creature, whose inward mind now, for some thirty years past, has ranged through a world of his own making, real and yet unreal, peopled by men and women whom himself knew, loved, laughed at, and hated, in the flesh; yet who, in the plays, are often lovelier in kind, as they are larger in stature, than is given to the muddy vesture of decay. The question may sound fantastic; but it can be answered, as I believe, in the most meticulous detail, by reference to one of the best known portraits of "Shakespeare," namely the "Ashbourne."

The "Ashbourne"—formerly owned by Mr. Eustace Conway of New York—has "no pedigree," according to Mr. Parker Norris, the author of *Portraits of Shakespeare*; but Mr. M. H. Spielmann, a recognized authority upon Shakesperean iconography, holds that it " may be genuine," and wrote the following admirable description of the picture in *The Connoisseur*, for April-May, 1910. The portrait, I must add, bears the inscription, " Ætatis suae 47. Ao 1611." Thus Mr. Spielmann, of a picture which " at first glance wins the sympathy of the beholder."

"The three-quarter length standing figure is of the size of life. The high forehead, auburn hair, light beard and general aspect, and the fairness of the skin with its delicate flush of carnation bloom upon the cheeks, belong notably to one of the most favoured types of Shakespeare—the Jansen portrait and its copies—but are in sharp contrast with the swarthy face and dark hair of the Chandos portrait. The eyes are a nondescript brownish grey, dark in tone; The ear has no ring. The multifold ruff, zigzagged, yellowish in tint, with high lights of a stronger yellow, almost seems to be by another hand, and is certainly the most, and indeed the only, scamped part of the picture. The doublet is of black or grey-black material approximating to *velvet* with warm grey lights on the folds. Round the waist, with a downward point in the middle of the body, is a narrow sword or dagger belt—*a "dress" belt—embroidered with gold*, and in the left hand is held a *glove with gauntlet of crimson richly embroidered with bands of gold*—just such a dress belt and glove as we see in the portrait of James Douglas, Earl of Morton, who died in 1581— that is to say, thirty years before the date of this picture. At the corner of the rather crude red table cloth . . . stands a skull upon which rests the right lower arm, and around the wrists are small figure-eight edged ruffs (rather than ruffles) with small white corded edging. Upon the left-hand thumb, a member of unusual length, is a *gold signet-ring;* and held in the right hand *a gold embroidered book with broad red silk* tie-ribbons of the same colour as the table cloth, its pages kept slightly open by the insertion of the forefinger. This book might be, from its style and luxurious binding, a missal or similar devotional volume, save for what is claimed for a mask and cross-spears appearing upon it. The hands are yellowish in tone, not mellow, like the face, but are delicate in form, and correspond in character to the *elegance and ideality of the head* with *its refinement, its almost effeminacy of expression, plaintive, sad and rather startled* in its look. . . .

"We have thus the presentment of a *handsome, courtly gentleman, well formed and of good bearing, and apparently of high breeding, thoughtful and contemplative ;* so sincere in expression and presentation that *the picture cannot be regarded in any sense as a theatrical portrait.*[1]

Let us examine, for a moment, this careful description, written, be it remembered, by an expert who is convinced that the man of Stratford and "Shakespeare" are the same person; and see what results emerge.

In an earlier chapter of this book, as readers may remember, I discussed briefly the Grafton portrait of "Shakespeare," which turned out, upon examination, to be, apparently, a portrait of the Earl of Oxford, painted when he was about twenty-three or twenty-four years old; and I mentioned also the Welbeck Abbey portrait of Edward de Vere, probably painted by a Flemish artist, in Paris, during the Earl's stay there in 1575.

The Welbeck Picture represents a somewhat effeminate-looking, beardless young man, elaborately dressed in the fantastic fashion then affected by de Vere. At the moment of writing these words, I have beside me, upon my desk, a reproduction of that picture, and also of the "Ashbourne" portrait of "Shakespeare," which, as we have seen, is that of a bearded and very distinguished gentleman in middle life. Now after examining,

[1] All italics mine

and measuring, the relative positions and shapes of the features, and after making allowance for the passage of some twenty-two years of time, including change of appearance due to the growing of a beard, I have no hesitation in asserting, categorically, that the two portraits represent the same individual. Shape of head, contour of face, eyes, nose, and mouth, are all almost identical; and having obtained two reproductions of almost exactly the same size, we find that the two faces, including eyes, nose, and mouth, when cut out, can be transposed from one picture to the other, without substantially affecting either. I repeat my conviction, that they are portraits of the same man:[1] and I request the reader to examine carefully the two portraits which can be seen together at the beginning of this book.

Now there is no mystery attaching to the Welbeck (1575) portrait of Edward de Vere, nor is there reason for any, since, at that time, the Earl, though already known as a poet, had done little, if any, dramatic writing; and certainly did not adopt the pseudonym, "William Shakespeare," before the late 'eighties; but when the Ashbourne portrait was painted—judging by the inscription, and apparent age of the subject, during the Earl's forty-eighth year—de Vere, under strict oath of secrecy, as I have argued, had already been "Shakespeare" for about ten years; and—since his plays were then passing from the court, for which they were originally written, to the common stages—must perforce maintain his *incognito*, since neither he nor the Queen

[1] The Rev. Father, C. S. de Vere Beauclerk has sent to me a number of similar composite portraits of the Welbeck picture of de Vere, and the Grafton, Felton, Droeshout and Ashbourne portraits of "Shakespeare." Indiscriminate interchange of faces shows them to be all portraits of the same man—Edward de Vere.

would allow it to be publicly known, that the Lord Great Chamberlain of England was actively engaged as a working playwright for the public theatres.

Directly, then, that this Ashbourne portrait was kindly called to my attention, by Father de Vere Beauclerk as representing actually the Earl of Oxford, it became probable that, if we were right, there must have been some later manipulation of the portrait, both in the fashion of the ruff—which would change as between 1597 and 1611—and in the ascribed date of the painting. I turn, accordingly, to Mr. Spielmann's article, and find, as I had expected to find, that the picture, in his judgment, is "pure except in the ruff," and that, concerning the date, 1611, and the decoration of cross spears upon the book held in the right hand—of which more anon—" it would be *injudicious to decide that these are not of a later date, yet at the same time ancient additions.*" Mr. Spielmann, be it added, writes these words with no suspicion of the Oxford theory in his mind, although they fit exactly into such an hypothesis. My inference, therefore, was, and is, that these alterations were effected in 1611, to match the portrait with the original plot connived at in high places, to father the plays upon William Shaksper of Stratford.

Returning now to the "Ashbourne" portrait of Shakespeare, and its description—the first point we observe is, that feature after feature suggests a great nobleman for its original, whether we consider the gold-embroidered dress-belt, the gauntleted, embroidered gloves, with bands of gold, the gold-embroidered book,[1]

---

[1] Cf. Lady Capulet in *Romeo and Juliet*, I, iii.
   That book in many's eyes doth share the glory,
   That in gold clasps locks in the golden story.

with silk tie-ribbons, the gold signet-ring upon a delicate hand, the rich grey-black velvet doublet, the ideality of a thoughtful, contemplative head, or the general " presentment of a handsome courtly gentleman well formed and of good bearing, and apparently of high breeding." What compatibility is there here—if this, indeed, be Shakespeare—with the obscure provincial, of whom we know nothing, save dismal records of petty lawsuits, and dubious traffickings in malt? Mr. Spielmann, moreover, openly compares this portrait with another picture, not of a commoner, but of an Earl—the Earl of Morton, who died in 1581, some five years before young Shaksper had left Stratford—thus again, though without fathoming the significance of his words, throwing the portrait back just as our researches have, correspondingly, thrown the plays also back—into the style of the fifteen-'eighties, rather than of the eleventh year of the seventeenth century, which is the date recorded upon it. As for the plaintive, sad, effeminacy of the expression, to which marked attention is called, let me say that the very first comment made to me, by a highly intelligent American woman journalist, to whom I showed the 1575 portrait of de Vere, was, " What a feminine face ! " Moreover, all readers of my two last published books, *The Case for Edward de Vere as " Shakespeare "* and *The Oxford-Shakespeare Case Corroborated*, know that I have therein called attention, again and again, as I have also in these pages, to the repeated taunts of melancholy and " womanishness " levelled by Chapman, Jonson, and others, against Oxford as " Shakespeare."

We are getting " warm," as the children say, in our grown-up game of Elizabethan hide-and-seek ; yet evidences of identity, every whit as convincing, remain yet to be examined. Consider, for instance, that richly bound volume which "Shakespeare" holds in his hand. That hand wears on one of its fingers, a sealed ring, which Mr. Conway, in a written statement deposited by him with the portrait, at the time of the sale, in December 1929, claimed to be identical with that used by the Stratford man, upon the purchase-deed of the house in Blackfriars, 10 March, 1612–13. Unfortunately for his contention, however, the letters upon that seal, H.L., are the initials of Henry Lawrence, the scrivener who drew the deed in question, and who, therefore, if Mr. Conway be correct, is the historic original of this picture! Here is the old, old circumstance reappearing—that any attempt to identify plays, or portraits, with the Stratford man breaks down directly the ascertained facts, and resulting inferences, are honestly and intelligently faced and analysed.

Returning to this mysterious book held in "Shakespeare's" right hand, there confronts us immediately another remarkable point, namely that its inscription, and embroidered cover, "are painted as if of an orange tone of gold; and, unlike the rest of the paint, the orange gold stands in slight relief on the surface"— facts which develop the suggestion, already hinted at by the same writer, in his article in the *Encyclopædia Britannica*, that the inscriptions, including the date, the decoration of the book, the mask, and the cross spears, were added some years later; my inference from these facts being that such modifications of the original picture were made subsequently, for the sole purpose of transforming a portrait of "Shakespeare," the Earl of Oxford, into one of "Shakespeare," the spurious dramatist of

Stratford-on-Avon. Now, in quest of supporting evidence, let us further examine the book, with its rich binding, and crimson silk strings. From its style and luxurious make-up, Mr. Spielmann would set it down as a missal, or devotional volume, of some kind. Personally, for reasons which will immediately appear, I regard the book as a copy of Shakespeare's Sonnets, which were being written in 1597, about the time that I believe this portrait to have been painted. My reasons for so thinking are as follows.

In the year 1929 I published a book entitled *Shakespeare and Chapman as Topical Dramatists*, already quoted from in these pages, in which I showed, conclusively as I think, that Chapman's tragedy, *The Revenge of Bussy d'Ambois*, was a counterblast to Shakespeare's *Revenge of Hamlet*, and is packed with attacks upon Hamlet's philosophy, against and among which, in III, 4, of *Bussy*, is set an enigmatic, yet strangely eulogistic, reference to the Earl of Oxford himself. When writing that book, however—chiefly because I had not yet comprehended Chapman's practice, in common with some other Elizabethan writers, of inserting such words as "ever" and "never," by way of punning clues to concealed references to Edward Vere (E. Ver)—I overlooked the meaning of this important passage in *The Revenge of Bussy d'Ambois*, II, i :

"As these *high men* do love in all true grace,[1]
Their height being privilege to all things base
And as the foolish poet that still writ
All his most self-loved verse in paper royal,

---

[1] "High men" equals high-born men. "True" is probably a Vere pun.

Of parchment ruled with lead, smoothed with the
    pumice,
Bound richly up, and strung with crimson strings:
Never so blest as when he writ and read
The *ape-loved* issue of his brain, and never
But joying in himself, *admiring ever.*
Yet in his works behold him and he show'd
Like to a ditcher. . . ."

The manner of this attack—set, as it is, among obvious digs at " Shakespeare," and referring to a " foolish poet," a " high man "—meaning a man of high birth and position, and evidently of a dandified, theatrical type, since he wrote, on royal parchment, verses beloved by the apes, or actors, and, when he had finished them, sat back in his chair, " admiring E. Ver "—made it, to me, almost positively certain that the poet here referred to was Oxford, as " Shakespeare," and that the Sonnets, therefore—and Chapman, be it remembered, is the " rival poet " therein—were, as here described, richly bound up by their author, and " tied with crimson strings."

At the time of making that discovery, I did not so much as know the existence of the " Ashbourne " portrait; but a few weeks later, by a strange stroke of chance—if chance it be—I received from my friend and co-worker, Col. B. R. Ward, a copy of Mr. Robert Smith's article upon the " Ashbourne " picture, quoted from above, together with a reproduction of the portrait, in which I saw, for the first time, the hand holding the richly bound book, and read, with intense interest, though without surprise, the fact, foretold by myself a few weeks before, that Shakespeare's poems were

" Bound richly up and strung with crimson strings,"

and that, as usual, all the inferences were fitting in correctly with the assumption that Oxford was "Shakespeare," that Chapman knew him to be so, and that the "Ashbourne" portrait was simply a picture of Edward de Vere, painted, probably, in 1597, and "faked" a little, in 1611, to fit in with the elaborate plot, which fathered plays and poems alike upon William of Stratford. I had even, by a happy guess, foretold, to Col. Ward, that the crimson strings would be of *silk*!

The "Ashbourne" portrait of "Shakespeare," then, appears to be an original painting of the Earl of Oxford, done in 1597, one year before he wrote *King Lear*. Further, though the matter cannot be elaborated here, the Droeshout portrait, which was published twenty-six years later, at the head of the Folio "Shakespeare," seems to be a clumsily "faked" likeness of Oxford, with marked resemblances to the "Grafton," "Ashbourne," and "Flower" portraits of "Shakespeare," as well as to the "Welbeck" portrait of Edward de Vere. The Folio itself, be it not forgotten, is dedicated to two brother Earls, of whom one, Philip, Earl of Montgomery, was husband to Edward de Vere's daughter Susan; while the other, William, Earl of Pembroke, was her brother-in-law, who had once been engaged to another daughter of the Earl of Oxford, namely Lady Bridget Vere. Their mother, Lady Pembroke, who seems to have become one of the principals of the group responsible for the Shakesperean works, after Oxford's death, lived at Wilton House on the Avon, and may thus have been responsible for what many of us regard as Ben Jonson's reference, in the Folio, to the "Sweet Swan of Avon." All that, however, is "another story."

CHAPTER ELEVEN

CLOSING YEARS AND DEATH: 1599–1604

Lady Bridget Vere marries Francis Norris, 1599—Death of Burleigh 4 August, 1598—Relations between Burleigh and Oxford—The Earl's fame as Dramatist spreading—His Petition for Governorship of the Isle of Jersey—The Essex Rising—Oxford one of Essex's Judges—" Richard II " and the Essex Conspiracy—Oxford revises " Measure for Measure," with himself as the Duke—Jonson burlesques Oxford as Amorphus in " Cynthia's Revels " 1600, and lauds him as Virgil in " The Poetaster " 1601—Full recognition by Jonson of Oxford-Shakespeare Plays—Death of Queen Elizabeth—" Shakespeare's Company becomes the King's Players; and the Oxford-Worcester Company the Queen's Players—Oxford at the Welcoming of King James—His Salary confirmed by the new King—The Lord Great Chamberlain's Official Privileges at the Coronation—" Shakespeare" present at Performance of " As You Like It " at Wilton House 1603—Death of Edward de Vere, 6 June, 1604—Conclusion.

DURING the autumn of this year 1599, on 8 September, Oxford wrote to Burleigh:

"I do perceive how both my Lord and Lady (of Pembroke) do persevere which doth greatly content me, for Bridget's sake, whom always I wished a good husband, such as your Lordship and myself may take comfort thereby."

The proposed marriage, however, fell through; and in 1599 Lady Bridget Vere married Francis Norris, who succeded to the Barony of Rycote in 1600, upon the death of his grandfather, Lord Norris of Rycote.

We have reached a point in our story when many of its principal figures have left, or are about to leave, the world's stage. At the conclusion of Oxford's letter to Burleigh, above quoted, we read:

> "I am sorry that I have not an able body which might have served to attend on Her Majesty in the place where she is, being especially, there, whither, without any other occasion than to see your Lordship, I would always willingly go."

Oxford, then—himself evidently in weak health—was now wholly reconciled to his father-in-law, and, it would seem, so remained until the Lord Treasurer's death, which took place on 4 August, 1598, after a still unparalleled career of forty unbroken years, as Elizabeth's right-hand man and chief Minister to the Crown. Bitterly, and often, had Burleigh and Oxford disputed, in the Earl's young and headstrong days; bitterly also, in the characters of Hamlet and Pandarus, had the dramatist gibed at that "tedious old fool," his father-in-law, in language which travesties with cunning skill the style of Burleigh's own talk and letters; yet, despite these disputes and insults, despite the perpetual exasperations which Oxford's headstrong caprices and eccentric ways, his stormy tempers, and his biting tongue, his incurable addiction to the society and employment of "lewd" players, poets, and playwrights—a costly habit financed in part, by sales, for a song, of "goodly manors," the revenues of which, should, by evident right, have gone towards the maintenance of the three daughters, who become, instead, a charge upon Burleigh himself—despite such wrongs, inflicted by a son-in-law who had proved himself as bad a husband as father, Burleigh, it would seem, had always been as kind and considerate to Oxford as the difficult circumstances would allow.

CLOSING YEARS AND DEATH

He had been so, I think, less by way of willing concession to an æsthetic temperament, that himself was incapable of understanding, than from innate kindliness, and desire for peace, at any price, with a relative so gifted, and of so high degree. Also the Lord Treasurer was genuinely fond of his granddaughters, whom he remembered, in his will, as follows.

> "To Lady Bridget and the Lady Susan Vere, the daughters of my deceased daughter, the Lady Anne, Countess of Oxford, all my goods, money, plate and stuff that are or shall be remaining, at my death, within my bedchamber at Westminster, and in my two closets and any chambers thereto adjoining."

Bridget, Susan, and Robert Cecil were each to have an equal third of this, less £1,000 value to go to Elizabeth, Countess of Derby, and £1,000 to the expenses of Burleigh's own burial. In addition, the three granddaughters received, under Burleigh's will, specified gifts of plate, and half the residue of his money. Sir Robert Cecil took over from his deceased father the guardianship of the three young women, and, so far as we can judge from such correspondence as exists, remained, to the end, on friendly terms with his brother-in-law.

Oxford's fame as poet and dramatist, meanwhile, is fast spreading through London. In 1598 Francis Meres, who seems not to have been wholly in the secret of Oxford's identity with "Shakespeare," writes of the Earl as "the best for comedy among us," in a book, *Palladis Tamia*, which includes a list of "Shakespeare's" plays.[1] In 1599, John Marston wrote in *The*

---

[1] See Appendix C, Dr. Hotson's *Shakespeare versus Shallow*.

Scourge of Villainie (ninth Satire) concerning a concealed poet, Mutius:

> "Far fly thy fame
> Most, most, of me belov'd, whose silent name
> One letter bounds. Thy true judicial style
> I ever honour, and of my love beguile
> Not much my hopes, then thy unvalued worth
> Shall mount fair place, when Apes are turned forth—

lines which, I feel certain, refer to the secret works of Edward de Vere, whose unvalued worth, and silent name as hidden author, is, in fact, bounded by the single letter E; and the same allusion, I suppose, lies behind the words in the letter which Oxford's nephew, Robert Bertie—eldest son of Lord Willoughby and Lady Mary, Oxford's sister—wrote to his uncle, from the Continent, on 3 March, 1599, "Je n'ay trouve encores aucun subject assez digne de vous divertir de vos plus serieux affaires." The £1,000 a year that Oxford was receiving for his dramatic work did not go far enough; and in July 1600, we find him petitioning Sir Robert Cecil to obtain for him the appointment of Governor of the Isle of Jersey.

> "Although my bad success in former suits to Her Majesty have given me cause to bury my hopes in the deep abyss and bottom of despair, rather than now to attempt, after so many trials made in vain and so many opportunities escaped, the effects of fair words or fruits of golden promises; yet for that I cannot believe but that there hath been always a true correspondence of word and intention of Her Majesty, I do conjecture that with a little help that which of itself hath brought forth so fair blossoms will also yield fruit. . . . First for that I know Her Majesty doth give you good ear; then, for that

our houses are knit in alliance; last of all, the matter itself is such as nothing chargeth Her Majesty, sith it is a thing she must bestow upon some one or other. . . . If she shall not deign me in this, in an opportunity of time so fitting, what time shall I attend which is uncertain to all men unless in the graves of men there were a time to receive benefits and good turns from princes."

Oxford's petition, however, did not succeed. The plums of office, in this opening year of a new century, were falling into younger mouths; and it was to Sir Walter Raleigh that the appointment went. Undeterred, and still importunate, Oxford, in February 1601, wrote to his brother-in-law again, petitioning, this time, for the Presidency of Wales; and, having received an encouraging, though non-committal, answer from Cecil, wrote again, during the next month, to his powerful ally:

"My very good brother, I have received by H. Lok your most kind message, which I so effectually embrace, that what for the old love I have borne you—which I assure you was very great— what for the alliance which is between us, which is tied so fast by my children of your own sister: what for my own disposition to yourself, which hath been rooted by long and many familiarities of a more youthful time, there could have been nothing so dearly welcome unto me. Wherefore not as a stranger but in the old style I do assure you that you shall have no faster friend or well wisher unto you than myself, with either in kindness which I find beyond my expectation in you, or in kindred whereby none is nearer allied than myself, since of your sisters, of my wife only have you received nieces. I will say no more, for words in faithful minds are tedious; only this I protest, you shall do me wrong and yourself greater, if either through fables, which are mischievous, or conceit, which is dangerous, you think otherwise of me than humanity or consanguinity requireth."

This was the time of the Essex rising, an event which, though of much import to British drama, since it initiated a long vogue of conspiracy plays, extending over many years, is too well known to call for discussion in this book. All we need say here is that Oxford took no share whatever either in promoting or suppressing the rebellion, but was summoned from retirement to act as senior of the twenty-five noblemen who, after a trial the methods of which, judged by modern standards of justice, are open to strong criticism, unanimously found Essex and Southampton guilty.[1] Oxford's true feelings, concerning the whole sorry business, are not, and perhaps will never be, known, since he did not refer to it in any of his letters to Cecil, that have come down to us. It was to Oxford, however, that the Queen granted the lands of Sir Charles Danvers, executed for his share in the conspiracy; and there followed much correspondence upon the subject between Cecil and the Earl, who complains of the delay in getting his case, or "book," through the law-courts. We cannot be positively certain—though it is most probable—that Bacon and "Shakespeare" knew one another intimately well; but it is noteworthy that this correspondence, concerning Danver's lands, provides the only documentary link

---

[1] I agree with Capt. Ward that this jury of peers was probably "packed" by Cecil, who knew that Oxford had already thrown over the Essex-Southampton Section.

CLOSING YEARS AND DEATH

between the pair that we possess, when the Earl wrote to Cecil:

> "I am advised that I may pass my book from Her Majesty, if a warrant may be procured, to my cousin Bacon."

The escheat, however, did not pass to Oxford, through Bacon or any other.

Oxford, we have seen, excepting as judge, took no part whatever in assisting, or in suppressing, the Essex conspiracy; yet the trend of English drama, nevertheless, was affected, for many years, by that upheaval. Conspiracy plays became popular; one of the earliest of them, strangely enough, being Shakespeare's *Richard II*, of which the first two Quartos had appeared in 1597 and to which I have already alluded in this connexion. That play, dealing with the deposition of an English monarch, Elizabeth, very naturally, did not approve; since, as she pithily put it, "Know you not that myself am Richard," or, in other words, "If one monarch may be deposed, so also may another," yet *Richard II* was the very play performed by the Lord Chamberlain's Company upon the eve of the Essex conspiracy, under subsidy, it would seem, of the Earl of Southampton, himself a chief conspirator, and the peer to whom *Venus and Adonis* and *Lucrece* had been dedicated, about the same time that he had been named as a probable husband for Elizabeth Vere. These are dark matters, concerning which the whole truth has never come to light; but the letters that I have quoted, as also, it would seem, the internal evidence of the play, show conclusively—as also have other evidences brought forward in these pages—that Oxford, at this time, was dissatisfied with his treatment by Elizabeth. I cannot but draw the conclusion that though, psychologically considered, King Richard, and Achilles in *Troilus and Cressida*, are originally and at bottom de Vere himself, yet both characters were subsequently made to aim also at Essex—a conclusion strongly enforced, when we remember that Chapman's *Biron's Tragedy*, which I have shown elsewhere to be, in some sort, a counterblast and rival conspiracy play to *Richard II*, not only reveals close verbal imitations of that play, but twice mentions the Earl of Essex by name in the text; just as that counterblast to Hamlet, *The Revenge of Bussy d'Ambois*, makes elaborate personal reference to Oxford.[1]

Upon yet another play, I think, Oxford's mind was brooding at this time, when his aforetime friend, Southampton—escaped, almost as by miracle, from the block—was imprisoned in that very Tower of London, wherein Oxford, some twenty years before, during the most critical and dangerous year of his own life, had conceived, or written *Measure for Measure*, with its dark broodings upon death and after. Oxford, I feel sure, revised this play in 1600, writing into it, as I believe, among other passages, certain key-lines, in the form of a duologue, in III, ii, between Lucio, who is Arundel, and the Duke, who is Oxford himself, and who, exactly as does Kent in *King Lear*, returns, disguised for the purpose of better service, into his own country, at the age of fifty—that is in 1600—Kent's corresponding reappearance in *King Lear* having taken place at the age of forty-eight, in the year 1598.

---

[1] See my *Shakespeare and Chapman as Topical Dramatists*.

CLOSING YEARS AND DEATH

Lucio. Who, not the Duke ? (i.e. " detected for women ") yes, your beggar of fifty . . . the Duke had crotchets in him. He would be drunk too ; that let me inform you.

Duke. You do him wrong, surely.

Lucio. Sir, I was an inward of his : a shy fellow was the Duke and I believe I know the cause of his withdrawing.

Duke. What, I prithee, might be the cause ?

Lucio. No, pardon ; 'tis a secret must be locked within the teeth and the lips : but this I can let you understand, the greater file of the subject held the Duke to be wise.

Duke. Wise ! why, no question but he was.

Lucio. A very superficial, ignorant, unweighing fellow.

Duke. Either this is envy in you, folly, or mistaking : the very stream of his life and the business he hath helmed must, upon a warranted need, give him a better proclamation. Let him be but testimonied in his own bringings forth, and he shall appear to the envious a scholar, a statesman and a soldier ; or if your knowledge be more, it is much darkened in your malice.

Here, Lucio, this former " inward " or close friend of the Duke, provides unmistakable clues, including Oxford's impecuniousness (" your beggar "), his age, his " crotchets " or eccentricities, and his tendency to occasional drunkenness. All this is unmistakable, and no whit less significant is Lucio's point-blank refusal to answer the disguised Duke's question concerning the " cause of his withdrawing " :

" 'Tis a secret must be locked between teeth and lips."

We do not know to-day, any more than the mass of Elizabethans, I take it, knew, in their day, the determining cause of the Duke's withdrawal into private life; but I am positively certain, and have already argued, that the decision was not, at bottom, voluntary, but was a submission to the expressed wish of the Queen, whose private, and not yet penetrable, relations with Oxford supply, as I believe, the reason. Another cause, hinted at in both of what I have long believed to be the Earl's two favourite plays—*Hamlet* and *King Lear*—may be the occasional swelling, or overthrow into temporary dementia, of that vivid, and exuberant imagination, too often clouded by fits of deepest melancholy, that was always "Shakespeare's" mind. In *Hamlet*, the Prince of Denmark does but assume madness; in *King Lear*, the aged monarch, who is, in part, Oxford himself, becomes definitely and increasingly insane.

The duologue between Lucio and the Duke, however, makes it quite clear that, whatever may have happened, the mass of the Earl's contemporaries still held Oxford "to be wise," while the knowing ones recognized that "the business he hath helmed," namely the writing of the Shakesperean plays, "upon warranted need gives him a better proclamation," since those works, "his own bringings forth"—such, for example, as *Hamlet*, which *Measure for Measure*, as we have seen, again and again recalls—proclaim him "scholar, statesman and soldier," three of the qualities expressed in Ophelia's phrase concerning,

"The courtier's, soldier's, scholar's eye, tongue, sword."

It is regrettable that, in this matter, for three hundred and more years past, so many have spoken of Oxford, in the

CLOSING YEARS AND DEATH

Duke's own words, "unskilfully"; or even, when possessing knowledge, have permitted that knowledge to be "darkened in their malice," to the obscuring and complete distortion of the memory of Edward de Vere. The Duke's short soliloquy, following upon Lucio's departure, echoes exactly Hamlet's words to Ophelia concerning slanders:

> "back-wounding calumny
> The whitest virtue strikes."

These years 1600 and 1601 provide two more topical revues, of paramount literary interest and importance, in which Ben Jonson—becoming increasingly bold, as he realizes that the stars of Queen Elizabeth, and her Lord Great Chamberlain, are both descending the firmament—openly satirizes or applauds his former rival. Those two plays are *Cynthia's Revels*, and *The Poetaster*.

I cannot repeat here the elaborate analysis which I have made elsewhere[1] of the first-named of these plays; but, bearing in mind what we have just read, in *Measure for Measure*, concerning the Duke who "would be drunk," it is interesting to find, among the first references to Amorphus the Traveller, who, quite evidently, is Oxford, that, according to Crites, who is Jonson himself, de Vere has "become a water-drinker," and evidently, therefore, "means not to write verses"; from all of which I conclude that, though the "fountain of self love," from which Amorphus drank, be metaphorical, the Earl did in actual fact add physical temperance to those spiritual reforms which we have seen adumbrated in *Measure for Measure*, and also in the closing sublimities of *King Lear*.

---

[1] *The Oxford-Shakespeare Case Corroborated.*

As for the "entertainment," "cashiering," "countenancing" and "catechizing" of that "page of good timber," from Arden Forest, Cos, the Whetstone, we have already deciphered the meaning of such references by Amorphus to him; and for the talk of Mercury, concerning Oxford, in II, i, of *Cynthia's Revels*, we have a vivid, if burlesqued, picture of the eccentric Earl, now bearded, as we have seen him in the "Ashbourne" portrait of "Shakespeare," strolling, tooth-pick in mouth, into a London ordinary—"the first Sunday of his silk stockings when he is most neat and new"—and therefore still the dandy at fifty—and with elaborate manner, and in the very mint of compliment, addressing "the wife of the ordinary," exactly as though she were a court lady; just as Touchstone and Autolycus do the rustics in the plays; and—as one would expect of "Shakespeare"—usurping to himself rather more than an even share of the talk. This still fantastic Earl even interests himself, at fifty, in strange Italian sauces and dishes, such as anchovies, maccaroni, bovoli, fagioli and caviare, "because he loves them," as again we should expect to be true of "Shakespeare" thoroughly italianized.

The third act shows us the Earl, in Hamlet-guise, as a coach and patron of his actors:

" 'Tis well enter'd sir. Stay, you are come on (the stage) too fast; your pace is too impetuous. . . First you present yourself thus"—

and so forth. There follows another burlesque of the balcony-scene in *Romeo and Juliet*, already burlesqued, a year before, by the same author, in *Every Man Out of His*

Humour; and evidently with success, or the trick would not have been so soon repeated.

"I am at your beauty's appointment, bright angel"

is almost the exact expression used by Romeo to Juliet in II, ii, following which we get the central, and most illuminating, point of the whole jest—that subtle game of *Riddles or Purposes*, played by the principal characters, and taking the form of "substantives and adjectives"; the episode comprising a series of elaborate witticisms upon certain extremely popular (Shakesperean) plays, which, "not content to be generally noted in courts,' where they were first produced, will:

"press forth on common stages and brokers' stalls [i.e. the plays offered for sale in quarto form] to the public view of the world"—

that last word standing, I take it, for the Globe Theatre, now, in this year 1601, completed, and presenting Shakesperean plays, with great success. Lastly, we are informed that the man who "did it" was "a traveller," otherwsie the individual who is described as a Traveller in this play, namely Amorphus the Deformed, otherwise Oxford himself, the star about which the whole satire revolves.

To conclude, we are given a palpable burlesque of the duel-scene in *Hamlet*—"the Dor the palpable Dor"—which is Jonsonese for "a hit a palpable hit," followed by a very charming confession, spoken by Crites-Jonson, that however much rivalry, and other reasons, including —though we are not specifically told so—a little jealousy, may have led him to deride Shakespeare, and to burlesque the plays, which are here symbolized, once more, as a lady, Philautia or Self-love—nevertheless,

> "I do love you in some sort do you conceive? and though I am no monsieur, nor no signior, and do want, as they say, logic and sophistry and good words, to tell you why it is so; yet by this hand and by that candle it is so: and though I be no bookworm, nor one that deals by art, to give you rhetoric and causes, why it should be so, or make it good it is so? yet, d—n me, but I know it is so."

This, with its obvious parody of Hamlet's style and phrase:

> "I have of late—but wherefore I know not lost all my mirth,"

is interesting, as affording proof of the skill with which Jonson had learned to borrow his rival's thunder, who, only some three years before, had mocked at Ben's own bluntness of style, as Ajax in *Troilus and Cressida*.

Cynthia's Revels, then, closes upon a note of mildly patronizing, yet quite acceptable, kindness, upon Jonson's part, towards Oxford—a feeling which, now that the Earl is drawing near to the close of his life's work, will deepen as time goes by; the passage of years naturally diminishing rivalries and personal feuds. Jonson's qualified, and almost grudging, approval of "Shakespeare," expressed in *Cynthia's Revels*, will develop, in *The Poetaster*, to whole-hearted, though keenly discriminating praise.

The occasion—for reality, I feel sure, lies behind the episode which I shall try here to interpret—is Virgil's—otherwise Oxford's—visit to Cæsar, whom I take to stand for the Queen, or some other great personage—Virgil having specially left the Campagna, which is just outside Rome, for that purpose, just as Oxford must leave Hackney, which is at about a similar relative distance from the English capital.

Our recluse, as my readers know, has been working, at intervals, upon the Sonnets, probably ever since his second marriage in 1593. By 1601, the date of *The Poetaster*, he has, it would seem, finished these " Æneids," as Cæsar calls them[1]; and the Emperor longs, " like another soul," to enjoy verses in which the poet unlocks not the minds of other men, but his own heart, for the delectation of his private friends. Oxford, then, is coming to London to read them ; and before his arrival Cæsar asks Horace-Jonson to tell him his " true thought of Virgil." This is the answer that he gets :

> *Hor.* I judge him of a rectified spirit,
> By many revolutions of discourse,
> (In his bright reason's influence), refined
> From all the tartarous moods of common men ;
> Bearing the nature and similitude
> Of a right heavenly body ; most severe
> In fashion and collection of himself ;
> And then, as clear and confident as Jove."

Gallus, standing for I know not whom, echoes, as follows this fine eulogy of our poet, whose " bright reason " has been tutored, both technically and spiritually, in the school of long experience. The lines are aimed obviously at the Sonnets :

[1] Long before interpreting *The Poetaster*, I had satisfied myself, from other evidence, that the Sonnets were substantially completed very soon after 1600.

> "And yet so chaste and tender is his ear,
> In suffering any syllable to pass,
> That he thinks may become the honor'd name
> Of issue to his so examined self,
> That all the lasting fruits of his full merit,
> In his own poems he doth still distaste."

I commend those lines to the attention of all who suppose that Shakespeare, as a poet, cared nothing for the verdict of posterity; and I follow them with these words of Tibullus, written in praise, not of the Sonnets, but of the plays:

> "But to approve his works of sovereign worth,
> This observation, methinks, more than serves,
> And is not vulgar. That which he hath writ,
> Is with such judgment labour'd and distill'd
> Through all the needful uses of our lives,
> That could a man remember but his lines,
> He should not touch at any serious point,
> But he might breathe his spirit out of him."

Such, so far as I know, is the first contemporary criticism of Shakespeare that recognizes the applicability of some line or other in the plays, to almost every conceivable circumstance of human life. Another interesting opinion, expressed by Horace-Jonson, concerns Shakespeare's learning; his conclusion being identical with ours, that, though the poet's scholarship is not of the academic type, and shines with no "school-like gloss," his poetry is "so ramm'd with life," that it must needs gather strength with the passing years,

> "And live hereafter more admired than now."

How much more admired than "now," Shakespeare was destined, in the fullness of years, to be, not even Jonson could possibly conceive or foretell.

Virgil-Oxford himself then enters—all present rising to receive him—and is led by Cæsar to a chair, "of purpose set" for him to read his poem in; which he consents to do, after protesting that, but for Cæsar's insistence, he "would not show them," because of their essentially intimate and private nature. Cæsar, in fact, describes them as being precisely what modern judgment has almost unanimously declared them:

> "A human soul made visible in life,
> And more refulgent in a senseless paper
> Than in the sensual compliment of kings."

It is a significant fact that Oxford, who, some two years before, in 1599, had taken partisan action in the battle of the poets, by "purging" Jonson and Chapman in *Troilus and Cressida*, is here made, by that same Jonson, to act as judge between himself (Jonson) on one side, and Crispinus and Demetrius on the other; the last named couple, I take it, being Marston and Dekker, both of them prominent warriors in the "Poetomachia," and part authors of *Histriomastix*, another Troilus-and-Cressida play of 1599, in which burlesqued allusion is openly made to the screened poet, who *shakes* his furious *speare*. Attacks and counter-attacks, in the War of the Poets, were, however, always, to some extent, a mere dramatic game, played for purposes of notoriety and advertisement, especially among the smaller fry.

The Poetaster, then, probably reflects an actual reconciliation between Jonson and Oxford, in the year 1601, celebrated, it may be, by a convivial meeting or two, at the "Boar's Head," a hostelry that now hangs out its sign prominently into our story.

Among the eulogistic comments passed by Jonson upon Oxford's plays, this one will be remembered, that his poesy—a word meant, I take it, to include his *dramatis personæ*—is " ramm'd with life." Now of all the multitudinous characters in the plays, the one individual to whom that description most fully applies is Falstaff; and it is precisely to the Falstaff comedies, and to their setting, that we are taken by a noteworthy event of 1602.

The Shakesperean plays, by this time, have, in Jonson's phrase, pressed forth from the court to the " common stages and broker's stalls," or, in other words, are not only being acted now in the public, as well as the private, theatres, but are also being sold, in quarto editions, by the London book-sellers ; and among those quartos the King Henry plays have been prominent. *Henry IV*, Part One, was first printed in February 1598, and Part Two in 1600; *King Henry V* appeared also in 1600, and a pirated edition of *The Merry Wives of Windsor* in 1602; this last having been written, according to tradition, at the request of Queen Elizabeth, who wanted to see Falstaff in love.

Now I need hardly remind my readers that, in connexion with the escapades of Falstaff, Prince Hal, and their boon companions, as set forth in the above-mentioned plays, there is one building in London, namely the " Boar's Head " tavern, in Eastcheap, which instantly comes to mind : though the Editors of the First Folio, very significantly, and for obvious reasons, have suppressed all mention of the tavern, in their stage directions, without, however, eliminating hints that remain plainly intelligible in the texts.

CLOSING YEARS AND DEATH

"You shall find me in Eastcheap," says Falstaff; "I shall command all the good lads in Eastcheap," says Prince Hal [1]; and in the second part of the same play, the Prince asks, concerning the fat knight, "Doth the old boar feed in the old frank?" Further, Gayton's *Festivous Notes*, 1654, alludes to "Sir John of the Boares Head in Eastcheap"[2]; nor must we forget that the Boar was one of the supporters of Oxford's own coat-of-arms, and one of the names by which he had been known at Court. It is, surely, therefore, a most remarkable fact, that, in this year 1602, the Earls of Oxford and Worcester amalgamated their companies; and, at the Earl of Oxford's particular request, the Queen is now "requiring" the Lord Mayor of London to allot officially, to the joint company, their favourite playing-place, "The Boar's Head." On the last day of March 1602, Lords Buckhurst, Worcester, and others, write from the Court at Richmond:

> "And as the other companies that are allowed, namely of me the Lord Admiral and the Lord Chamberlain, be appointed their certain houses, and one and no more to each company, so we do straitly require that this third company be likewise to one place. And because we are informed that the house called the Boars Head is the place they have especially used and do best like of, we do pray and require you that the said house, namely the Boar's Head, may be assigned unto them, and that they be very straitly charged to use and exercise their plays in no other but that house."

Now the Lord Chamberlain's Company, mentioned in

---

[1] *1 King Henry IV*, I, iv, and II, ii.
[2] J. T. Looney, "*Shakespeare*" *Identified*, pp. 398-403.

this letter, and, apparently, at this time, in what Mr. Looney calls "a state of suspended animation," is the company traditionally associated with Shakespeare's plays, and destined to be honoured, in May 1603, by transference to the patronage of the new king, with corresponding bestowal of the name, The King's Players; while, in the autumn of 1603, the united Oxford-Worcester companies, after acting for a while, under Henslowe, at the Rose, are transferred to the patronage of Queen Anne, and become the Queen's Players: in other words the two companies connected with "Shakespeare," and with Oxford, are taken over, respectively, by the new King and Queen, immediately upon their accession to the throne! Reverting to the "Boar's Head," it would be deeply interesting to know what particular play it was, that Oxford's actors were thus putting on? We cannot, of course, definitely say; but probabilities point to its being a new version of *Merry Wives*.

In November 1602, Lady Oxford was the victim of a little accident, due, no doubt, to the then appalling state of the public roads, and, perhaps, worth recalling, in days when, though the roads are almost perfect, the rivers of traffic that roar and hurtle along them are so imperfectly controlled that far more lives are lost upon them, yearly, than were sacrificed in any pitched battle of Elizabeth's day. Thus Lady Oxford, in a letter to Dr. Julius Cæsar, concerning a Cause in the Court of Requests, of which he was then Master. The Countess expresses her regret at "now being by a late mischance in my coach prevented from the hope of any present opportunity to meet you at the court." Coaches, as Capt. Ward reminds us, in this connexion, were first introduced into England about 1566, by the Earl of

CLOSING YEARS AND DEATH

Arundel—the uncle of the Earl of Arundel at whose trial, in 1589, Oxford had been one of the judges—and were promptly welcomed by the Queen, who was one of the first to use the then equivalent of a Rolls Royce.

Elizabeth, who was already ailing at the time of Lady Oxford's little mischance, died in March 1603. We have seen Oxford bearing the canopy over the living, and victorious, Queen, when she trod the aisle of St. Paul's on the occasion of the Armada Celebration, in 1588; and it may be taken as almost certain that, though the names are not mentioned, he was one of the six Earls who bore the canopy over the coffin, within which lay the body of the dead monarch.

Shortly before Elizabeth's successor, James, King of Scots, reached Theobalds, after first setting foot upon English soil on 5 April, Lord Oxford wrote to his brother-in-law, Robert Cecil, now Lord Burleigh, inquiring as to what arrangements were being made to receive the new king in London, and explaining that although, by reason of his "infirmity," and of the distance of his house from London, he cannot "at every occasion be present as were fit," he had, nevertheless, on receipt of an urgent summons to Whitehall,

> "hasted so much as I came to follow you into Ludgate, though through press of people and horses I could not reach your company as I desired, but followed as I might."

A vivid picture this, of that same frenchified nobleman, whom we have seen, at thirty-one years of age, about the time that he was writing *Romeo and Juliet*, airily riding down the Strand, towards Westminster, possibly from the theatre at Blackfriars, "on a footcloth nag, apparelled in a French ruff, a French cloak, a French hose, and in his hand a great fan of feathers, bearing them up (very womanly) against the side of his face"—

now, at fifty-five years of age, becoming infirm, with his work for England done, and only one year of life before him—no longer extravagantly clothed, in Gallic fashion, but in black velvet, rich yet sober—a somewhat frail yet proud and noble figure, pushing his horse along that same street, from Ludgate towards Whitehall, through the swarming, jostling throngs gathered boisterously to welcome the new monarch, whose general and ready acceptance has lifted from the land all threat and shadow of dreaded civil war. Thus Oxford's letter concludes:

"I cannot but find great grief in myself to remember the Mistress which we have lost, under whom both you and myself from our greenest years have been in a manner brought up; and although it hath pleased God after an earthly kingdom to take her up into a more permanent and heavenly state, wherein I do not doubt but she is crowned with glory, and to give us a Prince wise, learned, and enriched with all virtues, yet the long time which we spent in her service, we cannot look for so much left of our days as to bestow upon another, neither the long acquaintance and kind familiarities wherewith she did use us, we are not ever to expect from another Prince as denied by the infirmity of age and common course of reason. In this common shipwreck mine is above all the rest, who least regarded though often comforted of all her followers she hath left to try my fortune among the alterations of time and chance, either without sail whereby to take the advantage of any prosperous gale, or with anchor to ride till the storm be overpast. There is nothing left to my comfort but the excellent virtues and deep wisdom wherewith God hath endued our new Master and Sovereign Lord, who doth not come amongst us as a stranger but as a natural Prince, succeeding by right of blood and inheritance, not as a conqueror but as the true shepherd of Christ's flock to cherish and comfort them.

"Wherefore I most earnestly desire you of this favour, as I have written before, that I may be informed from you concerning these points. And thus recommending myself unto you, I take my leave.

"Your assured friend and unfortunate brother-in-law

"E. Oxenford."

Exactly when Lord Oxford first met his new sovereign we do not know; but this, I think, may be taken as certain, that the acceptances of Fortinbras and of Albany, as the rightful heirs, in the closing scenes of *Hamlet*, and of *King Lear*, read with the letter above quoted, all point to the Earl's whole-hearted acceptance of the accession of King James; and although Oxford's phrase, "In this common shipwreck mine is above all the rest," reveals deep-seated anxiety concerning the treatment to be meted out to him by the son of that Mary Queen of Scots, among whose judges Oxford had sat, his fears happily proved to be unfounded. Almost immediately, indeed, after the accession of James, the Earl's letters to Cecil take on a more optimistic tone, when he realizes that his title to the Stewardship of the Forest of Essex, vainly sought, and long since abandoned by him in despair, has been laid before the new king.

"Till the 12th of Henry VIII," de Vere reminds his brother-in-law, "mine ancestors have possessed the same, almost since the time of William Conqueror ... but Her Majesty refused the same and by no means would hear it. So that by this and the former means I have been thus long dispossessed. But I hope truth is subject to no prescription, for truth is truth, though never so old, and time cannot make that false which once was true."

The Earl's optimism was justified; for on 18 July, the King granted to him Bailiwick or custodianship of the Forest of Essex, and the Keepership of Havering House, and further, appointed him, about the same time, to the Privy Council, and in the following year renewed his annual salary of £1,000 a year from the Exchequer, in exactly the same words used by Elizabeth in the original grant. James who was himself, at least, a dabbler in letters, a patron of literary men, and a keen enthusiast of stage-plays and masques, thus proved himself more generous to his most gifted courtier and subject than ever that royal lady, his predecessor upon the throne of England, had been. When, on July 25, 1603, King James and Queen Anne were together crowned and anointed at Westminster, by Archbishop Whitgift, the Earl of Oxford, as Lord Great Chamberlain, claimed, as follows, his *ex-officio* rights in the matter of personal attendance upon His Majesty, on the morning of the Coronation.

"Edward de Vere Earl of Oxford, asks that as he is Great Chamberlain of England of the fee of our most dread Lord the King, that it should please the King that he should likewise at the Coronation, as formerly he was permitted, to do the said office

CLOSING YEARS AND DEATH

and services as he and his ancestors have formerly done. . . . that the said Earl on the day of the said Coronation, on the morning before the King rises, ought to enter into the chamber where the King lies, and bring him his shirt, and stockings, and underclothing. And that the said Earl and the Lord Chamberlain for the time being together on that day ought to dress the King in all his apparel. And that he may take and have all his fees, profits, and advantages due to this office. . . . That is to say forty yards of crimson velvet for the said Earls robes for that day . . . then the Earl should have the bed where the King lay on the night before the Coronation, and all the apparel of the same, with the coverlet, curtains, pillows, and the hangings of the room, with the King's nightgown, in which he was vested the night before the Coronation. He also asks [that he should have the same privileges] as his ancestors [who] from time immemorial served the noble progenitors of our Lord the King with water before and after eating the day of the Coronation, and had as their rights the basins and towels and a tasting cup . . . as appears in the records of the Exchequer.

"My Lord Steward adjudicates to the aforesaid Earl the fees, services . . . of presenting water to the Lord the King before and after dinner on the day of the Coronation; and to have the basins, tasting cups and towels. As for the other fees the said Earl is referred to examine the records of the Jewel House and the Kings Wardrobe."[1]

One autumn day, in 1603, between October 24 and 12 December, as we know from a note made by William Cory during a visit at some time in the nineteenth century,

[1] Col. S. P Dom. James I (July 7, 1603)

there were notable doings at Wilton House, the ancestral home of the Pembrokes.

"This house," said Lady Herbert to Cory, "is full of interest: above us is Wolsey's room: we have a letter from Lady Pembroke to her son, telling him to bring James I from Salisbury, to see *As You Like It;* 'we have the man Shakespeare with us.'"

Lady Pembroke, it seems, wished to cajole the King, in Raleigh's behalf: and his Majesty duly came to Wilton House.

That letter was never printed, and is now, unfortunately, lost; but it is evident that "Shakespeare," whose name seems to have been underlined in the original, did, in the autumn of 1603, make a journey from Hackney, to visit his old friends the Pembrokes, with whom his own house had been so nearly allied in marriage, and who are to be named, twenty years later, in the Folio edition of the plays. Thus de Vere saw acted—apparently in the King's presence, and probably for the last time—his own comedy of Arden, written some fourteen years before, and presenting himself in the double characters of Jaques and Touchstone. We have seen, when considering *Troilus and Cressida*, a reference to certain "great possessors" of the Shakesperean manuscript plays. One of these was, probably, Lady Pembroke herself, the script of *As You Like It* having come into her possession, it may be, during the late fifteen-'nineties, when she had come near to being mother-in-law to Bridget de Vere.

This is the last record that has come down to us of any journey from home by Oxford; and the end is now at hand. The Earl left no will; but on 18 June, 1604, he granted the custody of the Forest of Essex—prized by him, because his ancestors had held it "almost since

CLOSING YEARS AND DEATH

the time of William Conqueror" on to Henry VIII—to his son-in-law, Francis, Lord Norris, and to his (Oxford's) cousin, Sir Francis Vere, who had just returned to England, after twenty years of continuous campaigning in the Low Countries. It is, surely, a remarkable thing, that during these last days of his life, de Vere's thoughts seem, instinctively, to turn towards those favourite cousins of his, Francis and Horatio, whom I take to be Francisco and Horatio of the *Hamlet* play: and, if I am right, there is much more than mere coincidence in the fact that to Horatio, at the close of the tragedy, he commits the charge of his "wounded name," and that the Prince whose soul's election had sealed Horatio for itself, should select the same tongue also " to tell my story " to an else uncomprehending world. Nor again is it by chance that, at the close of the other longest and most nobly wrought Shakesperean tragedy, *King Lear*, that plaintive fool, " Lear's Shadow," lies dead, and will jest no more, in rhyme or prose; or that his royal master, soon to go the way his fool has gone, finds all " dark " and " cheerless " here: nor even that Kent, though not yet fifty years of age, as he tells us, will accept, at the new King, Albany's, hand, no rule, nor any charge for the sustainment of the " gored state "; answering simply, when requested, by King Albany, to share the governmental authority with Cornwall:

"I have a journey, Sir, shortly to go;
My master calls me, I must not say no."

On 6 June, 1604, Edward de Vere died at Hackney, and was buried in the Church of St. Augustine, of which the tower alone now stands. The immediate cause of death may have been the plague, since the words, "ye plague," are written in the margin of the page of the Parish Register, in which the entry of his burial occurs. The Earl's grave was marked by neither stone nor name; but when his widowed Countess died in 1612, she intimated in her will her desire

> "to be buried in the Church of Hackney . . . as near unto the body of my late dear and noble lord and husband as may be: only I will that there be in the said church erected for us a tomb fitting our degree."

This must be the tomb described by John Strype, lecturer in the Church of St. Augustine, from 1689 to 1723, in his *Continuation* of Stow's Survey (1721):

> "On the north side of the chancel, first an ancient Table Monument with a fair grey marble. There were coats-of-arms on the side, but torn off."

A drawing of that monument, made during the eighteenth century, and showing the place originally occupied by the two coats-of-arms, which were probably those of Vere and Trentham, still exists, and can be seen in the Public Library at Hackney. It is a circumstance wholly consonant with the facts, and the issue, of a mysterious life, that, excepting the two coats-of-arms, no inscription or other declaration of identity seems to have been marked upon the tomb.

Shakespeare has gone; but our story is not quite finished yet. Some four months after the Earl of Oxford's passing, on 12 October, 1604, William Herbert, now Earl of Pembroke, wrote to his father-in-law, the Earl of Shrewsbury, a letter telling how, "after long love and many changes, my brother (Philip Herbert)

CLOSING YEARS AND DEATH

on Friday last was privately contracted to my Lady Susan (Vere)," and how, "yesterday the King, taking the whole matter on himself, made peace on all sides."

King James, besides establishing himself peace-maker, became also royal provider; for on 24 October, Rowland White informed the Earl of Shrewsbury, by letter, that the King had ordered the grant of " certain lands to above the value of one thousand pounds per annum for Sir Philip Herbert and his heirs for ever." By 18 December, there is made " great provision for Cockpit, to entertain the King at home, and of masks and revels against the marriage of Sir Philip Herbert and Lady Susan Vere," which took place on St. John's day. Further there must be set down here the significant fact that, during the season of 1604-5, beginning four months after Oxford's death, there were given eight court-performances of Shakesperean plays, including *Othello, Merry Wives of Windsor, Measure for Measure, The Comedy of Errors, Love's Labour's Lost, Henry V*, and *The Merchant of Venice*, which is three times as many as had ever been given at court during any previous season; and that, soon after 9 April, 1604, William Shaksper of Stratford-upon-Avon withdrew from the King's Players, and " quitted that department of the (theatrical) professsion."

Nineteen years after the marriage above recorded, namely in 1623, that same Philip Herbert who, with his wife, Susan de Vere, King James had thus delighted to honour, received, with his brother, William, Earl of Pembroke, the dedication of the first Shaksperean Folio, containing opposite to Ben Jonson's enigmatic verses, a portrait of " Shakespeare," which turns out, upon examination, to be a clumsily contrived mask-portrait of Edward de Vere. Can any doubt exist, henceforth, concerning the names of those noble families, who were the " grand possessors " of now vanished manuscripts of Shakespeare's plays ?

At precisely the same time, during the years 1622 and 1623, appear works by Francis Bacon, Viscount St. Alban, a cousin of Oxford's first wife, Anne Cecil, and related, therefore, to Susan, Countess of Montgomery and her sister. In 1625 Ben Jonson, who, as we have seen, was, from the first, deep in the secret of Shakesperean authorship, and had contributed enigmatical introductory matter to the Folio, drafted his comedy *The Staple of News*, wherein, with the publication of the Folio topically in mind, he seems to hold up to comparison the respective literary merits of Francis Bacon and Edward de Vere ; certain characters of the play, apparently being partisans of the scientist-lawyer, others favouring rather the claims of that " vain oracle of the bottle," who—the bottle being one of the many de Vere badges—seems to stand for the 17th Earl of Oxford.[1]

. . . . .

Several times of late I have visited Hackney, where " Shakespeare " completed his life's work, and lies buried. Here, within that populous borough, standing on the north side of the railway bridge that crosses Mare Street, just where, two hundred years ago, the road ran through a pond, at which you might water your horses, looking left and right, up the slope and down, one's view comprises, on either side of the steel bridge, a double line of shops, banks, and flaming cinemas, before which moves a sliding frieze of busy foot-passengers obstructed, at many hours, by lounging groups of

[1] Ben Jonson and the First *Folio*, pp. 36-39, by W. L. Goldsworthy.

dark uniformed bus-conductors off duty. Within the carriage-way itself, burly blue policemen halt, with one gesture, and let loose upon you with another, whole fleets of snorting vehicles, and rattling and roaring lorries, swirling purple trams, and thunderous scarlet omnibuses. No vestige at all of the antique world, one would say, can exist among these clamorous trappings of modernity; and yet, not so; for turning here, behind the formal opulence of the Midland Bank's façade, stands one grey, weather-beaten Gothic tower, all that remains of the parish church of St. Augustine, at Hackney, within which were laid the bodies of the Earl of Oxford and his Countess.

A delectable spot to linger in, on this morning of May, are these green encircling lawns, hushed and stilly, after the strident clamour of the street; its quietude broken only by a group of children playing about the paths, and shying an occasional surreptitious stone at the chestnut-trees, leafy all, and in full flower, though altogether fruitless as yet. For the rest, no other visible animation saving an old Adam-gardener or two, each with broom in hand, leisurely gleaning a sprinkle of cut grass from the lawns; a few loiterers dawdling beneath the plane trees; a pair of neat nursemaids gossiping beside their sleeping charges, in the dappled shadow of poplar and elm; and, drowsing here and there upon the seats, those nondescripts in degree, who always, and in a very place, have upon their hands a surplus of that elusive commodity, Time.

The minutes pass; midday clangs from the steeples and towers of Hackney; but none here, I suppose, ever dream, or would even greatly care to know, that the tower above them, upon whose face, seen through idly swaying boughs, flickers the spring sunlight and shadow, is the tower beneath which " Shakespeare " worshipped ; and that the very ground, upon which they tread, has been pressed by his feet, and now covers his coffined dust.

No more than a few minutes distant from St. Augustine Church, at the corner where Kenninghall Road runs into the Upper Clapton Road, stands the last home of Lord Oxford and his Countess—" King's Place," now known as Brooke House, modernized, and much altered by the insertion of a wide-gabled front, of much later date than the rest; yet some parts of the red-brick façade, a few of the chimney-stacks, perhaps, especially the long, tiled ridge of the Elizabethan roof, are still, in some degree, recognizable for what is shown upon the old drawings of the mansion in which kings once held their courts. Within, though " fallen and changed," certain structures of de Vere's day yet stand ; so that, by the elimination of ten or a dozen partitions, there could be restored the great open gallery, some one hundred and sixty feet long, in which, it is no fantastic guess to suppose, many of the later sonnets may have been written, and some of the world's noblest plays revised.

To-day, Brooke House, for so long time Shakespeare's home, is fulfilling its strange and perverse destiny, as an asylum for mental deficients ; and not very long since, I read, scrawled with a lump of white chalk upon one of its doors, by some errand-boy innocent so far as Shakespeare is concerned, of ironic intent, the words : " This is the door of the barmy house."

Neither in greatness, nor in less than greatness either, must madness unwatched go ; yet, if I have written truth in this book, England should show gratitude enough for her noblest national possession, which is "Shakespeare," to win back, from such a decadence, the home in which, probably, he wrote *King Lear*, and in which, quite certainly, his dying faculties exerted themselves to weave into that play, as also into *Hamlet*, his farewell messages to a world, which, alike through numberless failures, immeasurable sufferings, and triumphant, though then unrecognized achievements, had never fulfilled his heart's desire.

Surely we have some responsibility in this matter; and thereupon, not long since, my fancy lingered, musing, while the midday sun splashed the paths with leaf-shadow, while the morning breeze scattered, over those trim footways, the last, pink blossoms of the May, and swayed the fresh green boughs of the lime-trees overhanging the grim and formidable boundary walls of Brooke House.

APPENDIX A

THE RELATIONS BETWEEN OXFORD AND QUEEN ELIZABETH

EVER since beginning an intensive study of the Life of Edward de Vere as "Shakespeare," it has been more and more insistently borne in upon me that, if we could fully understand them, Oxford's personal relations with Queen Elizabeth would provide the clue to a complete understanding of his life, and particularly to his mysterious withdrawal from court in 1589, the secret of which, as Lucio phrases it in *Measure for Measure*, must be "locked between teeth and lips."

The references, in the plays and poems, to love affairs between de Vere and Elizabeth are many; but they are self-contradictory, and difficult wholly to reconcile with one another.

First of all, there is *Two Gentlemen of Verona*, obviously dealing with incidents closely following upon Oxford's return from Italy in 1576, and dramatizing himself as Valentine and Silvia as Queen Elizabeth. In II, i, Speed and Valentine duologue thus concerning Silvia, the possessor, by the way (as Queen Elizabeth, I mean) of a notoriously painted face, which was already, by reason of years, being denied the too candid truth of the mirror.

> *Val.* I mean that her beauty is exquisite, but her favour infinite.

APPENDIX A 363

Speed. That's because one is painted, and the other out of all count.

Val. How painted? and how out count?

Speed. Marry, sir, so painted, to make her fair, that no man counts of her beauty.

Val. How esteem'st thou me? I account of her beauty.

Speed. You never saw her since she was deform'd.

Vale. How long hath she been deform'd?

Speed. Ever since you loved her.

Vale. I have loved her ever since I saw her; and still I see her beautiful.

Speed. If you love her, you cannot see her.

Vale. Why?

Speed. Because Love is blind. O that you had mine eyes.

Vale. What should I see then?

Speed. Your own present folly, and her passing deformity.

Now in my last book, *The Oxford-Shakespeare Case Corroborated*, I argue, conclusively, I hope, that it was de Vere's persistent habit to drive home his identity, in important passages, by the insertion into his texts of such words as "ever" and "never," by way of puns upon his name, E. Ver, a trick of which I have already given an instance in this book (pp. 83-4). The passage above quoted seems to be one of these; four of its lines, in my opinion, being correctly readable thus.

Speed. You, E. Ver, have not seen her since she was deformed.

Vale. How long hath she been deform'd?

Speed. Since you, E. Ver, loved her.

Vale. I, E. Ver, have loved her since I saw her.

Here you have the usual "E. Ver" puns linked with use of the word "deform'd," which I have shown to be one of the stock names for Oxford. Connect the now, I hope, obvious meaning of these words with Speed's subsequent remark concerning :

> "Your own (Valentine's) present folly, and her passing deformity—

and what other conclusion is possible than this—that Silvia-Elizabeth's "passing deformity," or, in other words, maternity, was the work of Edward de Vere. Several married ladies, to whom I have submitted this passage, agree with me that, accepting my general method of Shakesperean interpretation, no other meaning is possible. I am aware that Chamberlin's *Private Character of Queen Elizabeth* has convinced many that the Queen could not, and never did, bear a child ; but, in that case, I ask why did de Vere insert such a passage into his play ; and what did he mean by it, if not what I suppose ? It should be remembered, in this connexion, that the fashion of dress of great ladies, in those days, made concealment relatively easy, and that the birth, if it took place, would, of course, be rigorously concealed from all the world. At the close of *Two Gentlemen of Verona* a closely analogous idea is repeated, when Proteus who is simply another side of Valentine-Oxford, threatens a criminal assault upon Silvia—"I'll force thee yield to my desire"—an idea strangely echoed, as we shall see, in *Venus and Adonis*, which I believe to have been first drafted during the late 'seventies, about the same time as *Two Gentlemen of Verona*.

That the Queen was fond of Oxford is undeniable. Such phrases as those quoted in this book, concerning

Elizabeth's delight in his dancing and valiantness, and Talbot, (1571) "there is no man of life and agility in every respect in the court but the Earl of Oxford," make this absolutely certain, nor have I the slightest doubt that Oxford reciprocated, to some extent, at least; firstly because it was the fashion for all young courtiers to adore, or to pretend to adore, Gloriana; secondly, because Romeo's first love, Rosaline, is undoubtedly, Elizabeth; and thirdly because Mary Queen of Scots, writing a gossipy letter to Queen Elizabeth, about 1584, says that she has been told, by the Countess of Shrewsbury, "Bess of Hardwick,"

> " que mesme le comte d'Oxfort n'osoit ce rappointer avecque sa femme, de peur de perdre la faveur qu'il esperoit pour vous fayre l'amour—"

We have seen that the Howard-Arundel charges against Oxford, in 1580-81, together with the seduction, by him, of Anne Vavasour, had infuriated the Queen, who, apparently, sent him twice to the Tower, and readers of my books know that the balcony-scene in *Romeo and Juliet*, between Oxford-Romeo and Anne-Juliet, opens with a vicious counter-attack upon Elizabeth, who is therein described as "the envious sun."

Taking all these facts into consideration, it seems to me probable that the Earl's withdrawal from court in 1589—evidently done, as the plays conclusively show, at the Queen's request, and for some profoundly secret reason—must have been due, in part at least, to some change in his relations to her; and we have seen that, by 1593, Oxford is definitely named by the Spaniards as being among the discontented lords, in that very year when de Vere is on good terms with the Essex-Southampton faction, and is negotiating a marriage between Southampton and his own daughter, Elizabeth. At the same time we find him publishing *Venus and Adonis*, in which he pictures the Queen as making wanton, shameless, and unrequited love to himself as Adonis—matters all suggesting that the cause of his withdrawal in 1589 may have been the fury of a woman scorned. A recent reading of Mr. H. T. S. Forrest's book, *The Original Venus and Adonis*, strengthens an impression, already, for a long time past, present to my mind, that the poem was first written somewhere about the period of the late 'seventies, when the Queen was actually making love to Adonis, and was added to, before publication, by another and imitative hand, which introduced the concealed identity of "Shakespeare," and the glory of the plays under the guise of the "death" and resurrection of Adonis. The ascription, by Venus, of her lover's "death" to a clumsy demonstration of affection on the part of the boar—who is again Oxford[1]—fits in again very closely with the Proteus-Silvia episode of *Two Gentlemen of Verona* to which I have already called attention; nor, in this connexion, must we forget Hatton's letter to Elizabeth (1572): "Reserve (your favour) to the Sheep (Hatton), he hath no tooth to bite, where the Boar's (Oxford's) tusk may both raze and tear." Here is obvious suggestion of the possibility of physical violence from de Vere.

In 1598 Oxford writes *Troilus and Cressida*, wherein Achilles-Oxford, withdrawn into his tent, is accused, by Ulysses, of being in love with "one of Priam's daughters," whom I take to be, once more, that daughter of Henry VIII named Elizabeth. We need not suppose that the

---

[1] P. 176 of Mr. Forrest's book.

APPENDIX A

Earl, in his forty-ninth year, was passionately in love with the aged queen, but those words of Ulysses must surely mean that the private relations between Elizabeth and her Lord Great Chamberlain had supplied a principal reason for the latter's withdrawal.

The matter, it will be agreed, is difficult and contradictory. Valentine and Romeo are both, obviously, in love with the queen, and themselves make the running; Valentine, it would seem, actually becoming the father of her child; while Proteus, who is Oxford-Valentine again, has threatened Silvia-Elizabeth with physical assault. Romeo also has been maudlin with unrequited love for the cold and chaste Rosaline-Elizabeth; but turns from her instantly, when Juliet floats into view. Queen Mary's letter, and *Venus and Adonis*—the latter especially, if written in the Earl's early manhood, as suggested above—both strongly suggest that the Queen flirted with, and even made passionate love to, Oxford on her own account; while the Sonnets, written about the mid-'nineties, suggest that Oxford may well have dreamed of intimate relations with his Queen, when he writes:

"In sleep a king, but waking no such matter."

When all is so contradictory, so dependent upon circumstance, and upon the variable moods of two notoriously fickle and capricious creatures, it is impossible to form any precise or definite conclusions upon this delicate matter; but I have, I hope, set down enough here to justify my innate conviction, that de Vere's relations with Queen Elizabeth—could they be sufficiently known—would completely solve the mystery that still hangs about "Shakespeare's" paradoxical and enigmatic career.

APPENDIX B

COUNTS OF FLANDERS

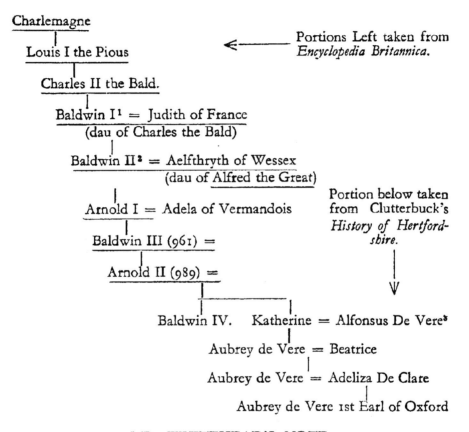

MR. WHITEHEAD'S NOTE

If Clutterbuck is correct this establishes a long line of princely ancestors underlined.

This does not necessarily upset the Danish theory of Majendie. An earlier ancestor may have come from Denmark to Holland. And of course, if true Normans they must have come from Norway, Sweden or Denmark originally in any case.

Many of the Countesses of Oxford had Royal Blood but in all these cases there was no surviving issue.

[1] Widow of Ethelwulf King of Wessex and of Ethelbald King of Wessex.
[2] Step-daughter of Judith.
[3] Of the town of Veer in the Island of Walcheren in Zealand.

APPENDIX C

DR. LESLIE HOTSON'S "SHAKESPEARE AND SHALLOW"

DR. LESLIE HOTSON'S new book, *Shakespeare versus Shallow* has fluttered the Shakesperean dovecots, and has provided certain of the orthodox, with the thought—fathered of course by the wish—that his book destroys the Oxfordian case. Thus Mr. Desmond McCarthy, in the *Sunday Times* of 4 October, 1931:

> "And what will the Baconians say now? The strength of their case such as it is—and it can be entertained by *no one who is a judge of either probability or psychology*—has always rested on the fact that it has been impossible to link any matter in the plays with any known incident in Shakespeare's life. To Baconians, or to those who favour the Earl of Oxford as the author of the plays, this negative fact has always seemed a sufficient reason for supposing that they must have been written by some one famous for other reasons. What will they say now?"

Baconians can speak for themselves. Oxfordians—I beg to inform Mr. McCarthy—are saying now that Dr. Hotson's discoveries support their own case as strongly as they damage that of their opponent.

The discoveries are these. Dr. Hotson, searching the roll of the Queen's Bench, came upon this:

"England be it known that William Wayte craves sureties of the pece against William Shakespeare, Francis Langley, Dorothy Soer . . . and Anne Lee, for fear of death and so forth."

Dr. Hotson knew that Langley was the individual who in 1594–95 had built on the Bankside the Swan Theatre, of which de Witt's sketch is so well known, and he drew the justificable conclusion that Shakespeare's company in 1596 was already playing *Twelfth Night*—a scene from which is the probable subject of that sketch—not, as has been supposed hitherto, at the Theatre in Shoreditch, but at the Swan on Bankside. Dr. Hotson promptly sought further information concerning William Wayte, and discovered from the Exchequer Rolls and other sources that he was " a certain loose person of no reckoning or value," wholly under " rule and commandment " of his step-father, William Gardiner, a rascally Justice addicted to all forms of chicanery and theft. Why this insignificant Wayte believed himself to be in grievous danger from Shaksper Dr. Hotson cannot inform us ; but his further discovery, upon which he built the book, is that this knavish Justice Gardiner, by marrying in 1558 the daughter of Robert Lucy, earned the right to impale with his own coat that of Lucy, which, in common with Sir Thomas Lucy's of Charlecote, bore " three luces haurient."

Dr. Hotson, to whom such identifications as that of Burleigh as Polonius are apparently unknown, jumped to the conclusion that, *for the first time*, he had revealed Shakespeare as a satirist of his contemporaries, Justice Gardiner being pilloried by Shakespeare, as Justice Shallow of *Henry IV* and *Merry Wives*, with Slender

APPENDIX C 371

standing for Wayte. Against such an inference, however, the arguments are overwhelming.

Gardiner is a London Justice—twice Sheriff elect of London—aged about 65; Shallow is a countryman, a Gloucestershire Justice, of the slippered pantaloon variety, and over eighty years of age. Gardiner is an unscrupulous man-of-affairs, usurious and grad-grinding; Shallow is a garrulous old boaster, foolish and gullible enough to lend £1,000, without security, to Falstaff, of all people in the world! Further, Dr. Hotson's contention that Shakespeare makes Shallow " sufficiently corrupt to countenance the arrant knave Visor," is instantly challenged by Shallow's answer, "I say he shall have no wrong," or in other words, " Full Justice shall be done to him." Shallow, therefore, is, quite certainly, *not* Gardiner; and could never have been so identified by Shakespeare's audiences.

Turning to the question of dates, Dr. Hotson's discoveries again support the Oxfordian, rather than the Stratfordian thesis; and for these reasons. Dr. Hotson seems to have made out a good case for *Twelfth Night* having been played at the Swan at least as early as 1596, and for the ascription of *Merry Wives* to 1597, since he shows the last-named comedy to contain an allusion to the Count of Mompelgart's election to the Garter, in April of that year; thus continuing the tendency of all modern research to push farther and farther back the dates of the plays, until there is exercised upon them a process of compression which is fatal to the orthodox view, since the Stratfordians, by the necessities of their own case, are precluded from setting the plays farther back than about the year 1590.

There follow conclusions ruthlessly catastrophic to

orthodoxy. For instance, Sir Edmund Chambers knowing that neither *Twelfth Night* nor *Merry Wives* is included in Meres' list of Shakesperean plays in existence in 1596, assigns those two comedies to 1599 and 1600 respectively. Consequently, if Dr. Hotson is right, Meres' list of plays is no longer trustworthy; and with the passing of Meres, as a basis of orthodox chronology, there falls also one of the strongest Stratfordian props.

But worse remains behind; for a majority of Shakesperean students, whether orthodox or not, concur in Sir Edmund Chambers' opinion that *Merry Wives* is a comparatively late play, written not merely after the Henry plays, but after a number of others, including the Richard plays, *King John, Romeo and Juliet, Love's Labour's Lost*—all of which, upon style alone, are demonstrably earlier than *Merry Wives*—and including also those two court-comedies, *As You Like It* and *Twelfth Night*, also closely linked by manner and method. Approximately, therefore, it comes to this—that the Stratfordians are being compelled, upon their own showing, to cram some twenty plays into the years 1591-97, which, on an even distribution, is at the rate of three plays a year, with, however, a more probable congestion of *some five or six plays a year round* 1594-96, while the author, we are asked to believe, was actively engaged also, as actor and business-man, in the Swan and other London Theatres!

Which then is the more probable?—the thesis advanced in this book, that the plays were first drafted, in most instances, by Lord Oxford himself, during the fifteen-'seventies and 'eighties and were, revised, and added to, again and again, during the course of the years, or the orthodox theory, which compels the writing of an impossible number of them during the first half of the

APPENDIX C

decade of the 'nineties? Read, in this connexion, from the *Arte of English Poesie*, written in 1589:

> "For tragedy Lord Buckhurst and Master Edward Ferrys do deserve the highest price (praise?) *the Earl of Oxford* and Master Edwards of Her Majesty's Chapel for Comedy and Enterlude. . . . And in Her Majesty's time that now is are sprung up another crew of *Courtly makers*, Noblemen and Gentlemen of Her Majestys own servants, who have written excellently well as it would appear *if their doings could be found out and made public* with the rest, of which number is first that noble gentleman *Edward Earl of Oxford.*"

"What will the Oxfordians say now?" asks Mr. Desmond McCarthy. These pages, if he will honour me by reading them, may enlighten him upon those very points of "probability" and "psychology" in which he holds us to be so lamentably deficient.

INDEX

"Aery of children." 208
Agamemnon and Ulysses, 200
Agincourt, 12, 49
Alençon, Duke of (d. 1584); as Bassanio in *Merchant of Venice*, 134; as Bottom in *A Midsummer Night's Dream*, 285; as Cloten in *Cymbeline*, 91, as Orlando in *As You Like It*, 195; as Orsino in *Twelfth Night*, 33 34, 143, in *Love's Labour's Lost*, 128.
"Allowed fool," 36, 152, 159, 195
"All this to season a dead brother's love," 35
Alva, Duke of (1508-1583), 53
Anonymity, 48
Anjou, Duke of, 33, 35
Antonio, Don (the Portuguese Pretender), 147
Antwerp, 90, 228
Apology for Actors, 237n
Arden, District of, 261, 301, 340
Arden, Robert, 260, 261
Arden, Thomas, 260
Arden, Walter, 260
"Arise fair sun and kill the envious moon," 192
Armada, The, 247, 248
Arte of English Poesie, 261, 373
Arundel, Charles (1540?-1587), 188; his accusations against Oxford, 53, 75, 155-164; as Aaron in *Titus Andronicus*, 90; as Conrad in *Much Ado*, 64, 157-161, 170; as Iago in *Othello*, 230; as Lucio in *Measure for Measure*, 174; in *Cymbeline*, 163, in *Winter's Tale*, 115

Asbies, 260
"Ashbourne" portrait, vii, 56n, 319-328
Ashby, Gerard, 187
Audley End, 139
Audrey, 243, 256-259, 265, 304
"Authority," 239-241, 243, 254

Bacon, Francis (1561-1626), 334, 335, 358; as a member of the Shakespeare Group, xiv, 235, 310; as editor of the First Folio, 309; as author of the *Tempest*, 313; as Ulysses in *Troilus and Cressida*, 309
"Banishment" motive, 303n, 318
"Bath" portrait, 56
"Bear" motive, 239-241
Beauclerk, Rev. Fr. C. S. de Vere, vii, 322n, 323.
Bedingfield, Thomas, 44, 51, 53, 206, 216
Belchamp St. Paul's, 19
Bertie, Peregrine, Lord Willoughby de Eresby (1555-1601), 188, as Petruchio in the *Shrew*, 19, 94; in *Hamlet*, 205
Bertie, Robert (1582-1642), 332
"Best for comedy," 272, 331
Billesley, 259
Bilton, Manor of, 258
Blackfriars Theatre, 153, 199
Boar's Head Tavern, 216, 346, 347
Bothwell, Earl of (1536?-1578), as King Claudius in *Hamlet*, 203; As Macbeth, 29
"Bottle badge," 358
Bray, Sir Denis, 305
Breviary of Britain, 44

Brincknell, Thomas, 26
Buchanan, George, 236
Buckhurst, Lord (*see* Sackville)
Bull, The, 134
Burbage, Richard (1567?-1619), 299n
Burleigh, Lady 37
Burleigh, Lord (*see* Cecil)
Byron, Lord, 37

Cade, Jack, 30
Cambrai, 196
Campaspe, 199
"Candle-holder, A," 15
Canopy, Bearing the, 249, 250, 295, 305
Cardanus Comfort, 44-47, 207, 216
Case for Edward de Vere as Shakespeare, The, 139n, 324
Castiglione, Baldassare (1478-1529), 38-44
Castiglione, Note on, 42
Castle Hedingham, 7, 23, 269
"Cataian," 145
Cathay Company, The, 133-135, 145
Cecil, Anne, Countess of Oxford (1556-1588), 54, 58, 62, 83, 182, 246; as Adriana and Luciana in *Comedy of Errors*, 84; as Anne Page in *Merry Wives*, 32, 224; as Cressida, 65, 99; as Desdemona in *Othello*, 228, 248, 249; as Helena in *All's Well*, 96, 97, 181; as Hermione in *Winter's Tale*, 112; as Hero in *Much Ado*, 171; as Imogen in *Cymbeline*, 92; as Mariana in *Measure for Measure*, 21, 63, 115, 179, 181; as Ophelia in *Hamlet*, 27, 33, 65, 66, 67, 213, 248
Cecil, Thomas (1542-1622); as Laertes in *Hamlet*, 203
Cecil, William, Lord Burleigh (1520-1598), 25-29, 50, 331; his nickname "Pondus," 99, 202; his motto "Cor unum via una," 203; as Brabantio in

Cecil, William—(*contd.*)
Othello, 228, as Corambis and Polonius in *Hamlet*, 33, 66-75, 203, 207-213, 244, 330; as Pandarus in *Troilus and Cressida*, 32, 99, 245
Cecil, Robert (1563?-1612), 332 as Laertes in *Hamlet*, 203
Cecil House, 25
Chambers, Sir E. K., xii, 80, 145, 301n, 372
Chapman, George (1559?-1634), 165; eulogizes Oxford, 57; attacks Oxford, 276, 291-298, 305, 326; as Macilente in *Every Man Out*, 306; as Thersites in *Troilus and Cressida*, 310; in *Love's Labour's Lost*, 128
Chettle, Henry, 272
"Cheveril," 194
Churchyard, Thomas, 267
Clark, Mrs. Eva Turner, v
Clerke Bartholomew (1537?-1590) 39
Coligny, Gaspard de (1519-1572); as King Lear, 29, 317
Conspiracy Plays, 335, 336
Conway, Mr. Eustace, vii, 319
Coronet for his Mistress Philosophy, A, 165, 292
"Corrupter of words," 36
Cory, William, 354
Coucy, Sire de, 9
Courtier, The, 38-44, 171
Cynthia's Revels, 59, 263, 340-342

Dale, Dr. Valentine, 54
Darnley, Murder of, 203, 236, 317
Davis, Sir John, 235
Dawtrey, Captain Nicholas (1545?-1601); as Falstaff, 217, 218
De Beaumont, 196
De Bex, 196
"Deformed, The," 59, 157, 159 263, 341
Delves, George, 31
De Profundis, 24
Devereux, Robert, 2nd Earl of Essex (1566-1601), 249, 314,

INDEX

Devereux, Robert—(cont'd.) 334; as Achilles in *Troilus and Cressida*, 336
Derby, Countess of (*see* Vere)
Derby, Earl of (*see* Stanley)
"Desire" Poems, 85
Desmond, Earl of, 218
Detection, 236
Discourse of English Poetry, 232
Disintegration of Shakespeare, xiii, xiv
"Disvalued in levity," 65, 115
"Dog" motive, 130, 274, 306–309
Dogberry, 160
Donald, Rev. K. J. L., vii
Double Mask, A, 126
Drake, Sir Francis (1540?–1596), 152, 196, 247; as Antonio in *Twelfth Night*, 147
Droeshout portrait, 56, 328, 357
Dudley, Ambrose, Earl of Warwick (1528?–1590), 153
Dudley, Robert, Earl of Leicester (1532?–1588), 127, 219; in *Cymbeline*, 92
Dun, Sir John, 15

Earthquake, 172, 192, 270
"Echo" song, 80, 193, 281
Edward Bonaventure, The, 247
Elizabeth, Queen of England (1533–1603), 23, 33–38, 62, 141, 252, 350; patronises a company of actors, 198; orders anti-Spanish propaganda plays, 227; as Lavinia in *Titus Andronicus*, 90; as Olivia in *Twelfth Night*, 34, 143; as Portia in the *Merchant of Venice*, 134; as Rosaline in *Romeo and Juliet*,188–190, 365; as Saviolina in *Every Man Out*, 305; as Silvia in *Two Gentlemen*, 86, 362; as Titania in *A Midsummer Night's Dream*, 285; as Venus in *Venus and Adonis*, 279, 366
Elsinore, 205

Eresby, Lord Willoughby de (see Bertie)
Essex, Earl of (*see* Devereux)
Essex Rising, The, 334
Euphues Golden Legacie, 197
Euphues the Anatomy of Wit, 138, 207
Evans, Henry, 199
Every Man Out of His Humour, 31, 65, 222, 301, 305, 309

Faerie Queene, The, 261
Famous Victories of Henry V, The, 60, 48–52, 54, 77, 216
Fanner, George, 289
Farewell to Military Profession, 151
Farmer, John, 290
Farrant, Richard, 199
"Felo-de-Se," 27
Feuillerat, Prof. Albert, 187
Field, Richard, 262
First Rape of Fair Helen, The, 259
Fletcher, John (1579–1625), xiv.
Forrest, Mr. H. T. S., xiii
"Frailty thy name is woman," 206
Frederick II, King of Denmark, 205
French Fury, The, 228
Frobisher, Sir Martin (1535?–1594), 132
Fugger News-Letters, 169

Gad's Hill, 49–52, 216
Gascoigne, George (1542–1577), 24, 28, 79, 94
Gaston de Latour, 35
Gastrell, 187
Gerville, M. de, 3
"Glove" motive, 86, 162
Golding, Arthur (1536?–1606), 22, 25, 36, 85, 90, 263
Golding, Margery, Countess of Oxford (1525?–1568), 19; as Queen Gertrude in *Hamlet*, 203; in the *Merchant of Venice*, 135–137
Gorboduc, 92
Gorges, Sir William, 168
Gosson, Stephen (1554–1624), 134

"Grafton" portrait, 55, 56, 321
"Grand Possessors," 314, 358
"Grandsire phrase, A," 15
Gray, Lady Katherine, 92
Great Lord Burleigh, The, 207
Greene, Robert (1560?-1592), 234, 262, 272, 273, 294
Greville, Fulke (1554-1628), 137
Group Theory of Shakespeare authorship, The, xiii, xiv, 12, 328
Guise, Duke of, 236

Hackney, 287, 301, 358-361
Harriots, To M., 295
Harrison, Dr. G. B., 276
Harvey, Gabriel (1551?-1630), 41, 59, 139, 148-150, 264, 310
Harwich, 248
Hatcher, Dr. John, 153
Hatton, Sir Christopher (1540-1591), 30, 31, 151; his posy "Si fortunatus infelix," 79; his nickname, "the Sheep," 36; as Malvolio in *Twelfth Night,* 36, 79, 143, 144, 146, 243; in *Love's Labour's Lost,* 128; in *Two Gentlemen,* 85
"He is but a little fellow," 150
"He jests at scars that never felt a wound," 192
Henderson, Mr. Drayton, 42
Henry II, King of France (d. 1559); as Sir Rowland de Bois in *As You Like It,* 195
Henry III, King of France (d. 1589) 54, 60; as Oliver in *As You Like It,* 195; as Orsino in *Twelfth Night,* 143
Henry IV, King of France (d. 1610), 297, 317; as King of Navarre in *Love's Labour's Lost,* 126
Henry VIII, King of England (d. 1547), 134
Herbert, Philip, Earl of Montgomery and Pembroke (1584-1650), 328, 357
"Hercules be thy speed," 196

Hertford, Earl of (*see* Seymour)
Heywood, Thomas, 237n
Hidden Allusions in Shakespeare's Plays v
Historie of the Solitarie Knight, The, 88, 89
Historye of Titus and Gisippus, The, 89
History of the crueltie of a Stepmother, An, 91
History of Agamemnon and Ulysses, The, 309
History of Ariodante and Genevora, A, 172n
History of Portio and Demorantes The, 134
Histriomastix, 345
"Hob-goblin," 136
Holland, Admiral H. H., v
Honour in his Perfection, 17
Hotson, Dr. Leslie, 369
Howard, Henry, Earl of Surrey (1517?-1547), 22, 78, 79
Howard, Lord Henry (1540-1614), 63, 75, 155-164, 188; as Borachio in *Much Ado,* 64, 157-161, 246; as Iago in *Othello,* 230, 246; in *Cymbeline,* 163; in *Winter's Tale,* 115
Howard, Philip, Earl of Surrey (1557-1595), 77
Howard, Thomas, 4th Duke of Norfolk (1536-1572), 29, 33
Hundreth Sundrie Flowres, A, 79
Hunnis, William, 199
Hymns to the Night, 276

"I am proverb'd with a grandsire phrase," 15
"I am that I am," 228
"Ipse is he," 257
"Is this a dagger that I see before me?" 236
"It is a wise father that knows his own son," 136
Ivry, Battle of, 317

James I, King of England (1566-1625), 349; as Albany in *King*

INDEX

James, 1—(contd.)
  Lear, 351, 355; as Bottom in *A Midsummer Night's Dream*, 286; as Fortinbras in *Hamlet*, 351
Jew, The, 134
"Johannes Factotum," 273, 276
Jonson, Ben (1573 ?–1637); his evidences in the First Folio, xiii, xiv, Burlesques Oxford as Puntarvolo, 31, 60, 274, 301, and as Amorphus, 59, 165, 339; and praises him as Virgil, 343–345, Epigram to Lady Susan Vere, 246; burlesques William Shakspere as Cos, 263, 340; and as Sogliardo, 222, writes *The Staple of News*, 358; as Ajax in *Troilus and Cressida*, 310

Kind Hart's Dream, 272
King's Place, 287
Knevett, Mr. Edgar de, vi
Knyvet, Thomas (1543 ?–1622), vi; as Tybalt in *Romeo and Juliet*, 188–190, 226
Kyd, Thomas, 234
"Knighted on carpet considerations," 147

La Mole; as Viola in *Twelfth Night*, 34–36
La Mothe Fénélon, 33; as Moth in *Love's Labour's Lost*, 128
Lavenham, 20
"Laid great bases for eternity," 305
Lea, James, 247
Le Beau, 196
Leicester, Earl of (*see* Dudley)
Lepanto, Battle of, 226
"Lewd companions," 53, 216, 272, 330
Lock, Michael (fl 1578–1615); as Shylock in *Merchant of Venice*, 133
Lodge, Thomas, 197, 234
Lok, H, 333
London Stone, 30

Long Melford, 20, 91, 224
Long Tom, 188
Looney, Mr. J. T., v, viii, xi, 32, 78
Lopez, Dr., 284
Loss of Good Name, a parody, 65
Lucy, Sir Thomas, 223, 262
Lumley, Lord (1534 ?–1609), 261
Lyly, John (1554 ?–1606); writes *Euphues*, 126; Oxford's Private Secretary, 138, 139; and actor-manager, 153, 207; given lease of the Blackfriars, 199, 200; as a "University wit," 234

MacCarthy, Mr. Desmond, 369, 373
Machiavelli (1469–1527), 38
Mackail, Dr, 153
Majendie, Rev. Severne, 3, 9n
Manners, Edward, 3rd Earl of Rutland (1549–1587), 28, 32
Manners, Roger (1530 ?–1605 ?), 202
Manningham's *Diary*, 299n
Marchaumont, M de, as Le Beau in *As You Like It*, 196; as Malvolio in *Twelfth Night*, 146
Marguerite de Valois, as the Princess of France in *Love's Labour's Lost*, 126, 297
Markham, Gervaise (1568 ?–1637), 17
Marlowe, Christopher (1564–1593), 234, 284
Marprelate Controversy, The, 265
Marston, John (1575 ?–1634), 331
"Marry me to one Frances," 128
Mary Queen of Scots (1542–1587), 236, 365; as Queen Gertrude in *Hamlet*, 203; as Lady Macbeth, 29, as Tamora in *Titus Andronicus*, 90
Mask of Amazons and Mask of Knights, A, 126, 297
Massacre of St Bartholomew, The, 34, 144, 317
Masters, Dr. Richard (1530 ?–1588), 62

Medici, Catherine de' (1519-1589), 28; as Goneril in *King Lear*, 29; as Katherine in *Love's Labour's Lost*, 127
Melford, 20
Mendoza, Bernardino de, 156
Meres, Francis, 272, 331
Molyneux, 142
Mompelgart, Count of, 371
"More matter for a May morning," 142
Morrall of the Marryage of Mynde and Measure, A, 94
Muiopotmos, 265
Munday, Anthony (1553-1633), 234, 262, 290
"Muses that Fame's loose feathers beautify," 293
"Muses that sing love's sensual empery," 292, 294

Nashe, Thomas (1567-1601), 150, 234, 272, 310
Navy, Royal Commission on, 204
Nerac, 126
"Niggardly, rascally sheep-biter," 36, 146
Nigrone, Baptista, 58; as Baptista in *The Shrew*, 60, 94
"No Italian priest shall tithe and toll in our dominions," 8
Norfolk, Duke of (*see* Howard)
Norris, Colonel John (1547?-1597), 219
Norris, Francis (afterwards Earl of Berkshire) (1579-1623), 329
North-west passage, 132
Nowell, Laurence (d. 1576), 25

"Old Bill," 218, 235
"Our pleasant Willy, ah, is dead of late," 268
Ovid's *Banquet of Sense*, 292
Ovid's *Metamorphoses*, 22, 85, 90, 263, 279
Oxford Boys, 198, 208
Oxford, Countesses of (*see* Cecil, Golding, Trentham, and Trussell)
Oxford, Earls of (*see* Vere)

Oxford-Shakespeare Case Corroborated, The, 305n, 324

Paget, Charles (1545?-1612), 169
Paget, Lord (1540?-1589), 169
Paradise of Dainty Devises, The, 79
Parma, Duke of (1545-1592); as Charles in *As You Like It*, 196
Pater, Walter, 35
Paul's Boys, 153, 198, 265
Peele, George (1558?-1597?), 234
Pembroke, Countess of (*see* Sidney)
Pembroke, Earl of (*see* Herbert)
Penn, Mistress Julia, 268
Perez, Antonio; as Iago, 227
Philip II, King of Spain (1527-1598), 29; as Duke Frederick in *As You Like It*, 196; as Othello, 226; as Saturninus in *Titus Andronicus*, 90
"Picking teeth" motive, 98, 239, 340
Pilkington, Francis, 289
Poems of Edward de Vere, 78
Poetomachia, The, 278, 308, 345
Pompey, 177
Pondus, 100, 202
Portraits of Shakespeare, vii, 55-57, 319-328
Poetaster, The, 343-345
Prince, The, 38
"Privileged vicar for the lawless marriage of ink and paper," 145, 217
Privy Seal Warrant, 233
Propaganda, xiv, 181, 227, 232-237, 297, 217
"Proverb'd with a grandsire phrase," 15

Radcliffe, Thomas, 3rd Earl of Sussex (1526?-1583), 29, 152, 153
Raleigh, Sir Walter (1552?-1618), 201, 354; as Coriolanus, 202
Rape of the Second Helen, The, 96
Rendall, Dr. Gerald H., vii
Revenge of Bussy d'Ambois, The, 57, 291, 298, 302, 326, 336

INDEX

"Richard Conqueror," 299
Riche, Barnabe (1540?–1620?), 150, 275
Rising in the North, The, 29
"Romeo without his roe," 194
Rosalynd, 197
"Rude grooms," 274
Rysing, Manor of, 87

Sackville, Thomas, Lord Buckhurst (1536–1608); as Sir Toby Belch in *Twelfth Night*, 143–146
St John, Lord, 32
Sapho and Phao, 199, 200
Scott, Dr. Mary A., 41
Scourge of Villany, The, 332
"Scylla and Charybdis," 135
"Secret must be locked within the teethe and the lips," 181, 337
"Serpent before the fire," 202
Seven Shakespeares, 12n
Seventeenth Earl of Oxford, The, v
Seymour, Edward, Earl of Hertford (1539?–1621), 92, 286
Seymour, Lord, 51, 92
"Shakes a spear," 264, 345
Shakespeare and Chapman as Topical Dramatists, 57n, 299n, 326
Shakespeare's Environment, 260
Shakespeare Fellowship, The, vi
Shakespeare Identified, xi
Shakespeare's Plays in the Order of their Writing, v
Shakespeare: Truth and Tradition, 259
Shakespeare versus Shallow, 369
Shakespeare's Characters identified:
    Aaron, 90
    Achilles, 310, 312, 336, 366
    Adonis, 279, 366
    Adriana, 84
    Ajax, 310
    Albany, 351, 355
    Angelo, 65, 74, 174
    Anne Page, 32, 224
    Antipholus, 84
    Antonio, 16, 133, 147
    Armado, 128
    Autolycus 239, 254

Shakespeare's Characters—*(contd.)*
    Baptista, 60, 94
    Beatrice, 171
    Benedick, 42, 47, 162, 171
    Bertram, 51, 74, 96–98, 181, 240
    Biron, 128, 222, 298
    Borachio, 64, 157–161, 246
    Bottom, 285, 286
    Charles, 196
    Claudio, 171, 173
    Cloten, 91
    Conrad, 64, 157–161, 170
    Corambis, 33, 66–75, 203, 207–213, 244, 330
    Coriolanus, 202
    Cressida, 65, 99
    Desdemona, 226–228, 248, 249
    Dromio, 84
    Duke Frederick, 196
    Duke, The, 174, 336
    Emilia, 117, 231
    Fabian, 141, 143
    Falstaff, 217, 218
    Fenton, 32, 224
    Feste 36, 142, 143
    Ford, 224
    Fortinbras, 351
    Francisco, 76, 203, 355
    Ghost, 203
    Goneril, 29
    Hamlet, 27, 48, 66, 202–214, 355
    Helena, 96, 97, 181
    Hermione, 112
    Hero, 117
    Horatio 76, 203, 292, 355
    Iago, 227, 230, 246
    Imogen, 92
    Jaques, 59, 98, 142, 197, 253
    Juliet, 81, 175, 186–195, 365
    Katharina, 19, 94, 304
    Katherine, 127
    Kent, 318, 336, 355
    King Claudius, 203
    King Lear, 29, 317
    King of Navarre, 126
    Lady Macbeth, 29
    Laertes, 203
    Launce, 85
    Launcelot, 136

Shakespeare's Characters—(contd.)
  Lavinia, 90
  Le Beau, 196
  Leontes, 112, 120
  Lucio, 174
  Lucius, 90
  Macbeth, 29
  Malvolio, 36, 79, 143, 144, 146, 243
  Mariana, 21, 63, 115, 179, 181
  Moth, 128
  Old Gobbo, 136
  Oliver, 195
  Olivia, 34, 143
  Ophelia, 27, 33, 65–67, 81, 213, 248
  Orlando, 195
  Orsino, 33, 34, 143
  Othello, 226, 229
  Pandarus, 32, 99, 245
  Paulina, 117
  Perdita, 120, 239
  Pericles, 91
  Petruchio, 19, 94
  Poins, 218–220
  Portia 134
  Posthumus, 91, 92
  Prince Hal, 48–50
  Prince, the, 188–190
  Princess of France, 126, 297
  Proteus, 85, 364
  Queen Gertrude, 203
  Richard II, 335
  Romeo, 31, 190–195, 365
  Rosaline, 188–190, 365
  Saturninus, 90
  Shylock, 133
  Silvia, 86, 362
  Sir Andrew Aguecheek, 36, 143–147
  Sir Toby Belch, 143–146
  Sir Rowland de Bois, 195
  Slender, 32, 79, 224
  Sly, 299
  Speed, 85
  Tamora, 90
  Thersites, 310
  Timon, 88, 89
  Titania, 285

Shakespeare's Characters—(contd.)
  Touchstone, 59, 142, 197, 253
  Troilus, 99
  Tybalt, 188–190, 226
  Ulysses, 309
  Valentine, 85, 86, 362
  Venus, 279, 366
  Viola, 34–36
  William, 222, 241, 256, 257, 299
  William Visor, 221–223
Shakespeare's Plays analysed:
  All's Well that Ends Well, 96–98
  As You Like It, 195–197, 253–264
  Cymbeline, 91, 92
  Hamlet, 81, 82, 203–214
  King Henry IV, 215–222
  King Lear, 271, 317–319
  Love's Labour's Lost, 126–131, 297, 298
  Measure for Measure, 174–184
  Merchant of Venice, 132–137
  Merry Wives of Windsor, 224
  Midsummer Night's Dream, 285, 286
  Much Ado About Nothing, 157–162, 170–174
  Othello, 226–231
  Pericles, 90
  Richard II, 315
  Romeo and Juliet, 185–195
  Taming of the Shrew, 93–95, 299–304
  Timon of Athens, 89
  Titus Andronicus, 89, 90
  Troilus and Cressida, 99–112, 309–315
  Twelfth Night, 141–148
  Two Gentlemen of Verona, 85, 86
  Winter's Tale, 112–125, 238–243
Shakspere, William, (1564–1616); his relations with Lord Oxford, 223, 261; his penmanship, 265; buys New Place, 301; as the Clown in *Winter's Tale*, 241, 242; as Cos in *Cynthia's Revels*, 263; as Sly in *The Shrew*, 299; as Sogliardo in *Every Man Out*, 222, 242, 301, 305, 308; as

INDEX

Shakspeare, William—*(contd.)*
William Visor in *Henry IV*, 221–223; as William in *Merry Wives*, 222; as William in *As You Like It*, 241, 256, 257, 299
"Sheep" as Sir Christopher Hatton's nickname, 36, 85, 146
Shrewsbury, Earl of (*see* Talbot)
Sheffield, Edmund, 1st Baron (1521–1549), 22
Sidney, Mary, Countess of Pembroke (1561–1621), as a member of the Shakespeare Group, xiv, 12, 328, 354
Sidney, Sir Phillip (1554–1586), 28, 160; opposed to the Alençon marriage, 141; the Tennis-court quarrel with Oxford, 141, 220; knighted on "carpet consideration," 147; as Sir Andrew Aguecheek in *Twelfth Night*, 36 143–147, as Ned Poins in *Henry IV*, 218–220, as Slender in *Merry Wives*, 32, 79, 224
"So fortunatus infelix," 79, 146
Simier, M. de, 141
"Sir Francis, Sir Francis, Sir Francis is come," 152
"Sitting alone upon my thought in melancholy mood," 80
Slater, Dr Gilbert, 12n
Smith, Sir Thomas (1513–1577), 22
Smart, Dr. J S., 259
Snitterfield, 260
Some Account of the Family of Vere, 3, 9n
Somers, Will (d. 1560), 23
Songs and Sonnettes, Book of, 78, 79
Sonnets, The, 5, 6, 24, 46, 47, 59, 250, 291, 295–297, 304, 305, 326
Sorel, 127
Southampton, Earl of (*see* Wriothesley)
Southwell, Francis, 155
Southwell, Robert, 259, 287, 288
Spanish Fury, The, 89
Speculum Tuscanismi, 59, 148, 151

Spenser Edmund (1552?–1598), 261, 265, 268
Spielmann, Mr. W. H, 319
Spinola, Benedict, 94
Stafford, Sir Edward (1552?–1605), 169
Staple of News, The, 358
Stanley, William, 6th Earl of Derby (1561–1642), as a member of the Shakespeare Group xiv, 286, 287, and the Succession question, 289, marries Elizabeth de Vere, 285; "penning comedies," 289
Stopes, Mrs. C C, xii, 260
Stoke Newington, 270
Strange News, 272
Sturmius, John (1507–1589), 57, 218
"Suborned informer," 170
Suffolk, Duchess of (*see* Willoughby)
Suffolk Succession, The, 92, 286, 317
Surrey, Earl of (*see* Howard)
Sussex, Earl of (*see* Radcliffe)
Swan Theatre, 370
"Sweet Swan of Avon," xiv, 328
Talbot, George, 6th Earl of Shrewsbury (1528?–1590), 37, 249
Talbot, Gilbert, 37
Tears of the Muses, 268
Tennis-court quarrel, The 141
"The counterfeit presentment of two brothers," 205
"The courtier's, soldier's, scholar's eye, tongue, sword," 42, 183, 338
"The fortunate unhappy," 79, 146
Throckmorton, Sir Robert (*fl.* 1500), 260
Throgmorton Plot, The, 217
"Tiger's heart wrapt in a player's hide," 273
"Toe of the peasant comes so near the heel of the courtier," 142
To M. Harriots, 295

Tottel's *Miscellany*, 79
Tower, The, 167–170, 175, 302, 365
Townshend, 188
"Tragical-comical-historical," 209
"Traveller" as a Shakespeare pseudonym, 53, 59, 149, 157, 159, 164, 263, 339, 341
Trentham, Elizabeth, Countess of Oxford (1559?–1612), 270, 304, 348
Trentham, Sir Thomas, 270
Triumph over Death, The, 259
Trogus Pompeius, Th' Abridgement of the Histories of, 25
Trussell, Elizabeth, Countess of Oxford (1496–1559), 15, 16, 223, 259
Trussell, John, 259
Trussell, Thomas (d. 1517), 260
Turbervile, George (*fl.* 1567–1576) 24n
"Turk" as Oxford's nickname, 162, 189, 308
"Twelfth Day of December," 145
Twyne, Thomas, 44
"Tympanies of State," 295
Tyrrell, Charles (d. 1570); as King Claudius in *Hamlet*, 203 as Old Gobbo in *Merchant of Venice*, 136

Ubaldinas, Patruchius, 95
Underdowne, Thomas (*fl.* 1566–1587), 26
"University Wits," 234

Valois, Elizabeth de; as Desdemona in *Othello*, 227
Vaux, Thomas, 2nd Baron (1510–1556), 79
Vavasour, Anne (*fl.* 1580–1610), vi, 169, 225, 270, 365; as Juliet in *Measure for Measure*, 81, 175; as Juliet in *Romeo and Juliet*, 81, 186–195, 365; as *Ophelia* in *Hamlet*, 81
Vavasour, Thomas, 176, 225; as Laertes in *Hamlet*, 203

Vere, Some Account of the Family of, 3
Vere; history of the Family of, 2–18, 368; of Danish origin, 3, 205, 368; descended from the Counts of Flanders, 3; grants of land by the Conqueror, to Aubrey, 4; grant of the office of Lord Great Chamberlain, 5; origin of the Arms of, 5; grant of the Earldom of Oxford. 6; Aubrey (2nd Earl), 7; Robert (3rd Earl), 7; Robert (5th Earl), 8, 22; Robert (6th Earl), 8; John (7th Earl), 8; Robert (9th Earl), 9–11; Richard, (11th Earl), 12, 49; John (12th Earl), 13, 173; John (13th Earl), 13, 21; "Little John of Campes" (14th Earl), 14, 15, 21, 91; John (15th Earl), 15, 16, 21; John (16th Earl), (d. 1562), 16, 19, 23; as the Ghost in *Hamlet*, 203
Vere, Edward de, 17th Earl of Oxford (1550–1604); Portraits of, 54, 56, 319–328; as the most important member of the Shakespeare Group, xiv, xv; as actor, actor-manager, and playwright, 77, 131, 152, 153, 198–201, 340, 347, 348; as Queen Elizabeth's lover, 37, 38, 65, 164, 191, 312, 338, 362–367; his £1,000 a year, 233, 234, 352; as Achilles and Troilus in *Troilus and Cressida*, 99, 310, 312, 366; as Adonis and the Boar in *Venus and Adonis*, 279, 366; as Amorphus in *Cynthia's Revels*, 59, 157, 159, 165, 339; as Antipholus and Dromio in *Comedy of Errors*, 84; as Antonio and Launcelot in the *Merchant of Venice*, 16, 133–137; as Benedick and Claudio in *Much Ado*, 42, 47, 162, 171, 173; as Bertram in *All's Well*, 51; 74, 96–98, 181, 240; as Biron

Vere, Edward de—(contd.)
and Armado in *Love's Labour's Lost*, 128, 222, 298; as the Duke, Claudio, and Angelo in *Measure for Measure*, 65, 74, 173, 174, 336; as Fenton and Ford in *Merry Wives*, 32, 224; as Feste and Fabian in *Twelfth Night*, 36, 142, 143; as Hamlet, 27, 48, 66, 202-214, 355; as Kent and King Lear in *King Lear*, 317, 318, 336, 355; as Leontes and Autolycus in *Winter's Tale*, 112, 239, 254; as Lucius in *Titus Andronicus*, 90; as Othello, 229; as Postumus in *Cymbeline*, 91, 92; as Prince Hal in the Famous *Victories* 48-50; as Puntarvolo in *Every Man Out*, 31, 60, 131, 274, 301-306; as Romeo, 31, 190-195, 365; as the "Deformed" (see Deformed); as the "Traveller" (see Traveller); as Timon, 88, 89; as Touchstone and Jaques in *As You Like It*, 59, 98, 142, 197, 253; as Valentine, Proteus, Launce, and Speed in *Two Gentlemen*, 85, 86, 362; as Virgil in *The Poetaster*, 343-345; as Will Monox in *Strange News*, 272; In *Farewell to Military Profession*, 151; in *Pericles*, 90, 91; in *Speculum Tuscanismi*, 148

Vere, Anne, Lady Sheffield, 22
Vere, Bridget, Lady Norris (1584-1620), 328, 329, 331
Vere, Elizabeth, Countess of Derby (1575-1627), 62, 335; as Perdita in *Winter's Tale*, 120, 239
Vere, Frances, Lady Surrey, 22
Vere, Sir Francis (1560-1609), as Francisco in *Hamlet*, 76, 203, 355
Vere, Henry, 18th Earl of Oxford (1593-1625), 234; as the Fair Youth of the *Sonnets*, 283
Vere, Sir Horatio (1565-1635); as Horatio in *Hamlet*, 76, 203, 292, 355

Vere, Katherine, Lady Windsor (1541?-1600), 94
Vere, Mary, Lady Willoughby (1554?-1624), 19, 93; as Beatrice in *Much Ado*, 171; as Emilia in *Othello*, 231; as Emilia in *Winter's Tale*, 117; as Katharina in *Taming of the Shrew*, 19, 94, 304; as Maria in *Twelfth Night*, 143
Vere, Susan, Countess of Montgomery and Pembroke (b. 1587), 246, 328, 331, 357
Vere puns, 83, 84, 102, 104, 224, 314, 363
Venus and Adonis, 10, 252, 279-284, 291, 292, 366
Venice, in *Othello*, 226
Walsingham, Sir Francis (1530?-1590), 244
War Propaganda, xiv
Ward, Col. B. R., vi, 327, 328
Ward, Capt. B. M., v, vi, xi
Warwick Castle, 34
Warwick, Earl of (see Dudley)
Warwickshire, 258-261
Webbe, Edward (fl. 1566-1590), 61
Webbe, William, 232
"We have the man Shakespeare with us," 354
Welbeck portrait, 55, 56, 321
"Were't aught to me I bore the canopy," 250, 295, 306
"While the grass grows—the proverb is something musty," 214
Whitehead, Mr. L. H. Haydon, vii, 3, 20, 368
"Why didst thou promise such a beauteous day?" 24
"Why should a man whose blood is warm within, Sit like his grandsire cut in alabaster?" 16, 133
Wilkins, George (fl. 1607), xiv, 90, 93
Will Monox, 272
William Shakespeare: A Study of Facts and Problems, xii, 316

Willoughby, Lord (*see* Bertie)
Willoughby, Katherine, Duchess of Suffolk (1519-1580); as Paulina in *Winter's Tale*, 117
William the Silent (d. 1584), 218
Wilmcote, 260
Wilson, Mr. S. C., 259
Winchester, Marquess of, 249
Windsor, 78
Winstanley, Miss Lilian, 226
Wright's *History of Essex*, 96

Wriothesley, Henry 3rd Earl of Southampton (1573-1624), 276, 283, 315, 335
Wyatt, Sir Thomas (1503?-1542), 79

Year of Jubilee, 60
Yorick, 22, 204
"You have sold your own lands to see other men's," 8, 59

Zuccaro, 56

THE LIFE STORY OF EDWARD DE VERE AS "WILLIAM SHAKESPEARE"

By PERCY ALLEN,

Author of *The Oxford-Shakespeare Case Corroborated*, etc.

Crown 8vo.   *7s. 6d. net.*   *Cloth.*

The first authentic life of the real William Shakespeare. A book of profound human interest and of first-rate literary importance.

EDWARD DE VERE—A GREAT ELIZABETHAN

By GEORGE FRISBEE

Crown 8vo.   *7s. 6d. net.*   *Cloth.*

A valuable and indispensable contribution to the Shakespeare controversy. The De Vere theory is steadily gaining ground and Mr. Frisbee's work will further establish the claims of the Oxford Adherents.

EXIT SHAKSPERE

By BERTRAM G. THEOBALD

Author of *Shakespeare's Sonnets Unmasked*, etc.

Crown 8vo.   *2s. net.*   *Boards.*

Mr. Theobald's latest work is a well-reasoned, logical statement of the case against William Shakspere, of Stratford-on-Avon as the author of the plays and sonnets of Shakespeare. Here is an opportunity for the man in the street to judge for himself the merits of this important controversy.

THE EARL OF OXFORD AS "SHAKESPEARE"

By LIEUT.-COL. MONTAGU W. DOUGLAS, C.S.I., C.I.E.

Crown 8vo.   *5s. net.*   *Cloth.*

Some Contents : The Traditional Case. The Life and Personality of the Earl of Oxford, etc., etc.

CECIL PALMER   **LONDON**

A CHALLENGE TO THE STRATFORDIANS

THE CASE FOR EDWARD DE VERE (Seventeenth Earl of Oxford) AS SHAKESPEARE
By PERCY ALLEN

Crown 8vo.   7s. 6d. net.   *Cloth.*

Contents: Chapter I Introductory; III Shakespeare in the Lyrics of Lyly's Plays; IV Oxford in *Venus and Adonis* and *Lucrece*; VI Oxford in the Shakespearean Sonnets; VII Oxford's Connection with Elizabethan Drama; VIII Oxford in Some Shakespearean Comedies; XI Tragedies.

SHAKESPEARE JONSON AND WILKINS AS BORROWERS
By PERCY ALLEN

Crown 8vo.   7s. 6d. net.   *Cloth.*

"This interesting book should become a standard work, and is certainly indispensable to students of Elizabethan drama. A masterly series of analytical and parallel studies."—*Christian Science Monitor.*

SHAKESPEARE AND CHAPMAN AS TOPICAL DRAMATISTS
By PERCY ALLEN

Crown 8vo.   7s. 6d. net.   *Cloth.*

"Written with the critical insight and far-reaching learning that characterise its author's former treatise. . . . Clearly expounded, and skilfully and temperately argued, it makes out a convincing case in support of the thesis that Chapman is much more indebted to Shakespeare than is generally supposed."—*The Scotsman.*

THE CASE FOR EDWARD DE VERE AS WILLIAM SHAKESPEARE
By PERCY ALLEN

Crown 8vo.   1s. net.   *Boards.*

A brief summary of the principal arguments upon which the case for Oxford as "Shakespeare" is built up.

SHAKESPEARE AUTHORSHIP
By GILBERT STANDEN

1s. *net.*

Uniform with Mr. Percy Allen's 1s. pamphlet.

This pamphlet contains a summary of the Anti-Stratfordian claims to the authorship of the plays of Shakespeare.

SHAKESPEARE: NEW VEWS FOR OLD
By RODERICK L. EAGLE

Demy 8vo   5s. net   *Cloth.*

"The volume is well written, and contains much that is interesting, and often very cogently put."—*The Scotsman.*

"Judicious and convincing."—*Lewisham Journal.*

SHAKE-SPEARE'S SONNETS UNMASKED
By BERTRAM G. THEOBALD, B.A.

Demy 8vo   5s. net.   *Cloth.*

"Mr. Theobald's book on the Shakespeare Sonnets is intensely interesting but hardly satisfying. . . ."—*Manchester City News*

". . worth examination as a contribution to the Bacon-Shakespeare theory."—*Northern Echo.*

". . his clever book will prove most stimulating"—*Sunday Dispatch.*

". . presented with great care and diligence"—*China Mail*

FRANCIS BACON: CONCEALED AND REVEALED
By BERTRAM G. THEOBALD, B.A.

Demy 8vo.   7s. 6d. net.   *Cloth.*

FULLY ILLUSTRATED

Those readers of the Author's previous book, *Shake-speare's Sonnets Unmasked*, who may have hesitated to accept his conclusions as to Francis Bacon's authorship of these sonnets, should study the present work. Mr Theobald devotes one chapter to a consideration of the objections raised by those who have misunderstood his argument, and he sets forth clearly the grounds for regarding these demonstrations as being reliable.

THE SELF-NAMED WILLIAM SHAKESPEARE

The Prince of Wales Born Legitimate but Unacknowledged. Son of H M Queen Elizabeth and the Earl of Leicester. Baptised in the False Name of Francis Bacon; Philosopher, Dramatist, Poet and Arch-Martyr. Thereafter named Viscount St Albans

By ALFRED MUDIE

Demy 8vo   5s net   *Boards.*

"SHAKESPEARE" IDENTIFIED IN EDWARD DE VERE, the Seventeenth Earl of Oxford.—By J. THOMAS LOONEY. Demy 8vo. 21s net

THE POEMS OF EDWARD DE VERE, Seventeenth Earl of Oxford. With Biographical Notice, Introduction to the Poems and Notes by J THOMAS LOONEY Demy 8vo. 7s net.

SHAKESPEARE'S PLAYS IN THE ORDER OF THEIR WRITING
By EVA TURNER CLARK

Demy 8vo., cloth.   21s. *net.*   700 *pages.*

A study of the Oxford theory based on the records of early Court Revels and personalities of the times. A work of remarkable scholarship that must be essential to every student of the period and of the drama.

THE OXFORD-SHAKESPEARE CASE CORROBORATED
By PERCY ALLEN

Cr. 8vo.   7s. 6d. *net.*   370 *pages.*

In this volume Mr. Allen's case for Oxford as Shakespeare is substantially complete.

SHAKESPEARE—HANDWRITING AND SPELLING
By GERALD H. RENDALL, B.D., Lit.D., LL.D.

Cr. 8vo.   3s. 6d. *net.*   *Boards.*

A scholarly examination of the handwriting and spelling of Shakespeare as evidenced in the sonnets in the Quarto Text.

BEN JONSON AND THE FIRST FOLIO
By W. L. GOLDSWORTHY

Cr. 8vo.   2s. 6d. *net.*   *Boards.*

The reader is left to take his choice between the three alleged claimants—Player Shakespeare, Edward de Vere, and Francis Bacon.

COMPLETE CATALOGUE FREE ON APPLICATION

CECIL PALMER
49 Chandos Street, Covent Garden, London, W.C.2

CPSIA information can be obtained at www.ICGtesting.com
Printed in the USA
237392LV00004BB/72/P